A Century of Progress?
IRISH WOMEN REFLECT

A Century of Progress?
IRISH WOMEN REFLECT

Alan Hayes and Máire Meagher
EDITORS

ARLEN
HOUSE

A Century of Progress?
IRISH WOMEN REFLECT

is published in 2016 by
ARLEN HOUSE
42 Grange Abbey Road
Baldoyle, Dublin 13, Ireland
Phone: +353 86 8207617
Email: arlenhouse@gmail.com
www.arlenhouse.blogspot.com

978–1–85132–155–1, paperback

International distribution by
SYRACUSE UNIVERSITY PRESS
621 Skytop Road, Suite 110
Syracuse, New York
USA 13244–5290
Phone: 315–443–5534/Fax: 315–443–5545
Email: supress@syr.edu
www.syracuseuniversitypress.syr.edu

Typesetting by Arlen House
Index by Therese Caherty

Cover Artwork: 'Shapeshifter' by Diana Copperwhite
oil on canvas
175 x 235 cm
2016
Image credit: Gillian Buckley
Image courtesy of the artist and Kevin Kavanagh Gallery

The views expressed in this book are not necessarily those of
the editors, the Countess Markievicz School or Arlen House

Contents

JUSTICE, EQUALITY AND HUMAN RIGHTS

VOICES FROM THE FRONT LINE

A Century of Progress?
IRISH WOMEN REFLECT

FOREWORD
A Century of Progress? Irish Women Reflect

Catherine McGuinness

The centenary of the 1916 Rising has seen the publication
of a considerable number of books either closely or
peripherally related to the events of that crucial Easter
Week. New research and historical exploration has thrown
welcome light on the important part played by women
both directly in the military conflict, in the surrounding
events, and in the struggle for women's rights. *A Century of
Progress? Irish Women Reflect* is a most worthwhile addition
to these centenary publications.

The central theme of the contributions from the various
authors relates to the crucial question mark in the book's
title. The book looks at the rather uneven progress – and
lack of progress – that has been made in the hundred years
since the Rising. As expressed by historian Margaret Ward
in her contribution, a gender lens is applied to the
information and a more nuanced assessment is achieved.

The book contains three sections – 'The Historical Context', 'Justice, Equality and Human Rights', and 'Voices from the Front Line'. The book is introduced by what is entitled a 'Noble Call', a name derived from the customs of traditional music. This is an imaginary dialogue between Countess Markievicz and Rosie Hackett, which has been composed by (now Minister for Children) Katherine Zappone and Ann Louise Gilligan.

In the 'Historical Context' section Margaret Ward's account of Countess Markievicz's period as Minister for Labour is fascinating. It provides new and detailed information on the work of the Department of Labour during the period of the First Dáil, and shows the innovative and practical side of the Countess. She is described as looking after the rights of people before the rights of property, an attitude which was not necessarily shared by all her colleagues. Dr Ward firmly rejects the all too common view of Markievicz as being highly eccentric and overly emotional. While she was undoubtedly unconventional, she was also businesslike in her approach to her Ministerial role.

In a further interesting contribution Sonja Tiernan writes of the life and career of Eva Gore-Booth, and stresses the importance of her influence in women's fight for the franchise and for political rights. Senator Ivana Bacik surveys the historic and continuing impact of the Constitution on the rights of women, and Marie O'Connor tells a very personal and moving history of the impact of symphysiotomy on women.

The section entitled 'Justice, Equality and Human Rights' surveys many of the familiar inequalities and diminished rights which have affected women during the 'Century of Progress', and which still affect them today. In a book covering such a wide range of topics it is impossible to refer to all the contributions here, but among others there is an excellent survey by Jane O'Sullivan of Ireland and gender inequality under the international spotlight. Justine McCarthy casts an expert eye over the role of women in politics and Claire O'Hagan writes of the gendered order of caring. The National Traveller Women's Forum provides an account of gender issues in the traveller community. I was a member of the Second Commission on the Status of Women led by Ms Justice Mella Carroll in the 1980s. I clearly recall speaking to traveller women themselves about the double discrimination they suffered as travellers and as women; it is clear that this still prevails.

The section entitled 'Voices from the Front Line', as the title implies, consists in the main of personal accounts by a number of women who have experienced discrimination or suffering and have been failed by the 'Century of Progress'. Mariaam Bhatti's account of the experience of migrant domestic workers reveals a side of society of which too little is known. Ruth Riddick illustrates the long and weary road that often has to be followed by the political activist.

A Century of Progress? Irish Women Reflect taken as a whole is a substantial work. A particular strength is the careful listing of sources for all material. The Countess Markievicz School deserves congratulation for the initiation and organisation of this book, as do the joint editors Alan Hayes and Máire Meagher. I hope that the book will be widely read and that it will also spur on today's women to achieve needed progress during the coming century.

THE COUNTESS MARKIEVICZ SCHOOL: THE STORY SO FAR

Niamh Murray

In January 2011, in a bar in Dublin's north inner city, the first meeting of the Countess Markievicz School took place. Brigid Bergin Mooney and Áine Carroll joined Lucy Keaveney and myself that evening. We were all UCD Equality Studies students and it was via the School of Social Justice mailing list that Lucy first proposed the meeting. Coincidentally, and unbeknownst to us, the first political meeting that Constance Markievicz had attended in Dublin over 100 years earlier was on nearby North Great Georges Street. Her initiation into the women's political arena was courtesy of Helena Molony who, in 1908, invited her to a meeting of Inghinidhe na hÉireann, Maud Gonne's nationalist women's organisation. The aim of that meeting was to establish a women's newspaper and the radical journal *Bean na hÉireann* emerged as a result. In publishing *A Century of Progress? Irish Women Reflect*, we are seeking to emulate their example, by publishing a collection of essays which chronicle the lives of Irish women of our time.

From the outset of the Markievicz School our concern was the lack of women in public and political life in Ireland and the impact that this was having. The situation, particularly politically, seemed to be regressing for women, who are the largest population group in Ireland comprising some 51%. At the time, women represented only 15% of Ireland's national parliament, Dáil Éireann. The large gender imbalance at parliamentary level undoubtedly had a knock-on effect on public policy decisions affecting women. Statistically, women were behind in virtually every tenet of Irish society, the sole exception being participation in third level education where the positive statistics did not translate as easily into the workforce.

We decided to establish an annual forum on women in Ireland, to provide a platform for and raise consciousness about issues relating to women's equality. We envisaged that discussion panels would address aspects of gender inequality. But would simply talking go far enough in achieving change? We decided the school would be non-partisan and operate on an ethos of equality; admission was free to guarantee that money would not be an impediment to potential attendees. In our efforts to raise funds we were careful to avoid corporate sponsorship – thus we are grateful to the trade union sector for their support, particularly SIPTU, INTO, TUI, ASTI and the UCD School of Social Justice. We decided to video the Markievicz School to widen the audience by making the debates accessible for those not in a position to attend. Because they capture the issues of our time, the repository of videos on the website will serve as a valuable future archive.

We were complete novices at both organising committees and event management. Our early days were ad hoc, slightly unorthodox and characterised by a zero bank balance. One night shortly after our first meeting we attended a pre-general-election debate in the Button Factory, Temple Bar, chaired by journalist and broadcaster Vincent Browne. One of the speakers that evening was Mary Lou McDonald TD. Deciding that she would be an ideal speaker for our first event, I was given the task of 'door-stepping' the formidable Mary Lou. My mission was to hang around outside the bathrooms, hardly decorous and somewhat comical on reflection, but it was successful – Mary Lou agreed to take part.

We set our sights high that first year, looking toward Scandinavia, the bastion of equality, for inspiration. In retrospect, inviting an international speaker and offering to cover the mileage, a cost we could ill-afford, was a risky move, yet it proved pivotal. Arni Hole from the Ministry of Social Inclusion in Norway spoke about gender quotas and paid parental leave which seemed a long way off in the Ireland of 2011. Hole, who described 'gender equality as the smart economy' was 'astonished' at some of the statistics, likening the Irish experience to the Norwegian one of 35 years previously. Fortunately, Arni Hole was so taken aback at the status of gender inequality in Ireland that she waived her airfare in sympathy. The committee collectively emitted a sigh of relief.

Despite some rudimentary mistakes, including holding our inaugural event on a scorching June bank holiday weekend, the first Countess Markievicz School was a success. Over one hundred people attended the event and the energy was palpable in the Teachers' Club on Parnell Square. During the break, people sat on beer kegs outside in the yard, chatting and networking over coffee in the blazing sun. These connections, some rekindled and others newly sparked, had been inadvertently orchestrated by virtue of us holding the event. Geraldine Moane, lecturer in UCD School of Social Justice, encapsulates the importance of this: 'Creating connections ... where the emphasis is on building strengths and developing a sense of belonging to community ... can provide a positive focus for action'. What we were attempting to do was essentially pretty basic, but it was unique and many of the women in attendance felt an important space had been created. 'It reassured me that I am not alone in thinking we need a women's movement in Ireland today', one 2011 attendee remarked.

Since our inception attendees have provided regular feedback which subsequently has been used to determine future themes, many of which are reflected in the chapters of this book. We chose topics for discussion which we felt reflected the issues at a particular time – for example women and poverty was chosen to mark the centenary of the 1913 Lockout. That year, National Archive historian Catríona Crowe described life in tenement Dublin a century beforehand, whilst in echoes of the past, Graham Usher outlined the stark situation for residents of the Priory Hall apartment complex on the northside of Dublin, a modern day tenancy nightmare.

Six years on a myriad of unresolved issues remain; the sheer volume of articles in this book underscores the many issues which women in the Ireland of 2016 still face. Indeed, the short time since the inception of the Markievicz School in 2011 has seen the equality framework of the State itself being dismantled; with the abolition of the Equality Authority and the long delay in re-establishing its successor, the Irish Human Rights and Equality Commission (IHREC). These changes have occurred in tandem with the enormous budgetary cuts to the National Women's Council of Ireland and many other non-governmental organisations tasked with ensuring rights are upheld. The economic recession during these years resulted in political decisions being made which increased inequality in Irish society. Women, particularly single parents and those in precarious employment, were disproportionately affected by such decisions, so it is critical that there is a platform available for women to challenge, highlight or campaign on these issues.

There has been some progress. The introduction of gender quotas saw the recent general election return 22% female TDs to Dáil Éireann, a significant increase on the previous figure of 15%, yet the statistic still falls well short of the voluntary minimum 40% quota for either gender in Norwegian political parties. At the time of writing, a new Family Leave Bill is being progressed through the Houses of the Oireachtas which will provide for paid paternity leave. Since 2011, a number of women have been appointed to high profile roles in Irish public life, including Susan Denham as Chief Justice, Frances Fitzgerald as Minister for Justice and Joan Burton as Tanáiste. Symbolically, these are important appointments. It is particularly important for young girls to see female figureheads, they need role models as aspiration. The situation is a welcome contrast to my own childhood, growing up in the 1980s where it was predominantly grey-haired men in suits who talked politics on television.

Perhaps the most affecting moment for Irish women was the death of Savita Halappanavar, an event which has left an indelible mark on Irish society. Her death triggered a huge outpouring of public sympathy and saw thousands take to the streets for the March for Savita. The solemn candlelit procession with the refrain, 'Never Again', wound its way silently through the streets of the capital as darkness descended one cold Saturday afternoon in November 2012. Halappanavar's death was a watershed moment for contemporary Irish feminism as it instigated the campaign to 'Repeal the Eighth' amendment. Clare Daly, the first member of parliament to bring a private members bill to the Dáil on the issue, has written about it in this book. Indeed, the fact that several chapters address the issue is testament to the lack of reproductive choice in Ireland as an inequality which prevails.

Significantly, this book features women whose voices aren't often heard; women from minority groups who are living on the margins of Irish society. We were keen to highlight the issue of direct provision and its impact on women and children in particular. Upon inviting Kubby Olatilewa to speak at the 2015 school, we were ashamed to discover that we needed to send official invitations to Kubby and Pamela Kpaduwa, who has contributed a chapter to this volume. The women requested these to present to management at the direct provision centre, so that they could be given leave to attend the Markievicz School.

The struggle of women still seeking justice for past abuses is also addressed in this book. Chapters on symphysiotomy and the Magdalene Laundries provoke a sense of incredulity in the younger generation at the abuses suffered by women who came before us and the treatment they were, and continue to be, subjected to at the hands of the State. The strength and passion of women in the community sector fighting cuts in an era of public-private partnership and privatisation is told by some of its activists, many of whom have charted their course over decades of campaigning.

In 1937, many of Constance Markievicz's friends and comrades, including Maud Gonne MacBride, Dr Kathleen Lynn, Hanna Sheehy Skeffington, Kathleen Clarke and Helena Molony campaigned at the inclusion of Article 41.2, 'by her life within the home, woman gives to the State a support without which the common good cannot be achieved', in the new Irish Constitution. Remarkably, this archaic clause remains intact, despite vast societal changes and the recommendations of the Constitutional Convention.

Each year, our modus operandi is to invite a variety of speakers on an issue, attempting to create a fusion of ideas and perspectives. Grassroots activists, research academics, NGO campaigners, journalists and politicians as legislators are invited. The committee is always conscious of the importance of the 'experiential' expert – the person working on the ground, one who can best articulate an issue, yet is often excluded from debates – in the media, in the Dáil, in policy groups and so forth. The experiential voice is always considered to be of paramount importance, partly owing to the influence of our then Equality Studies lecturer, Professor Kathleen Lynch.

Indeed, over the years, the voice of experience has proven to be most powerful at the Markievicz School. In 2015, we listened to the harrowing testimonies of women living in direct provision, or what is often termed Ireland's modern day 'Magdalene Laundries'. Emily Logan, also a speaker that day, spoke about the hidden or silenced voices in Irish society, voices we were keen to amplify. In her role as Chief Commissioner of the Irish Human Rights and Equality Commission (IHREC), Logan herself had been stymied; she was unable to comment during the marriage equality referendum campaign which had just concluded. In a historic moment, the results of the referendum were announced to great applause in the auditorium that May afternoon, shortly after her speech concluded. The marriage equality referendum count affected our audience numbers. Oversubscribed with sandwiches, we delivered several trays via taxi to Panti

Bar where we delighted in briefly bearing witness to the festivities on Capel Street.

There have been emotional moments over the years, with tears shed both onstage and in the audience: moments of shame, such as when Mariaam Bhatti described life as a domestic worker in modern Ireland, moments of pride when Eileen Flynn spoke candidly about her life as a young traveller woman and moments of fury when journalist Una Mullally recounted vignettes of abusive comments women in the media are subjected to. Over the past six years we have hosted many people who have made a difference; in terms of legislation, former Supreme Court Judge Catherine McGuinness, women such as journalist Justine McCarthy who use the written word to challenge the status quo on gender inequality and women such as Rita Fagan who campaign to empower women in the community. Fagan was instrumental in ensuring the State play a role in commemorating the Women of the 1916 Rising. She lobbied for State involvement in the event which took place in the Royal Hospital Kilmainham on International Women's Day, 8 March 2016. Rita and the women of St Michael's Family Resource Centre in Inchicore paid tribute to the women of 1916 with their moving performance of *Flames Not Flowers*.

There have been innumerable highlights in the School's trajectory. Undoubtedly, the speaker who received the greatest response was Bernadette Devlin McAliskey. Constance Markievicz was the first woman elected to Westminster, Devlin was the youngest, so there was a symbolic resonance to her participation. In her maiden speech in Westminster in 1969, Devlin referenced Markievicz and speaking at the Markievicz School in 2014 it felt as if the circle had been completed. Both women fought for social justice and were (are in Devlin's case) deeply embedded in helping those in their communities.

Devlin spoke of her early life which was in homage to the maxim that the personal is political, and attendees were enthralled by her account. 'Nobody walked like the Devlin girls' was her description of how the five sisters had been encouraged to believe in themselves. Devlin had lost both parents by her late teens and attributed this to her politicisation, 'I got into the civil rights movement because, really, there was no parental control'.

We were delighted to move to Liberty Hall for our 2013 event where we have been resident since. Symbolically, Liberty Hall is Constance Markievicz's spiritual home. Originally headquarters of the Irish Citizen Army, in which she was a lieutenant, its basement was where Markievicz and Delia Larkin organised a soup kitchen during the 1913 Lockout. After the 1916 Rising, Markievicz was appointed honorary President of the Irish Women Workers' Union and significantly became Ireland's first Minister for Labour, so the headquarters of trade union activism and labour rights is the optimal venue to commemorate her legacy.

Aside from the present book which aims to capture the zeitgeist of life for women in Ireland a century after Constance Markievicz, there have been other notable 'spin-offs' from the Markievicz School. Brigid Bergin Mooney moved on from the committee to co-establish a sister school, the Sheehy Skeffington School, an annual event which focuses on human rights. Constance Markievicz's sister, the poet and human rights campaigner Eva Gore-Booth is buried with her partner Esther Roper in Hampstead, North London. Upon discovering the grave had fallen into disrepair, Lucy Keaveney instigated a campaign to have the grave restored. Lucy enlisted then Minister of State Jimmy Deenihan and, at a fitting ceremony in London in November 2015, the Irish

Ambassador Dan Mulhall read some of Eva's poetry at the graveside.

Fast forward to the present day and the sheer volume of issues around women's equality is testament to the need for a space for women. Our remit as an organisation remains providing a space for discussion and a platform to launch ideas. We intend to widen our scope, indeed, publishing this book is one such avenue. Expansion is resource dependent and like anything hinges on financial resources.

For the centenary year, we decided to commemorate Constance Markievicz by organising a wreath-laying ceremony. On Saturday 26 March 2016 a crowd gathered in Glasnevin Cemetery where Sabina Higgins, Ireland's First Lady, laid a wreath at Markievicz's graveside. Higgins was chosen as we were keen to have a woman in a high profile public role who was non-partisan lead the event. We also wanted to include Markievicz's own voice in the proceedings and employed an actress, Anne Doyle, who recited a speech Markievicz delivered on suffrage in Dáil Éireann in March 1922. Sabina Higgins referred to Markievicz as 'a true revolutionary and true radical'. She used the event to make a rallying call to Irish people to beware the perils of capitalism, something which the socialist Countess would have greatly approved of. The following day a number of newspapers referenced our event. Significantly, in organising the event, we managed to ensure Constance Markievicz was part of the commemorations narrative.

This book is an attempt to capture the diversity of women's voices and the complexity of issues faced by women in Ireland a century after Ireland's bid for independence. We are grateful to the Department of Arts, Heritage and Gaeltacht for providing funds. As outgoing chairperson of the Countess Markievicz School, I would like to say thank you to the voluntary committee of Máire Meagher, Lucy Keaveney, Alex Kirrane, Juliet Fleming, Niamh Crudden and Lisa Connell and also to Dolores Gibbons, Martin Saunders and Jane O'Sullivan who contributed to making the Markievicz School the success it has become.

Always in our endeavours to organise the annual event, we defer to the legacy of Constance Markievicz. To her we leave the final word:

> The old idea that a woman can only serve her nation through her home is gone, so now is the time, on you the responsibility rests. No one can help you but yourselves alone ... For each of you there is a niche waiting – your place in the nation. Try and find it. It may be as a leader, it may be as a humble follower ... but it is there, and if you cannot find it for yourself, no one can find it for you.[1]

SOURCE
1   Constance Markievicz, *A Call to the Women of Ireland* (Dublin, Fergus O'Connor, 1918), p. 12. Originally delivered as a lecture entitled 'Women, Ideals, and the Nation' to the Students' National Literary Society, Dublin, 1909.

A NOBLE CALL TO THE IRISH PEOPLE
FROM CONSTANCE MARKIEVICZ AND ROSIE HACKETT

Katherine Zappone and Ann Louise Gilligan

The Risen People ran in the Abbey Theatre from Thursday 28 November 2013 to Saturday 1 February 2014. This historical play, which depicts the plight of a group of working class Dubliners in the throes of the 1913 Lockout, has itself a long and rich history. The original text is the work of esteemed Irish writer James Plunkett and formed the basis of his iconic 1963 novel, *Strumpet City.* *The Risen People* was first staged at the Abbey in 1958 before being resurrected by Jim and Peter Sheridan in 1978. The 2013 adaptation, which was directed by Jimmy Fay, draws its influence from all of these sources, and served as a timely commemoration of the centenary of the lockout.

This version of the play was also highly unique in that each performance featured a 'Noble Call' from various cultural figures. Fiach Mac Conghail, Director of the Abbey Theatre, explained the idea behind the old Irish tradition of the 'Noble Call': 'it is essentially a party piece –

a time when you're at a party where you're asking all your guests to respond to the mood and the atmosphere of the day'. According to Mac Conghail, 'it could be anything. It could be to do with responding to the themes of *The Risen People*, or politics, or their own reflection of what's happened in the last 100 years'.

Following the performance of the play on 11 January 2014, we were invited to present our 'Noble Call'. We chose to adopt the personas of two of the most prominent women in Irish history, Constance Markievicz and Rosie Hackett. The two were friends, with the Countess serving as a mentor to the young Hackett.

Our desire was to remember the extraordinary leadership and courageous commitment to revolutionary change that these two women exemplified. We also imagined that their friendship with one another was integral to their perserverance and effectiveness as agents for cultural and social change.

While we conducted research to locate written correspondence between Constance and Rosie we were unable to unearth any letters. However, by accessing other materials, including some key speeches of Countess Markievicz[1] and Rosie's own original 'Witness Statement'[2] we felt confident to imagine what they might have said about those times and about each other.

We used our 'Noble Call' to highlight the remarkable accomplishments of these two women while also calling on all of us to follow in their footsteps. Here is a written record of our performance.[3]

ANN LOUISE GILLIGAN: We'd like to end with two stories. Now, as you all know, story is above all rooted in memory. Memories of times past. But story also flowers, the best stories, into images of the possible, which call us, in our time, to reflect on how we live.

I am Rosie Hackett. I was born in 1893. I was born into an ordinary family; working-class people. My father was a barber, my mother was a housekeeper. I just had seven years of schooling and after those very few years really, I got a job as a messenger in Jacob's factory. The biscuit factory, by and large, had women employees. I'm not sure where I got it, you probably have it, but I had a deep passion for justice and I could not stand the lack of terms and conditions, and the appalling pay that these women received.

And so, in 1909, I became one of the first members of the ITGWU (Irish Transport and General Workers' Union). I was an active trade unionist all my life and I believed in the absolute importance of the unions, above all for the poorest of workers. So, in 1911, I organised the women in the factory and 3000 of them came out. Yes, I was a very young woman. But out they came with me. And yes! We Won! We got them better terms and conditions.

I joined the Irish Women Workers' Union and I also became a member of the Irish Citizen Army. But of course, it all changed in 1913, with the Lockout. We all lost our jobs – I lost my job. But I got employment in Liberty Hall. One thing I wanted to say about Liberty Hall; it is my honest belief that it was, and maybe is, the most important building in the city. I worked there at everything. I ran a printing press, and in fact it was I who ran with a copy of the Proclamation, still damp off the printing press, to Connolly.

By 1970, I was given an award – never important to me. But in 1976, my life ended and I was given military honours. Now, as many of you know, they have decided to name a bridge after me – just very close to this theatre – that spans the Liffey, and all that I would ask is, as you cross that bridge, you would stand and remember what I stood for. Stand and imagine the possible. For female, poor, women workers, above all; that they could have different terms and conditions, proper pay, in this 2013.

Now, may I introduce to you, my great, great friend. A woman who was 25 years older than I. A woman who I greatly admired and who mentored me as a young woman. I always called her 'Madame'.

KATHERINE ZAPPONE: I am Constance Georgine Markievicz. I was born into a life of privilege in 1868. My parents were leading landowners and they entertained lavishly at Lissadell. I enjoyed country pursuits – hunting, driving, riding. But I became a republican, a labour activist and an advocate for women and their suffrage. With my friend Rosie, I served soup in Liberty Hall to the strikers and their families. I was an ardent supporter of the Irish Women Workers' Union, formed two years before the lockout, and as a member of the Irish Citizen Army, with my comrade Rosie, we helped to defend the workers during their demonstrations against and from police violence.

I was sentenced to death and imprisoned many times for my radical beliefs and activities. I was the first woman to become an Irish minister, named Minister for Labour in the first Dáil Éireann. And as I said in 1918:

> Our national freedom cannot and must not be left to evolution. Fix your mind on the ideal of Ireland free. Ireland needs each of you to build up our national life. Now is the time, and on you the responsibility rests. For each one of you, there is a niche waiting – your place in the nation. Try and find it. It may be as a leader. It may be as a humble follower. But, it is there and it is for you to find. No one can find it for you.
>
> To sum up in a few words, believe in yourselves. Arm yourselves with weapons to fight your nation's causes. Arm your minds with the histories and memories of your country

and her martyrs, her language and a knowledge of her arts, and her industries. Arm your souls with noble and free ideas.

The stories of these two extraordinary and ordinary women, Rosie and Constance, inspire in us images of the possible. They remind us today that many of Ireland's people are still not free. The young will leave our shores because there are not enough jobs. Women who desire public office will still face the barriers of a patriarchal order. Lesbians and gay men will not have the right to marry the person they choose to love. Refugees and asylum seekers will continue to be denied work permits. Children will grow up in the midst of intergenerational poverty.

And so, in memory of Rosie and Constance and all of the strikers and their families, we issue, all of you, all of us, a Noble Call to become the Risen People. Rise up, again and again. Rise up.

POSTSCRIPT

On 22 May 2015 the Irish people rose up to say 'Yes' to Marriage Equality – a twenty-first century cultural and social revolution.

SOURCES

1   Contained in Margaret Ward (ed), *In Their Own Voice: Women and Irish Nationalism* (Dublin, Attic Press, 1995).

2   Rosie Hackett, 'Statement by Miss Rosie Hackett', Bureau of Military History, 1913–21, Document No W.W. 546, 26/5/1951.

3   A video of the performance can be accessed at: bit.ly/kalnoblecall.

THE HISTORICAL CONTEXT

Constance de Markievicz
Minister for Labour

Margaret Ward

Constance Markievicz's political career was notable for many achievements. Not only did she play a role as a combatant in the Easter Rising, she was also the first woman in Ireland or Britain to be elected in 1918. When she was subsequently appointed Minister for Labour in the first Dáil Éireann she became the second woman in the world to hold a government appointment. As a prominent figure in political and public life she has been inspirational to many, yet little attention has been paid to her work as a minister. This occurred during the increasingly violent period of the War of Independence which saw Markievicz 'on the run', liable to arrest at any moment and, indeed, serve several periods of imprisonment. Her commitment to a government 'that looks after the rights of the people before the rights of property'[1] was not shared by all her colleagues who were happy for the Ministry to simply placate the demands of labour in the interests of the national cause. It may also be thought that there was little to record – the Dáil met only twenty one times in two and a half years and minutes of cabinet meetings were, of necessity, brief, but we have sufficient archival sources to see that, despite numerous difficulties, she remained an energetic champion for Labour. Her contribution to developing a democratic foundation for the fledgling Irish state deserves greater attention.

In the post-Rising era, with the huge loss of James Connolly, Markievicz was the republican figure most engaged with the labour movement. While in jail she read books on political economy, conscious that the work of developing an effective counter-state to British rule over Ireland was a task that the released prisoners would soon be undertaking. From Holloway jail she sent an election message that made it plain she regarded economic freedom as part of the goal of national freedom:

> Sinn Feiners affiliated or amalgamated with English Trade Unions should be recommended when possible to sever the English connection. That where Irish resources are being developed, or where industries exist, Sinn Feiners should make it their business to secure that workers are paid a living wage.[2]

She tried to educate herself in a variety of areas. Kathleen Clarke, in Holloway with her, said she ordered books on economics, labour, socialism and other topics, although she 'would skim through it, trying in her quick way to get the sense of it'. Her intention was to give them to the Labour Party as the nucleus of a Connolly Library when she was released.[3] However, although she was the Sinn Féin figure with the closest connection to Labour, her appointment as minister was not a foregone conclusion. Clarke knew from personal experience that 'the present leaders were not over-eager to put women into places of honour or power, even though they had earned the right to both'. When she asked Markievicz how it had happened, the latter declared that she had had to 'bully them', arguing that she had earned the right and 'if she was not made a minister she would go over to the Labour Party'.[4] One can conclude, therefore, that her cabinet colleagues were not necessarily wholehearted in their enthusiasm for their female colleague. In those early days of political organisation, Markievicz appears to have glossed over difficulties, writing to her sister Eva Gore-Booth:

> my conception of a free Ireland is economic as well as political; some agree with me, some don't, but it's not a sore point. Easter Week comrades don't fall out; they laugh and chaff and disagree.[5]

It is noticeable that those who most welcomed her appointment were women. The Irish Women Workers' Union declared 'We rejoice that the first woman elected to parliament in Ireland is one to whom the workers can always confidently look to uphold their rights and just claims'[6] and the *Irish Citizen* congratulated the Dáil for its appointment of Markievicz, while regretting that it had not cast off 'the whole system of British cabinet making and British parliamentary methods'.[7]

Markievicz's conception of policy was always rooted in the practical, wanting to see change happen as soon as possible. Throughout her ministry she stressed the importance of establishing cooperatives as a means of ensuring a just reward for labour and good prices for the consumer. From jail she had written to the Irish Women Workers' Union about a potential scheme whereby Sinn Féin clubs would supply milk from the country and send this to a cooperative shop in her constituency, selling the milk for 5d a quart instead of 8d. However, war conditions prevented this development.[8]

While appraisals of her performance as Minister vary widely, their diversity seems to be rooted in gender bias. Seán Ó Faoláin her first (and only male) biographer was fairly dismissive of her performance as Minister. Although he acknowledged that she was not 'generally popular with men in revolutionary circles' he did not consider whether misogyny might be an explanation.[9] His portrayal deeply upset Helena Molony, her friend and comrade from the Inghinidhe na hÉireann days, who unsuccessfully attempted to persuade him to make amendments to his text. She was withering in her explanation for the limitations of his approach:

> It is a curious thing that many men seem to be unable to believe that any woman can embrace an ideal – accept it intellectually, feel it as a profound emotion, and then calmly decide to make a vocation of working for its realization. They give themselves endless pains to prove that every serious thing a woman does (outside nursing babies or washing pots) is the result of being in love with some man, or disappointed in love of some man, or looking for excitement or limelight, or indulging their vanity. You do not seem to have escaped from the limitations of your sex … She allied herself with these later movements because they were advancing the ideals which she had accepted years ago. We were writing about Labour conditions, women's labour in particular – years before Larkin came to Ireland and she never 'abandoned' or 'drew away from' that cause.[10]

A short study of Markievicz in R.M. Fox's *Rebel Irishwomen* appeared in 1935, one year after Ó Faoláin's work. Fox, a socialist, also knew her, and wrote an account full of admiration for the woman whose meetings he often attended and whose oratory was capable of 'rising to great heights'. For him she worked, as Minister:

> under tremendous difficulties, to further the democratic ideas for which she stood … The demonstration of justice, the restriction of rents and profiteering went on, and in all these important activities Madame Markievicz played her part.[11]

Elizabeth Coxhead's short biography had the advantage of including reminiscences from a number of Markievicz's contemporaries. Although short on detail, Coxhead believed that her 'detractors' were 'much too ready to give credit' for success to substitute deputies appointed while Markievicz was in jail, ignoring the fact that 'the idealism, the vision, the directing brain were hers' and that foundation was what contributed to its successes.[12] Other biographers, in considering her period as Minister, have tended to emphasise her idealism and vitality, the hectic round of meetings she undertook and her love of dressing up in order to evade possible capture. Van Voris includes anecdotes of notable occasions, for example, Markievicz frightening one employer to agree to a settlement in an arbitration case by pretending to have a tip off that the premises were about to be raided by the crown forces[13] and Diana Norman recounts her brainwave in hiding departmental papers from British forces by placing a trunkful of papers in a second-hand shop.[14] Haverty follows this pattern and does not analyse the everyday work of the department. However, she believes that, while much of the Dáil work was 'merely propaganda', Labour was among the 'more effective in its practice'.[15] She adds that Markievicz, 'almost alone in her sympathy with Labour ... had little power to develop the more radical tendencies of the revolution, try as she might'.[16] Sari Oikarinen's more academic study emphasises the paucity of archival material and the fragmentary nature of her ministry due to imprisonment (mid-June until mid-October 1919 and from 26 September 1920 to July 1921) but concludes that Markievicz wanted to establish a nationally-organised Labour movement, to act as arbitrator between nationalists and socialists, to get the Dáil to back more radical reforms, and to have:

> an Ireland where the sexes would be equal, where the land would provide a living for every family and where all the different sections of the population would solve their problems together.

As Oikarinen admits, this was 'difficult to achieve in time of peace, and almost impossible to further in time of war'.[17]

In contrast, the impression given by some historians of the period is that her contribution was insignificant. Either the real work was done by the men who substituted for her during her periods of imprisonment, or she, as Minister, had no real understanding of the type of work that should be carried out. Arthur Mitchell, who has produced the most comprehensive study of the work of Dáil Éireann in setting up its 'counter-state' emphasizes the 'firebrand' qualities of Markievicz, quoting British officials to the effect that her imprisonment would be 'a relief' to Sinn Feiners.[18] However it could be argued that the British reactions were a product of misogyny rather than based on any kind of hard evidence and Mitchell relies on hearsay for this anecdote. Bizarrely, when outlining the backgrounds of the cabinet members, he describes her only as a former actress and youth organizer, with inherited wealth.[19] While he has doubts about the achievements of some of the departments, his contrast of Markievicz with Ernest Blythe, the Minister for Trade and Commerce, is breathtaking in its dismissal of one and understanding of the difficulties facing the other – when the reality is that the difficult conditions impacted equally on all departments of the Dáil:

> As Minister for Labour, she made no effort to establish standards for employment or anything of the sort ... Given the conditions under which the Dáil government operated, it is not surprising that Blythe's department achieved little.[20]

While Mitchell also states that her department initially had little to do and requested an appropriation of only £400 for the second half of 1920, he does not add that as she was in jail from September she was therefore not responsible for expenditure at this period.[21] Nor does he give any information regarding later expenditure of the department.

As we shall see, on her release from jail she had to conduct a vigorous campaign with the cabinet office in order to obtain increased finances for her department in 1921.

Most recently, Diarmaid Ferriter makes reference to her contribution as Minister for Labour, stressing the degree of social and economic turmoil that existed at this period, and the efforts of Sinn Féin politicians to prevent class conflict through emphasizing 'cross-class alliances' in the national interest. It is evident that Markievicz did not dispute this approach, but at the same time she made plain her sympathies with the struggling working class. While Ferriter appears to be understanding of the circumstances in which she operated, providing an example of a letter she wrote to Limerick County Council in which she criticized them for not supporting a motion that the council employ only trade union labour, 'Far from being a coercive measure, it is a measure for the protection of the worker against the constant encroachment on their liberties by the employing classes', he then goes on to question whether 'this devotion to the labour cause' was widely shared, asking 'was it meaningful in the first place or was it just a sop to SF's allies?'[22] This approach appears to imply that the establishment of the Labour Ministry was more or less a ploy to placate the labour movement at a period when the nationalist cause had to take precedence and its activities were of little account. It is clear that most members of the Dáil, many from middle class or rural backgrounds, had little interest in the cause of labour (the lack of any discussion on the Democratic Programme made that clear), but in assessing Markievicz as Labour Minister one cannot simply criticize the lack of interest evidenced by her colleagues.

How can one provide a more nuanced assessment of Markievicz's short career as Minister for Labour? While the historical records provide information that contradicts much of what has been written to date, we also need to apply a gender lens to that information so that we can contextualize the experience of our first female cabinet minister.

There were ten men and one woman in the Cabinet, and altogether sixty nine members of the Dáil, sixty eight of whom were male. The average age was mid-forties. What could it have been like for a middle-aged woman (she was fifty-one-years old in 1919), under-educated as all upper-class women were at this period (and trying to educate herself through reading while in the quietude of prison), entering Dáil Éireann after serving a period of more than a year in jail, to be the only woman in the chamber? The brief minutes of proceedings indicate that she was determined to ensure that her voice would be heard. The second session of Dáil Éireann took place between 1–11 April 1919 (after the release of the prisoners), with an attendance of 52 members. The first day was concerned with procedural issues. Of seven amendments of standing orders, Constance Markievicz seconded four. They were not particularly significant, being concerned with how deputies addressed each other; provision for expenses of 3rd class rail 15/- a day; the need for a quorum, but they showed an eagerness to make a contribution and a determination to ensure that the sole female voice would be heard. The following day, 2 April, she was formally appointed as Minister for Labour, proposed by Liam de Roiste and seconded by Sean Etchingham. On that day too she was nominated, along with ten men, onto a Select Committee to report on children kidnapped by British agents and the condition of absent deputies and other prisoners of war in jails in Ireland and England. Significantly, she also seconded a motion that was moved by Alex McCabe (Sligo), 'that the Assembly pledges itself to fair and full redistribution of vacant lands and ranches of Ireland among the uneconomic holders and landless men'. In its simplicity and in its good intentions, this motion was quintessentially of the woman. But wholescale redistribution would have entailed a much more radical agenda than had been promised in the Democratic Programme. After discussion, the motion was withdrawn, but a committee to consider land policy was formed. McCabe, although not Markievicz, was nominated.[23] This initiative must have been the reason why, also that April, Sinn Féin established a sub-committee to create a plan for cooperative 'land acquisition and working'; and the defining of a proper land policy.[24] By December 1919 the Dáil had set up a National Land Bank to lend money to cooperatives of landless farm labourers. This was not a social revolution, but it was a constructive programme that helped in some areas to quell discontent through providing help with land purchases. When there were disputes over land, however, it would seem that it was the landlords who were favoured by the courts.[25] It was not, however, an area of responsibility for Labour, but was entrusted to the Department of Agriculture.

During the few days of the second session of the Dáil, Markievicz also took part in a debate on the League of Nations, giving her support to President Wilson (wrongly as it turned out, because Wilson, needing the support of Britain to achieve a League of Nations, prevented discussion on the Irish question at the Peace Conference) and also in a debate on the 'Freedom of the Seas', where deputies debated the dominance of Britain to the detriment of Irish trade. Markievicz believed, somewhat idealistically, that the issue should be looked at from a 'world point of view', and that it might be possible that the nations of the world would come together against Britain 'on the question of the trading of the world or the freedom of the seas'.[26]

She was also, at this time, one of a number of people who supported the members of the American Commission on Ireland on a fact-finding mission, and who later, on 9 May, addressed the Dáil in a public session, talking of their findings and of their horror at discovering the conditions under which elected members were forced to operate. Van Voris claimed that the influence of Markievicz was apparent 'in their reports of attacks on women and children, the kidnapping of children for interrogation, in information on education, infant mortality figures and the appalling destitution and hunger'. In addition, the substantial section on labour 'bears signs of her indignation' as it praised 'the best organized and most coherent labor movement in the world [which] is being thwarted and suppressed by the army and constabulary'.[27] Members of the Commission, after being in her company, were concerned to discover that she was shadowed everywhere, with threats made against her.

On 13 June Markievicz was arrested and charged with sedition, serving four months imprisonment in Cork jail as a result. Tom Kelly was a brief substitute before he too was arrested. She was released on 16 October and the report of Dáil Éireann on 27 October stated she would again take up the work of the department. Arthur Griffith, as Acting President, added that 'The department has, in its brief existence, a good record to show'. The report from Labour declared that a Central Conciliation Board had been established for the settlement of trade disputes and 'a large number of disputants' had already availed of its services. On a strategic level it was reported that statistics regarding food prices, costs of production, wages, hours and conditions of employment were being prepared 'with a view to scheduling Area Groups showing an approximate level of conditions and thereby promoting stability in the employment of labour'.[28]

In 1920, as the war intensified, the Dáil was driven underground. Dáil Éireann met only on 29 June, 6 August and 17 September, but the cabinet continued to meet, in a variety of locations, mainly in the private homes of sympathizers. Meetings were short, to reduce the possibility of the ministers being caught together and the minutes, in their brevity, reflect these difficulties. Markievicz, appearing at a cabinet meeting in the disguise of a charwoman, caused much amusement amongst colleagues.[29] Very differently, Robert Barton recalled her attending a meeting 'cleverly disguised as an attractive young girl'.[30] A scrawled hand-written note from Markievicz (with the heading of Department of Local Government crossed out and Ministry for Labour handwritten on top) dated 27 February 1920 gave details of what she wanted to have included at the cabinet meeting the next day.[31] Diarmuid O'Hegarty, who was Cabinet Secretary and a person of considerable influence, sent her the Cabinet response: It was not feasible at the present to make grants to hospitals that have treated 'the suffering soldiers of the Republic' (Markievicz's words); on the issue of the non-cultivation of land by farmers, she was instructed to cooperate with the Minister for Agriculture in order to form a Central Conciliation Board composed of representatives of the Farmers' Union and Labour and the Ministers. The specific example of land in Maynooth was deferred until a report on the situation was received. On queries regarding wages in local authorities, the Secretary for Local Government would obtain any necessary information for the Minister and finally, payment was agreed for the expenses of Art O'Connor's work regarding the Tralee labour dispute.[32] Dáil records later noted the 'successful intervention of the Minister in association with Mr Art O'Connor TD in serious disputes in the counties of Kerry, Kildare, and Meath'.[33]

The scrawled hand-written note of February would seem to indicate that the Ministry had not yet been fully established with regards to staffing. That was delayed until June 1920, when the Ministry was in a position to submit a lengthy 5-page foolscap report of its work, starting with the establishment of Arbitration Courts for trade disputes. Markievicz was careful not to undermine the significance of the trade union movement, nor to attempt to usurp their role in arbitration. She recognized that trade unions were dealing with cases every day, and advised the Dáil that arbitration should only occur when both employers and workers recognized the authority of Dáil Éireann and where the matter could not be settled directly by trade union officials and employers. She explained the importance of urging the establishment of Irish trade unions – it was not only a nationalist objective, they had found that in some cases disputes could not be settled as unions with English executives were unable to come to decisions that were separate from that agreed in England. The Ministry was encouraging the development of an Irish Engineering Trades Union. Those who wanted to start one had received £100 to launch their scheme at a meeting in the Abbey Theatre. There were practical benefits to having an Irish union as payment of benefits was easier and union dues would be retained within Ireland and no longer lodged in English banks. An Irish Musician's Union also formed at this time. While Arthur Mitchell condemned her inactivity on setting a national pay scale, her report explained that the Ministry was discussing a 'scale for a minimum rate of wages on which to base labour arbitration; to take the place of the British document at present in use'. She added that the Ministry also intended to draw up a scheme of insurance, to be ready for the time it will be possible to get it adopted. She ended by urging Dáil members to 'press on the people in their constituencies the importance of using Irish goods' – four hundred girls were thrown idle in Dublin 'owing to the decrease in smoking of Irish cigarettes alone'.[34]

None of this evidence substantiates claims that disputes were settled in the employer's favour, or that Markievicz, as Minister, made no effort to establish national wage levels. What is evident is that war conditions limited the implementation of strategies being devised by the Ministry to help improve working class conditions and economic conditions – particularly the post-war agricultural depression and trade slump – limited the power of the Irish labour movement. One anecdote, from Louie Bennett of the Irish Women Workers' Union, would indicate that Markievicz was firmly on the side of the workers. When an employer refused to make any concessions regarding a wage demand, Markievicz rushed into the meeting at the Sinn Féin offices in Harcourt Street with the news that the military were on their way to raid the office. Louie Bennett would make no concessions either, as 'this was one of the worst firms'. Only when the military had almost reached the door did the employer agree to pay the same wages as other firms. R.M. Fox, who told this story in his biographical study of Louie Bennett, concluded 'The Black-and-Tans unwittingly helped to get a rise in pay for sweated workers that day'[35] but one is left with the impression Markievicz had deliberately used the threat of an imminent raid to pressurize the employer.

Now that we have witness statements from the Military Archives we can hear the voices of some of those with whom she worked. Testimony from individual staff members in the Ministry of Labour reveal Markievicz as a person who was capable and involved. They describe a woman who was business-like (if unconventional) and down to earth. Cumann na mBan member Eilis Ryan was a member of staff from the outset, recalling that 'Madame welcomed me in Irish and offered me a cigarette'.[36] Dick Cotter, who had been a civil servant before fighting in Jacob's Factory during the Rising, was a highly effective departmental secretary, operating under the *nom de plume* of 'Mr Kennedy'. He was appointed on 7 July 1920 and he and Eilis Ryan organized the Ministry office, which was based at 14 North Frederick Street (with a cover address in 61 Highfield Road, Rathgar used for communications). Furniture was bought at auction and curtains made to screen the inhabitants from the street. Within a week the office was fully functioning. Ryan recalled Markievicz arriving with 'terrific knocking – three times at the door', congratulating Cotter 'on the magnificent appearance of the premises and the general atmosphere of the surroundings and said she looked forward to splendid work being done in her Department'. As camouflage, a few pianos were placed in the office so female staff could masquerade as teachers and students of music in the event of a raid. Two planks of wood reached from the garden to the back window of the second storey so that staff could make a quick escape if necessary.[37]

Cotter reported that the first real work of the department occurred at the beginning of August 1920, when the Minister for Labour 'circularised all the Public Authorities in Ireland suggesting a scheme for the amicable settlement of disputes that might arise between such bodies and their officials or employees'.[38] At the Dáil session of 6 August 1920 Markievicz announced that a scheme to set up Conciliation Boards had been developed 'to settle disputes between local councils and their employees'. She asked deputies to send in names of individuals who would be willing to act as chairmen of Conciliation Boards or as Arbitrators in ordinary labour disputes. Terence McSwiney seconded her motion, which was carried.[39] Most Public Authorities had pledged allegiance to Dáil Éireann and adopted the scheme, which was designed to challenge British machinery for settling salaries and wages of public officials. Markievicz, Cotter and Joseph McGrath also attended a conference held to consider the question of state insurance. Given the conditions under which they were operating, this was not considered feasible, but it was recommended that approved societies should transfer their investments from government stocks to Irish trustee stocks.[40]

That July, Markievicz, along with Michael Collins, Erskine Childers and others, had met some members of the RIC who had been involved in a police mutiny in Listowel the month previously when they had refused to hand over their barracks to the British army, subsequently resigning from the police force. They claimed that Chief Inspector of Constabulary Smyth had incited the police force to shoot without warning men and women who were challenging the British forces. The issue received enormous publicity, illustrating as it did the depth of resistance to British policy in Ireland, and ex-Constable Jeremiah Mee was to play an important role in symbolising that resistance. Although Mee had met with several leading figures in Sinn Féin, it was Markievicz who invited him to join her department, where she appointed him to run an employment bureau for former RIC members, to encourage further resignations from the police. His memoirs recall 'Madame' 'doing things in dramatic style' as she insisted on administering to him the oath of allegiance to the Irish Republic:

> Having completed the ceremony of oath-taking she sat down, handed me another cigarette and said: 'Thank God at least one R.I.C. man has taken an oath to the Irish Republic'. I afterwards discovered that the book was a book of poems by William Butler Yeats.[41]

His testimony again reinforces the impression of a woman full of warmth and a sense of humour, even in the dangerous conditions of wartime as she received Mee 'in the most friendly manner' and took 'great delight' in introducing IRA men who visited the office to the 'RIC man from Kerry', going into 'a fit of laughter at the shock the visitor would get'. According to Mee, Collins opposed his appointment as a 'dangerous man' while Markievicz retorted that she would take him into her own office and if he proved to be 'a wrong un', she would herself 'do the shooting'.[42] The Cabinet minutes note that 'Madame may get extra staff if necessary to cope with this work but must provide for Volunteers also'.[43] Mee's appointment was not ratified by the Dáil until 10 September, when Lily O'Brennan, sister of Áine Ceannt and a Cumann na mBan member, was appointed to organise an employment bureau for out of work republicans.[44] Early in September a circular under the name of Countess de Markievicz, Minister for Labour, was sent out to all local bodies and those who employed large numbers of workers, asking for their help in coming to the aid of men victimized because they would not participate in the 'outrages' of creameries and homes being burnt and the daily terrors and callous shootings that people were forced to endure:

> I wrote to ask you to co-operate with me in finding work for these men, and I would ask you, if there are any vacant jobs under your patronage for which they would be suitable to communicate with me. The majority of these men seek employment as clerks, stewards, agents, motor drivers, etc.[45]

While few employers were in a position to offer employment, the circular appears to have been successful in encouraging resignations from the force, as by November 1,100 men had left in protest against British atrocities in Ireland. Mee paid tribute to Markievicz's intelligence as well as her personality, 'She was a grand person to work with and was one of the few who understood the question of the RIC as an economic rather than a political one'. That month, Markievicz was again arrested and Mee felt her arrest to be 'a great blow'.[46] Although he acknowledged that they were able to carry on under the various substitute ministers, one has a strong impression that she was an inspirational force to her small staff. His involvement with the General Employment Agency did not last for long. It is possible that Markievicz's imprisonment left him without a champion. At any rate, he then moved to working more with Michael Collins and by late October had become an organizer for the campaign to boycott British goods, retaining his link with the Labour Ministry.

In September 1920 the Ministry reported that it had been involved in 27 arbitration cases: 8 were successful, 5 unsuccessful, 14 were being dealt with and £500 was required for the fees and expenses involved. By January 1921 Lily O'Brennan had thirty Volunteers employed out of fifty-eight applications and sixteen Cumann na mBan members had been found employment, with twenty one still unemployed.[47] Markievicz was self-deprecating about her achievement, writing to her sister Eva as she went to prison, 'Well – I got it underway so that it goes on just as well without me. That wasn't too bad for an untried fool, was it?'[48]

Dick Cotter, as Departmental Secretary, was the person who held things together in this time of uncertainty and danger. He reported to the Cabinet on McGrath, her substitute, appointed in November, 'He had scarcely time to get a grip of the details of what had been previously done before he himself was arrested on 2 December'.[49] Joseph MacDonagh became Substitute Minister in February 1921. His primary focus was the organisation of the Belfast Boycott, although he also wanted to develop a labour policy that would be 'suitable to the ideals and requirements of the Irish people', and to that end he attempted to establish a Commission to consider the matter. Louie Bennett and Hanna Sheehy Skeffington were amongst those invited[50] but only one meeting took place, the second lacking a quorum of members. It then disappeared without trace.[51] It was an indication of the difficulties of trying to operate in wartime conditions.

The Belfast Boycott was a response to pogroms against nationalists in the north, targeting banks, insurance companies and goods manufactured in Belfast and goods going from Dublin to Belfast. Several of her colleagues reported that Markievicz was not in favour of the boycott and she was vocal in opposition in the Dáil, arguing that she was not convinced a blockade could be made effective and she feared it 'would be playing into the hands of the enemy and giving them a good excuse for partition'. She seconded an unsuccessful motion of Ernest Blythe's which favoured a commercial embargo 'against individuals responsible for inciting to the recent pogroms in Belfast'.[52] It is an interesting example of a moment when Markievicz was not in favour of the most militant possible policy, contradicting the impression given by many that she was always in favour of the most extreme action and would happily resort to the gun to achieve her goal. Ernest Blythe, Minister for Trade and Commerce, and the one Northerner in the Cabinet, corroborated her dislike of the boycott, including in his statement another memory of Markievicz. While ministers 'received each other's reports without much comment and without bothering to enter on much discussion', they once devoted considerable time to reviewing a death sentence imposed for a shooting committed during a land dispute. A local Volunteer courtmartial had been held and the gunman was found guilty of murder and sentenced to death. Blythe remembered that 'the matter came up before the Cabinet as the authority vested with the prerogative of mercy. Madame Markievicz, I remember, was disinclined to sanction the carrying out of the sentence', but the Cabinet eventually agreed that the sentence should be carried out because the man 'had been tried by the only sort of court possible and had undoubtedly been guilty of murder'.[53]

Máire O'Byrne, who began work in the Ministry for Labour in mid-1921, also provides evidence for Markievicz as a woman who thought twice before resorting to force. While MacDonagh had most to do with the conduct of the Boycott, which was at its height while she was in jail, O'Byrne recalled that 'the countess took it up enthusiastically' on her release. However, when the staff discussed organizing a raiding exhibition on a shop situated opposite Dublin Castle that had transgressed the boycott order by stocking numerous household items made in the north, they were conscious that they were likely to be fired on, given the location of the shop. Markievicz then declared 'Is it worth losing even one soldier's life for a few British goods? I think we can do it some other way'. The eventual alternative was that Máire volunteered, believing that she would be safer from violent retaliation because she was a woman. Overruling the protests of the men, Markievicz backed her and she was successful.[54] We can see in this the sense of camaraderie within the department, and the Minister's disregard for gender conventions.

Markievicz's return to the Ministry following her release from prison during the Truce of July 1921 showed her to be determined to re-assert her authority by putting in a request for substantial extra resources. In her opinion, the estimate submitted by Acting Minister MacDonagh, 'does not provide by any means sufficient funds for the efficient working of this department'. Her revised estimate was a substantial increase, reflecting increased office costs, greater levels of activity and a desire to increase pay levels as well as to acknowledge the amounts of overtime that had been worked, 'particularly since I resumed office, and none of them up to the present have been paid for any overtime'.[55] Arbitration costs were steadily rising and she believed that they would increase even more for the months October to December. There was a considerable difference between the £1244 estimate submitted by MacDonagh and the £1586.0.0 being claimed by

Markievicz. Staffing levels in the department had risen from three to seven people, a reflection of the increased volume of work. Her request was not immediately complied with. Correspondence between Cotter and O'Hegarty continued for almost one month, as the President's Department demanded to see the original and revised estimates while the Finance Department, under Collins, failed to produce their report on the issue for cabinet meetings on 11 and 15 November. On 17 November the Accountant General in the Department of Finance finally reported that in his opinion 'the matter could be put right' by having a contingency vote of £300. He recognized the increase in staff and concluded that the salaries were 'none too large, if the quality and quantity of the work is up to standard'.[56] There was eventual victory for Markievicz on 18 November when a contingency vote for £350 was passed by the Dáil. One wonders if all departments had this level of scrutiny for what were not extortionate amounts of money?

Having obtained additional resources, Markievicz continued to develop the work of her department. No longer having to work underground, she was able, on 29 November, to write to Edward Stephens, a Dublin solicitor, who was a nationalist but not a republican, to ask for his help with arbitration:

> Dear Mr Stephens
> I am writing to ask you if you would consent to act occasionally for me as Arbitrator in Labour disputes. I believe that your name would be one that would inspire confidence to both sides. I am very anxious to have a few such names as yours on our panels, that I can call on in important and delicate cases, men too with either general knowledge of business or with a technical knowledge of any certain business.[57]

A Second Dáil had been returned unopposed in May 1921 (and Markievicz was now joined by five other women), but, as Diarmuid O'Hegarty commented, 'The task of bringing together ninety members including several well-known ladies will be a big one'.[58] As a consequence the new Dáil did not meet until August, when the more favourable conditions of the Truce enabled deputies to appear in public. The difficulties in obtaining office costs had its origins in something greater than what appears to have been a deteriorating relationship between Markievicz and some of her colleagues. De Valera had decided to reorganize his cabinet. He wanted a smaller executive and in August the Ministry for Labour was one of those demoted. Being outside of the Cabinet and unable to appeal directly to influential colleagues must have contributed to the protracted negotiations on future resources. Robert Brennan, a Wicklow landowner, appointed to a newly-created ministry, stated that 'Agriculture, Commerce and Labour were under me as Minister for Economic Affairs' as de Valera considered they 'should be better co-ordinated in this manner'.[59] When the new structure was announced in the Dáil on 23 August, Kate O'Callaghan rose to declare she 'regretted that the only woman member of the Cabinet would not be given Cabinet rank in the new arrangement'. Mary MacSwiney agreed, adding that in her view 'it was creating a precedent'. Cathal Brugha, Minister for Defence, who had proposed the motion for re-organisation on the President's behalf, joked that 'no one knew yet who was going to be on the new cabinet. It might be all ladies (laughter)'[60] Throughout, Markievicz stayed silent. Two days later Joseph MacDonagh, still listed as Substitute Minister of Labour, presented the financial estimate for the Department for the coming six months. One wonders why, as Markievicz was also present, she had not undertaken that task. On 26 August she was proposed as Minister by Sean T. O'Kelly and seconded by Kathleen Clarke. The Belfast boycott grouping was detached from the Labour department to become a separate organisation with Joseph McDonagh continuing as director.[61]

Correspondence between Diarmuid O'Hegarty, who held a crucial position as Cabinet Secretary, and the Labour Ministry reveals a difficult relationship. For example, Markievicz missed a meeting on 14 October, due to a crucial ambiguity in the letter she received. O'Hegarty replied in smooth terms:

> so sorry you misunderstood the notification summoning you to the meeting of the Ministry for today. The mistake may have arisen owing to the fact that I used the words 'the Ministry' instead of 'all Ministers'. I hope you will accept this as explanation.

In other words, she was expected to attend when all Ministers were invited, but she was no longer a member of 'the Ministry', the more usual name given to the Cabinet.[62] Thereafter, terse communications between the two were normal. Markievicz wrote to O'Hegarty on 17 October, 'Re your letter of 17 October, it is the custom of this office to acknowledge letters as soon as they are received'. The antagonism appears to have been shared by her staff. Letters on 29 and 30 November from O'Hegarty, asking the Department to take away paper that had been ordered but was waiting at the printer, produced a sharp retort from Dick Cotter:

> I am directed by the Minister for Labour to acknowledge yours … and to inform you that I have sent for the paper that was for this department. There is some paper in this office belonging to the President's department. Will you kindly let me know what you wish done with it.[63]

Cotter was also capable of sending acrimonious letters on his own behalf, as this indicates, 'a messenger came to this office with the enclosed three letters … I never heard of the lady but it seems to be a very peculiar way to send messages'.[64]

O'Hegarty was a close ally of Michael Collins. Both were IRB members and both had been civil servants before 1916. Hanna Sheehy Skeffington, now working for Sinn Féin, had direct experience of working with Collins and in her estimation he 'had the usual soldiers' contempt for civilians, particularly for women'.[65] It is obvious, from messages conveyed by O'Hegarty, that Markievicz's conduct was scrutinized by the leadership and attempts made to dictate what she should say. Now outside the cabinet, she was unable to speak directly on her own behalf. On 26 November 1921 she was informed that she could 'speak strongly on the bad treatment of prisoners *but not to mention release* [underlined in letter] or report on their living conditions'.[66] Around the same period, after some criticism of remarks made by Markievicz at the 1921 Sinn Féin Ard Fheis, O'Hegarty wrote that the President advised her to take no notice of the criticism, but if she was taking action, she was to consult with him 'before taking any steps in the matter'.[67] She replied that she had already dealt with the matter by the time she had received his letter and enclosed her correspondence with the editors of *Young Ireland* and the *Voice of Labour*. They reveal a woman who was measured in tone, but firm in her understanding of the ethical behaviour of journalists:

> … Luckily no harm was done as labour know me better than to believe what they read. Of course I appreciate your difficulties as you probably are not acquainted with all the intricacies of labour's history and the policies that have evolved from it, also I know that I am a very difficult person to report as I talk very quickly, but I would ask you in the future to submit any notes of speeches by me that you may wish to publish in the future and there will be then no danger of any misunderstanding.

To the editor of the *Voice of Labour*, organ of the Irish Transport Union, she explained what she had tried to convey:

> I spoke generally on our position during the truce, and I anticipated that we should have to face hard times during the coming winter owing to the general depression of trade,

possibly we might even have to face the continuance of the war. I appealed to both workers and employers to each shoulder their share of suffering for Ireland and to try to avoid strikes and lock-outs during this coming winter by first trying to arrange their difficulties amicably by conference under the auspices of men appointed from my ministry.[68]

While this may appear neutral regarding the rights of workers and employers, the situation she was attempting to address was extremely difficult. As Mitchell has said, 'It sometimes seemed that the Irish social fabric was beginning to come apart' as factory seizures and agrarian violence increased. She had warned the Cabinet in October that social revolution was imminent, with:

small outbreaks growing more and more frequent and violent, the immediate result of which will be destruction of property and much misery which will tend to disrupt the Republican cause.[69]

She proposed that the government introduce measures such as investigating farm profits and establishing co-operatives, 'to show the workers that we [have] their interests at heart', but the Cabinet rejected her advice.[70]

Between July 1920 and January 1921 the Ministry reported sixty eight disputes, forty six of which were settled. Labour disputes escalated in 1921 as the economic situation worsened. The Labour Ministry was a buffer between labour and employers, and it seems that this was the role the Sinn Féin leadership wanted Markievicz to undertake, rather than anything more radical that would call into question the ownership of the means of production. Correspondence to Labour now followed a pattern of instructions for future action, 'I enclose for your information a list of the decisions affecting your department that were made at the meeting of the Ministry'. Her responses were very formal, 'I am directed by the Minister for Labour to thank you for having forwarded to her the decisions of the Ministry, relative to

Labour ...'[71] On 25 November Labour was instructed to intervene with the Secretary of the Trades Union Congress and the Irish Engineering Union to settle the Cork rail dispute; to report on a dispute in Donnelly's bacon factory, and to develop terms of reference for a dispute in the flour mills. On 6 December 1921 the Minister for Home Affairs was to instruct Volunteers acting as police to eject strikers from Mackey's in Castleconnell while at the same time the Minister for Labour was 'to interview Liberty Hall officials with a view to having an organizer sent down to settle the dispute'.[72]

At this period political life in Ireland became convulsed over the issue of acceptance of the Treaty. Negotiations with Britain had begun in London on 11 October 1921 and Lily O'Brennan was chosen to accompany the Irish delegation in order to provide secretarial assistance. The Labour department appears to have wound down some of its activities. As the terms of the Treaty were announced, Dáil members began to consider the contents. Ernest Blythe, strongly pro-Treaty, remembered one meeting, attended by himself, Sean Etchingham, Art O'Connor and Markievicz, at which:

Madame Markievicz [said] that she found nothing difficult except the Oath. She said that if it were not there she would not mind a bit about anything else in the Treaty.[73]

While that might have been the case, she soon emerged as a vocal opponent, basing her objections not only on the hated Oath of Allegiance to the British monarch, but also because she believed it was capitalists in England and Ireland who were 'pushing this Treaty to block the march of the working people in Ireland and England'. Speaking in the Dáil she declared her ideal was the 'Workers' Republic for which Connolly died' and she vowed she would remain 'a rebel, unconverted and unconvertible'.[74]

What followed was civil war, more bloodshed and, for Markievicz, a life lived on the run again, with one final spell of imprisonment. She would be dead before the anti-Treaty side, under de Valera's Fianna Fáil, entered the Dáil. In the immediate post-Treaty period, when the Labour department was being run by Joseph McGrath, a substitute minister who had taken the pro-Treaty side, (Dick Cotter also supported the Treaty) it was reported that the work of the department is 'more or less confined to settlement of Industrial Disputes', with 'on the whole gratifying results' as fifty one disputes were concluded during the period.[75] In 1924, when the Irish Free State reorganized its structures, the Ministry for Labour was abolished.

SOURCES
1   Jacqueline Van Voris, *Constance de Markievicz in the Cause of Ireland* (Massachusetts, 1967), p. 269.
2   *Ibid.* p. 251.
3   Kathleen Clarke, *Revolutionary Woman* (Dublin, 1991), p. 163.
4   *Ibid.* p. 170.
5   Elizabeth Coxhead, *Daughters of Erin* (Gerrard's Cross, 1979), p. 106.
6   Van Voris, p. 259.
7   *Irish Citizen*, May 1919.
8   Van Voris, p. 259.
9   Seán Ó Faoláin, *Constance Markievicz or The Average Revolutionary* (London, 1934), pp 188–9.
10 Helena Molony, Bureau of Military History Witness Statements, WS 391.
11 R.M. Fox, *Rebel Irishwomen* (Dublin, 1935, reprinted 1967), p. 20.
12 Coxhead, p. 107.
13 Van Voris, p. 260.
14 Diana Norman, *Terrible Beauty: A Life of Constance Markievicz* (Dublin, 1988), p. 214.
15 Anne Haverty, *Constance Markievicz: An Independent Life* (London, 1988), p. 198.
16 *Ibid*, p. 199.

17   Sari Oikarinen, *'A Dream of Liberty': Constance Markievicz's Vision of Ireland, 1908–1927* (Tampere, 1998), p. 145.

18   Arthur Mitchell, *Revolutionary Government in Ireland: Dáil Éireann 1919–1922* (Dublin, 1995), p. 162.

19   *Ibid*, p. 33.

20   *Ibid*, p. 162.

21   *Ibid*, p. 161.

22   Diarmaid Ferriter, *A Nation and Not a Rabble: the Irish Revolution 1913–1923* (London, 2015), p. 218.

23   Dáil Éireann, *Minutes of Proceedings of the First Parliament of the Republic of Ireland, 1919–1921*: Official Record, 2nd session, 1–11 April 1919.

24   Mitchell, p. 48.

25   *Ibid*, pp 134–7; see also Liz Curtis, *The Cause of Ireland: from the United Irishmen to Partition* (Belfast, 1994), p. 327.

26   Dáil Éireann, *Minutes of Proceedings of the First Parliament of the Republic of Ireland, 1919–1921*: Official Record, 2nd session, 11 April 1919.

27   Van Voris, p. 262.

28   Dáil Éireann, *Minutes of Proceedings of the First Parliament of the Republic of Ireland, 1919–1921*: Official Record, 6th session, 27 October 1919.

29   Ernest Blythe, Bureau of Military History Witness Statements, WS 939.

30   Robert Barton, Bureau of Military History Witness Statements, WS 979.

31   National Archives of Ireland, DE 2/5, 27 February 1920.

32   National Archives of Ireland, DE 2/5, 28 February 1920.

33   Dáil Éireann, *Minutes of Proceedings of the First Parliament of the Republic of Ireland, 1919–1921*: Official Record, 1st session of Second Dáil Éireann, 17 August 1921, Interim Report of Department of Labour.

34   National Archives of Ireland, DE 2/5, June 1920. Padraig Yeates acknowledges the role of Markievicz as a promoter of Irish craft unions in his article 'Craft workers during the Irish revolution, 1919–22', *Saothar*, 33 (2008), 37–54.

35   R.M. Fox, *Louie Bennett: Her Life and Times* (Dublin, 1957), p. 76.

36   Eilis ni Chonnail nee Ryan, Bureau of Military History Witness Statements, WS 568.

37   J. Anthony Gaughan, *Memoirs of Constable Jeremiah Mee, R.I.C.* (Dublin, 1975), p. 157.

38 Dáil Éireann, *Minutes of Proceedings of the First Parliament of the Republic of Ireland, 1919–1921*: Official Record, 1st session of Second Dáil Éireann, 17 August 1921, Interim Report of Department of Labour.

39 Dáil Éireann, *Minutes of Proceedings of the First Parliament of the Republic of Ireland, 1919–1921*: Official Record, 8th session of First Dáil Éireann, 6 August 1920.

40 Dáil Éireann, *Minutes of Proceedings of the First Parliament of the Republic of Ireland, 1919–1921*: Official Record, 1st session of Second Dáil Éireann, 17 August 1921, Interim Report of Department of Labour.

41 Gaughan, p. 154.

42 Jeremiah Mee, Bureau of Military History Witness Statements, WS 379.

43 National Archives of Ireland, DE 1/3, 15 September 1920.

44 Gaughan, p. 159.

45 *Ibid*, pp 160–1.

46 Jeremiah Mee, Bureau of Military History Witness Statements, WS 379.

47 National Archives of Ireland, DE 2/5, Report of Labour Department 7 July 1920–20 January 1921, 20 January 1920.

48 Coxhead, p. 108.

49 National Archives of Ireland, DE 2/5, Report of Labour Department 7 July 1920–20 January 1921, 20 January 1921.

50 National Archives of Ireland, DE 2/5, Report on the Working of the Labour Department, March 1921.

51 Mitchell, p. 243.

52 Dáil Éireann, *Minutes of Proceedings of the First Parliament of the Republic of Ireland, 1919–1921*: Official Record, 8th Session of First Dáil Éireann, 6 August 1920.

53 Ernest Blythe, Bureau of Military History Witness Statements, WS 939.

54 Maire Kennedy O'Byrne, Bureau of Military History Witness Statements, WS 1,029.

55 National Archives of Ireland, DE 2/5, Report of Department of Labour to Ministry of Finance, 19 October 1921.

56 National Archives of Ireland, DE 2/5, Accountant General, Department of Finance to Secretary of Dáil Éireann, 17 November 1921.

57 Coxhead, p. 109.

58 Mitchell, p. 285.

59   Robert Barton, Bureau of Military History Witness Statements, WS 979.

60   Blythe, Bureau of Military History Witness Statements, WS 939.

61   Mitchell, p. 304.

62   National Archives of Ireland, DE 2/5, Diarmuid O'Hegarty to Minister for Labour, 14 October 1921.

63   National Archives of Ireland, DE 2/5, Riseard MacCoitir, Department of Labour to Secretary, Dáil Éireann, 1 December 1921.

64   National Archives of Ireland, DE 2/5, Riseard MacCoitir, Department of Labour to Secretary, Dáil Éireann, 2 December 1921.

65   Leah Levenson and Jerry Natterstad, *Hanna Sheehy Skeffington: Irish Feminist* (Syracuse, 1986), p. 112.

66   National Archives of Ireland, DE 2/5, Diarmuid O'Hegarty to Minister for Labour, 26 November 1921.

67   National Archives of Ireland, DE 2/5, Diarmuid O'Hegarty to Minister for Labour, 18 November 1921.

68   National Archives of Ireland, DE 2/5, Markievicz letters to editor, *Young Ireland* and editor, *Voice of Ireland*, 19 November 1921; Constance de Markievicz to President, Dáil Éireann, 21 November 1921.

69   Arthur Mitchell, *Labour in Irish Politics 1890–1930* (Dublin, 1974), p. 141.

70   *Ibid*, p. 142.

71   National Archives of Ireland, DE 2/5, Richard Cotter to Diarmuid O'Hegarty, 27 October 1921.

72   National Archives of Ireland, DE 2/5, Diarmuid O'Hegarty to Minister for Labour, 6 December 1921.

73   Ernest Blythe, Bureau of Military History Witness Statements, WS 939.

74   Dáil Éireann, *Minutes of Proceedings of the First Parliament of the Republic of Ireland, 1919–1921*: Official Record, 5th session of Second Dáil Éireann, 3 January 1922.

75   National Archives of Ireland, DE 2/5, Report on Ministry of Labour, 11 January 1922–18 April 1922, 25 April 1922.

'THE REVOLT OF THE DAUGHTERS?'
THE GORE-BOOTH SISTERS

Sonja Tiernan

The single greatest influence on the personal and political life of Countess Constance Markievicz was her younger sister, Eva Gore-Booth. Constance and Eva were particularly close during their childhood at Lissadell. This bond was to be immortalised by the artist Sarah Purser who painted the two girls when Eva was ten years of age and Constance was twelve. In the portrait Eva is seated on the ground of a woodland admiring flowers and Constance stands behind her defiantly staring out of the picture, almost challenging the viewer.[1] The painting epitomises the complex and somewhat contradictory nature of the two sisters' relationship. In adulthood, Constance smoked cigarettes, took up arms against British rule in Ireland and was a flamboyant, dramatic character, both on and off the stage. In contrast, Eva was severely asthmatic, a steadfast pacifist and favored a contemplative life. Eva became a radical political activist but was more comfortable in the background rather than appearing center stage, like her sister. Despite such personal contrasts, the sisters held similar goals in life and they were to remain remarkably close throughout their lives, even believing that they had a telepathic connection.

Sir Henry Gore-Booth and his wife Georgina had five children; Constance was the eldest, followed by Josslyn, Eva, Mabel and Mordaunt. The Gore-Booth family owned one of the largest estates in the West of Ireland and they lived in Lissadell House, a seventy-two roomed Greek revival mansion set on the estate. Eva and Constance were born into a prestigious landed family which offered them privileges afforded to the Anglo-Irish aristocracy. The sisters' childhood took a dramatic turn during the winter of 1879-80 when famine revisited the Sligo area. The county had been devastated by famine during the Great Hunger of the 1840s and so the Gore-Booth family reacted quickly by distributing food and medical attention, to ensure their tenants were protected. This sense of responsibility had an impact on the Gore-Booth children who were old enough to witness the famine. Constance, Josslyn and Eva, all later exhibited an awareness of responsibility to others less privileged than themselves. Indeed, this traumatic episode may well have been the impetus which eventually led Constance and Eva to reject their aristocratic backgrounds in order to live amongst the working-classes.

There are only sketchy accounts regarding the girls' childhood at Lissadell. The Gore-Booth boys were sent away to be educated. Josslyn attended Eton and Mordaunt went on to graduate from Oxford University. The girls remained at home where they were educated by a private governess, Miss Noel, as was normal practice for the aristocracy. Noel provides the greatest insight into Eva and Constance's childhood. Noting how Eva was, 'a very fair, fragile-looking child, most unselfish and gentle with the general look of a Burne-Jones or Botticelli angel. As she was two years younger than Constance, and always so delicate, she had been, I think, rather in the background'.[2] Indeed, Eva remained in the shadow of Constance, even after death, often appearing as a mere footnote in histories written about her older sister. Constance is one of the few women to reach iconic status in Irish history. Mary Condren asserts that, 'when the history of those times was written, she herself [Eva Gore-Booth] was relegated to being a mere afterthought to her more famous sibling. For Irish schoolchildren, her sister was their role model: Constance Markievicz – the sole woman to appear, complete with military weapons, in the iconography of Irish revolution'.[3] However, it is now apparent that Eva was the driving force behind Constance and the person who first introduced her to political activism.

In their teenage years, Constance and Eva enjoyed roaming the local countryside on horseback and regularly stopped at cabins to speak with the local tenant farmers. During these visits Eva became enthralled with tales of Celtic legends and the history of Sligo. She thrived on folklore, in particular tales which recounted the legends of the High Queen of Connacht, Maeve, reputably buried on the cairn of Knocknaree Mountain not far from Lissadell. Constance was more aware of the faded pictures of Irish republican heroes, such as Robert Emmett, on the walls of the tenant's cabins. These early influences sparked Constance's interest in Irish republican history and Eva's dedication to the Celtic literary revival. Eva spent much of her early life at Lissadell writing poetry and reading the classics. Constance showed a flair for sketching and painting, often illustrating Eva's work with watercolour paintings or line drawings, a collaboration which was to continue for years to come.

Constance left Ireland in 1893 to attend the Slade School of Art in London. After pursuing her studies in London, she moved to Paris and furthered her studies at the Académie Julian. During this time Eva became quite ill and was sent to recuperate in Italy. It was while Eva was in Italy that she met her life-partner, Esther Roper, a young suffragist from Cheshire. Eva returned to Lissadell in 1896 enthused by ideas of suffrage politics and inspired by Esther's work on behalf of the factory women of Manchester. When Constance returned to the family home for Christmas celebrations, Eva convinced her to help bring the suffrage movement to Sligo. Eva organised a meeting at Breaghway Old School in Sligo. At the meeting Eva was elected secretary, Constance President and Mabel Treasurer of the Sligo branch of the Irish Women's Suffrage and Local Government Association.

Eva called the first official meeting of the Sligo Association on Friday 18 December at Milltown National Protestant School in Drumcliffe.[4] This was to be Constance's first political venture and she thrived on the experience. The sisters ensured that the hall was dressed with suffrage posters announcing messages such as 'Liberality, justice, and equality'. In what would become typical of their differing oratory styles, Constance opened the meeting by recounting light-hearted anecdotes about extending the vote to women explaining:

> I have been told amongst other things that it [the vote] will cause women to ape the other sex, to adopt their clothes, copy their manners and peculiarities, that it will cause women to neglect their homes and duties, and worst of all prevent the majority marrying. Of course this may be true; pigs may fly, as the old proverb says, but they are not likely birds.

Meanwhile Eva appealed to the audience to adopt a policy of cooperation calling on 'Irishwomen to follow the example of the farmers of Drumcliffe'. Sligo had never before witnessed such open debate about the, almost foreign, idea of votes for women. Women's suffrage was seen as too radical and even foolhardy by many people in a rural Irish town such as Sligo. As local bachelor, Percy Clarke, warned, 'enfranchisement of women would be Home Rule with a vengeance – petticoat government'.

As this was the first suffrage group established in Sligo, it is not surprising that the meetings drew attention not only from locals but also from the media. The *Sligo Champion* reported on the activities of the Gore-Booth sisters with respect, clearly conscious of the powerful position their father held locally. However, the British society magazine, *Vanity Fair*, known for its witty satire and for mocking members of the aristocratic classes, was not so wary. In the December issue of the magazine they published a humorous, yet condescending, sketch on the activities of Eva, Constance and their younger sister:

> The New Woman is still with us and shows herself where least expected. In the far-away regions of County Sligo, among the wives and daughters of the farmers and fishermen, the three pretty daughters of Sir Henry Gore-Booth are creating a little excitement (not to say amusement) for the emancipation of their sex. Miss Gore-Booth and her sisters, supported by a few devoted yokels, have been holding a few meetings in connection with the Woman's Suffrage (or, shall I say, 'The Revolt of the Daughters?') movement. Their speeches are eloquent, (un)conventional, and (non)convincing. They are given to striking out a line for themselves, in more senses than one; for Miss Gore-Booth has already distinguished herself as a lady steeplechaser, and public oratory is their newest toy. The sisters make a pretty picture on the platform; but it is not women of their type who need to assert themselves over Man. However, it amuses them – and others and I doubt if the tyrant has much to fear from their little arrows.[5]

Eva was not content with firing 'little arrows', shortly after her first taste of politics she moved to Manchester to live with Esther Roper.

When Eva arrived in Manchester in 1897 there were more Irish people living in that industrial city than in her entire home county of Sligo.[6] Eva devoted herself to organising women workers into trade unions and towards her ultimate goal of obtaining the vote for women in general elections.[7] While she was establishing herself as a formidable political activist in England, Constance continued to lead a bohemian life-style. While in Paris, Constance met a Polish Count, Casimir Markievicz, who was also studying art in the city.[8] The couple married in 1900 and they had a daughter the following year. Constance named her daughter Maeve after Eva's heroine, the High Queen of Connacht. The couple engaged in a vibrant social life, moving in an eclectic artistic circle across Paris, Dublin and London as well as spending periods of time at Casimir's family estate in the Ukraine. By 1908 the marriage was showing signs of stress and Constance placed her daughter in the full-time care of her mother, Lady Georgina, at Lissadell. While Eva and Constance remained close over the following years, they had little contact with the rest of the Gore-Booth family after this time. That same year Eva offered Constance a new direction which was to shape the remaining years of her life.

By 1908, Eva was an established and a respected trade union organiser. Her main focus that year was on protecting the employment of barmaids, a campaign that she had worked on since 1906. At this stage, the Liberal government produced a proposed Licensing Bill which would control the sale and consumption of alcohol. These controls were a welcome intervention at a time when alcohol abuse was causing major social issues, especially in industrial cities. However, a sub-section of the proposed Bill would exclude women from working in public houses. Eva estimated that if introduced 100,000 women would be forced into unemployment.[9] Barmaids were not unionised and previously had no cause to organise themselves. Eva established the Barmaids' Political Defence League. The controversy regarding the Licensing Bill would reach an all-time high after a cabinet re-shuffle. Amongst the changes, the newly-appointed Prime Minister, H.H. Asquith, promoted the young MP Winston Churchill to President of the Board of Trade. Under contemporary law a newly appointed cabinet minister had to resign his seat and stand for re-election. On his appointment, Churchill was forced to resign as MP for Manchester North-West and stand for re-election in the same constituency in April 1908. By then Churchill had become a central figure in the barmaid issue.

Mr. Winston Churchill escorted by police to a meeting.

Winston Churchill arriving in Manchester to begin his by-election campaign. He was confident of re-election. *Daily Graphic* (23 April 1908)

Eva was determined to overthrow Churchill and so she invited Constance to Manchester to help organise a campaign. This was Constance's first serious political venture. Her stepson, Stanislaw Markievicz, later recalled that 'without doubt Madame's debut into politics dates from this visit to Manchester'.[10] The sisters launched an intense campaign supporting the Conservative candidate, William Joynson-Hicks, in the by-election. Joynson-Hicks was a rather unlikely candidate for their support; he was staunchly evangelical and the *Manchester Catholic Herald* accused him of being anti-Catholic and anti-Irish.[11] Eva organised a striking coach, drawn by four white horses, to be driven around Manchester with the expert horsewoman Constance at the whip (as seen in illustration 2).

untess Markievic (driving) and her sister, Miss Eva Gore Booth—against the Liberal for the barmaids ("Daily Graphic" Photograph.)

The carriage driven by four white horses through the streets of Manchester by Eva Gore-Booth and Constance Markievicz. *Daily Graphic* (23 April 1908)

THE DAILY GRAPHIC, THURSDAY, APRIL 23, 1908.

THE FIGHT FOR NORTH-WEST MANCHESTER.

The barmaids' friends addressing the people from the four-in-hand, driven by the Countess Markievicz.

"Daily Dispatch" photo

Members of the Barmaids' Political Defence League addressing crowds during the Manchester North-West by-election, *Daily Graphic* (23 April 1908)

The women drew much attention (as seen in illustration three). The predominately male crowd gathered around the carriage to hear the deliberations of the women and the cause of the barmaids. When the coach stopped Eva and Constance took to the roof of the carriage and made rousing speeches. Eva also arranged a mass meeting in the Coal Exchange building in support of barmaids. At the meeting Constance took the stand, announcing:

> I have come over from Ireland to help because I am a woman. I am not a Conservative – I am a Home Ruler – but I have come over here to ask everyone to vote for Mr. Joynson-Hicks

because he, of the three candidates who are standing, is the only one who takes a straight and decent view of the barmaids' question.[12]

Through their consistent efforts, the Gore-Booth sisters successfully orchestrated the defeat of a prestigious politician at that by-election. Churchill lost his seat by a decent margin and was temporarily forced out of politics.[13] The following day the *Daily Telegraph* was jubilant in their headline, 'Winston Churchill is out, Out, OUT'.[14] Weeks later he sought a new constituency and stood as the Liberal candidate at a by-election in Dundee. Churchill was returned as an MP in May and his constituency remained in Dundee until 1922. Eva continued lobbying against the Licensing Bill. On 13 June 1908 she took her demonstration to the capital, holding a rally at Trafalgar Square in London. The event was attended by over two thousand people. Again Eva brought Constance to speak to the crowd. Constance was an inspiring and engaging orator, a fact which Eva was most aware. Constance addressed the crowd from the plinth, at the foot of the Nelson column, her speech reached a high when she announced how we are 'told the bar is a bad place for a woman ('So it is'), but the Thames Embankment at night is far worse'.[15]

Within months, the Barmaids' Political Defence League overwhelmingly won their campaign. 294 out of 355 MPs rejected the Bill. This was an immense victory, especially considering that two women had swayed a political decision without even having the power to vote in, or stand for, election. The actions of Gore-Booth sisters also inspired politicians to question the male dominated political system. In the House of Commons debate on the issue, Conservative MP Wilfrid Ashley questioned whether 'a body of men elected entirely by men had any moral right to prohibit the employment of women in a certain trade purely on sentimental grounds'.[16] Details of this campaign provide us with an insight into the early political life of Countess Markievicz, as influenced her younger sister. It is surprising to discover that Constance was electioneering on behalf of a Conservative, anti-Irish candidate the same year that she joined the Irish republican organisations, Sinn Féin and Inghinidhe na hÉireann.

Labour issues would eventually come to dominate Constance's life. In 1911, when the Irish Women's Workers Union (IWWU) formed, Constance was instantly supportive. She was nominated as honorary president and during a meeting to encourage women to join, she implored them 'if you join this union we will help you get an increase in wages but more than that it could help you get the vote and thus make men of you all'.[17] The main objective of the union was to 'improve the wages and conditions of the women workers of Ireland, and to help the men workers to raise the whole status of labour and industry'.[18] This was an objective welcomed by Eva. However, the development of trade unionism in Ireland would become intrinsically linked with the nationalist cause. In 1913 the Irish Trade and General Workers' Union (ITGWU) became embroiled in a battle of wits with employer William Martin Murphy. By the end of September that year twenty thousand labourers were out of work in an event now known as the Dublin Lock-Out. In a move reminiscent of the Lissadell food support of 1879, Constance and Delia Larkin organised soup kitchens to feed starving locked out workers and their children. In order to defend worker's rights to demonstrate, James Larkin, James Connolly and Jack White founded the Irish Citizen Army (ICA) in November 1913 and Constance became honorary treasurer. The ICA would later play a central part in organising the Easter Rising of 1916.

With the onset of World War in 1914, Eva concentrated her efforts on pacifism and supported conscientious objectors to the war. She now lived in London and visited Constance in Dublin regularly. However, Eva was unaware that Constance was becoming further embroiled in the Irish nationalist movement. Constance was of course centrally involved in the Easter Rising of 1916, taking up arms as second in command to Commandant Michael Mallin. Markievicz and Mallin, along with their troop of ICA combatants, originally based themselves in St Stephen's Green. When British snipers directed gun fire into the park from the roof of the Shelbourne Hotel, Mallin and Markievicz relocated their troops to the College of Surgeons nearby. Eva first learnt about the rebellion from newspaper reports in London. On Sunday morning, the final day of the Rising, Eva read an account in *Lloyd's Weekly Newspaper* that her sister's body had been discovered in the Green. It later transpired that Constance was unhurt but had been arrested after the surrender.

Constance faced a court-martial trial at Kilmainham Gaol on 4 May under a charge that she 'did take part in an armed rebellion and in the waging of war against His Majesty the King, such act being of such a nature as to be calculated to be prejudicial to the Defence of the Realm and being done with the intention and for the purpose of assisting the enemy'.[19] She pleaded not guilty to the charge but guilty of attempting to 'cause disaffection among the civilian population of His Majesty'.[20] In her statement to the closed court she did not plead for mercy, instead she remained defiant stating clearly that, 'I went out to fight for Ireland's freedom, and it doesn't matter what happens to me. I did what I thought was right and I stand by it'.[21] Under order of the court-martial president, Brig-General C.J. Blackader, Constance was sentenced to death by firing squad. Eva appealed the sentence, contacting Prime Minister Asquith on her behalf and her brother Josslyn lobbied his local Sligo MP, Charles O'Hara. Two days later a plea was inserted into Constance's charge sheet noting that 'the court recommend the prisoner to mercy solely and only on account of her sex'.[22] Her death sentence was commuted to penal servitude for life. Eva travelled to Dublin on board the same ferry as Prime Minister Asquith. She offered Constance support and visited her in prison. Although Eva was a committed pacifist she supported her sister's fight for Irish independence. Constance was transferred to Mountjoy prison before being sent to Aylesbury Prison in England, where Eva visited as often as she was granted permission.

During prison visits Eva gave Constance a section from a play, *The Triumph of Maeve: a Romance*, which she had originally published in 1905.[23] In the play, the warrior Queen Maeve unsuccessfully attempts to shield her daughter, Fionavar, from the atrocities of her brutal and bloody battles. When Fionavar witnesses the aftermath of the battle led by her mother, she dies from heartache. In the aftermath of the Rising, Eva resolved to publish the final three acts of the play separately, focussing on *The Death of Fionavar*.[24] Eva wrote the introduction in May 1916, which was dedicated 'To the Memory of the Dead. The many who died for Freedom and the One who died for Peace'.[25] This publication had a clear message, advocating pacifism. She asked her sister to illustrate the play and Constance agreed. She drew pen illustrations to accompany the text while she was imprisoned in Aylesbury prison. As Constance was not allowed art materials, she used quills fashioned from rook feathers to complete her task.[26] The play was published in October 1916 and the cover boasts that the book is, 'decorated by Constance Gore-Booth', and in brackets underneath is printed 'Countess Markievicz'.

The opening page is adorned with Constance's sketches of winged horses flying gloriously free. The remaining eighty-five pages of text are bordered with drawings of flowers, sunsets and horses. The *Manchester Guardian* newspaper was impressed with the publication and in their review they drew attention to how the illustrations 'form a kind of continuous accompaniment to the poetry, each page being enclosed in a charming border sympathetically responsive to its moods and changes'.[27] The reviewer also hoped that 'the little volume may serve the cause of peace in Ireland and help to convince English people that the Irish movement was not in essence revolutionary'. The volume was published in England and marketed in America by Laurence James Gomme, a publisher and book collector in New York. American reviewers were quick to note the obvious paradox with this publication. A play with a strong pacifist message was, after all, illustrated by a convicted armed rebel, from her prison cell.

The *New York Times* dedicated an entire page to the curiosity of the publication under the title 'Irish rebel illustrates non-resistance play'.[28] The newspaper announces that:

> There will soon be published a poetic drama destined to receive an amount of attention seldom bestowed upon this important but unpopular sort of writing. It is called 'The Death Fionavar', and the author is Eva Gore-Booth. The book is profusely illustrated, every page having its elaborate decoration of landscapes, flowers, and cabalistic designs. And these illustrations are the work of Eva Gore-Booth's sister, the Countess Markiewicz, now incarcerated in an English prison for her conspicuous share in the Irish uprising of last April.[29]

The reviewer concludes by noting that 'there is something ironical about the fact that the pages of this most passionately pacific work should be made by so convinced and practical a direct actionist as Countess Markiewicz'. It is indeed a remarkable publication especially considering the dedication poem written by Eva and printed on the inside cover:

Poets, Utopians, bravest of the brave,
Pearse and MacDonagh, Plunkett, Connolly,
Dreamers turned fighters but to find a grave,
Glad for the dream's austerity to die.

And my own sister, through wild hours of pain,
Whilst murderous bombs were blotting out the stars,
Little I thought to see you smile again
As I did yesterday, through prison bars …

The volume identifies how the close bond between the two sisters persisted even when the direction of their lives apparently contradicted. In fact during this time in prison the sisters became even more devoted to each other. Constance later described how during her time in Aylesbury prison, she and Eva made a pact to speak to each other every day, telepathically. Constance boasted that, 'I used to concentrate and try and leave my mind a blank, a sort of dark, still pool, and I got to her, and once I told her how she sat in a window, and I seemed to know what she was thinking. It was a great joy and comfort to me'.[30]

Eva persisted in her attempts to gain a release for Constance from prison and monitored how she was treated as a prisoner. By the end of 1916 hundreds of Irish people remained in prisons in England, most without any sentence. Due to a lack of support for Prime Minister Asquith he was forced to resign in December 1916. David Lloyd George was nominated to the role. One of his first actions as parliamentary leader was to grant an amnesty for all those Irish interned at Frongoch Internment Camp and at Reading Gaol, as well as the two women, Winifred Carney and Helena Molony, interned at Aylesbury. Constance remained in jail. In June 1917 an amnesty was called releasing the Irish rebel prisoners. Constance was released into Eva's care that month.

On release, Constance stayed at Eva and Esther's flat at 33 Fitzroy Square in London. In the years after the Rising this flat had become a base for Irish nationalists in London, Hanna Sheehy Skeffington described it as 'a home for all rebels'.[31] On 20 June 1917 Eva and Constance went to the House of Commons where they took to the terrace and ate strawberries and cream; the *Manchester Guardian* reported the event under the heading, 'strange times in the House'.[32] It was Eva who accompanied her sister back to Dublin for a triumphant homecoming. The women arrived into Kingstown (Dun Laoghaire) port and boarded a train to the city centre. People lined the railway track for miles along the route, cheering as the train in which the Countess was travelling passed. When they arrived in the city, Kathleen Lynn drove the women along a route, passing Liberty Hall, the GPO, the College of Surgeons and Jacobs' factory, key places of rebel occupation during Easter week. The *Irish Independent* reported excitedly that 'the crowd cheered themselves hoarse'.[33] A London newspaper the *Evening Standard* announced their surprise that Eva was present, even though she 'had little or no sympathy with Sinn Féin'.[34] The *Irish Independent* was quick to clarify that 'although she is not a Sinn Feiner, she is an Irishwoman in sympathy with all who love liberty'.[35]

Constance was imprisoned again the following year in an issue related to the conscription of Irishmen; again she sought support from Eva. Over 200,000 Irishmen voluntarily joined the British army during World War One. The British government wanted more. In March 1918, the Irish Convention established to resolve the Irish Home Rule issue, recommended the enactment of the Bill under condition that conscription would be extended to Ireland. On 16 April 1918 the extension of the Military Service Bill, enforcing conscription in Ireland, was announced. This new legislation would ensure that all Irish men between the ages of eighteen and fifty would be called to join the British army. Members of the Irish Parliamentary Party walked out of Westminster in protest. Political instability in Ireland again intensified as anti-conscription activities increased, including a general workers' strike on 23 April. In reaction British Intelligence in Ireland claimed to have uncovered a Sinn Féin plot with Germany and they arrested seventy three lead members of the organisation. Constance was amongst those sent to prison in England without trial. The arrests inspired a more effective propaganda campaign.

Eva had been organising on behalf of anti-conscription movements in England since the beginning of the war and she set about campaigning against the Irish conscription Bill. She wrote to British newspapers; 'the ruin preparing in Ireland' was published in the *Manchester Guardian* and received much attention. Her letter opens with the determined assurance that in Dublin, 'a resistance to the death is being undertaken in a spirit of passionate revolt and religious faith which may turn Ireland into a nation of rebels and martyrs, but never into an army of conscripts'.[36] Eva's campaign against the introduction of conscription in Ireland differs immensely from her previous campaigns in England. Her work there was based on ideals of pacifism and the promotion of choice for the individual. In her campaign against conscription in Ireland, Eva never mentions pacifist ideals but focuses instead on the fact that the introduction of conscription is yet another forced oppression of Irish people by British forces.

Despite efforts, forced conscription of Irish men into the British army was never introduced. Constance wrote to her sister explaining that:

> it wasn't talk blocked conscription: it was the astounding fact that the whole male population left at home and most of the women ... would have died rather than fight for England, and they simply did not dare exterminate a nation.[37]

While she was still in Holloway prison Constance was returned as an MP for St Patrick's Division of Dublin. This was the first British general election in which women could vote and Constance was the first woman ever to be elected to the House of Commons. In line with Sinn Féin policy she rejected her seat at Westminster. Significantly out of seventeen female candidates who stood for election that first year, Markievicz was the only one to be elected. She remained the only female candidate to be elected to Commons on her own record for a number of years.[38] The elected members of Sinn Féin formed the first Dáil Éireann on 21 January 1919 in the Mansion House in Dublin. Fittingly, Constance Markievicz was nominated as Minister for Labour. Constance proved herself as an effective Minister for Labour, one who possessed a unique way of solving employment disputes. Founder of the Irish Women's Workers Union, Louie Bennett, recounted a particularly difficult negotiation between her and a certain employer:

> When the meeting dragged on, with no sign of an outcome, Markievicz strode through the room pulled out her gun, pointed it at the terrified employer and said, 'ten minutes to settle or I shoot'.[39]

The employer settled within seven minutes.

Eva died in June 1926 and Constance was traumatised by the loss of her sister. Constance's own health deteriorated in the months that followed. In June 1927, Constance fractured her arm in two places while cranking her car. In July she became ill during a Fianna Fáil party meeting and was brought to Sir Patrick Dun's hospital in Dublin. Markievicz insisted on entering a public ward. She was operated on for appendicitis but her health weakened further over the coming days and she died on 15 July 1927. Constance had only outlived her sister by one year. A Catholic bible was found by her hospital bedside; it was inscribed in her own hand 'to Mother and Eva 1927 – They are not dead, they do not sleep. They have awakened from the dream of life'.[40] The Irish republican historian, Dorothy Macardle, attempted to summarise the bond between the sisters describing how:

> Constance had a way of talking about her sister as though Eva were her angel, and when the news of Eva's death came there came to some of us in Ireland a sharp apprehension that we would not have Madame long, for we knew how close and spiritual the bond between them had been.[41]

SOURCES

All images in this chapter have been reproduced by kind permission from the Lissadell collection.

1 The painting is currently on public display in the Merrion Hotel, Upper Merrion Street, Dublin 2. An auction catalogue describes the painting: 'a double portrait of Constance and Eva Gore-Booth as young girls in a woodland setting, Constance standing holding a blossom, Eva sitting on the woodland floor'. Medium Oil on Canvas, Size 59.8 x 41.3 in./152 x 105 cm. *Christie's Catalogue: Country House Auction* (25 November 2003).

2 Esther Roper, (ed.), *Poems of Eva Gore-Booth: Complete Edition* (London, Longmans, 1929), p. 6.

3 Mary Condren, 'Theology and Ethics: The Twentieth Century', in Angela Bourke, Siobhan Kilfeather, Maria Luddy et al (eds.), *The Field Day Anthology of Irish Writing Volume IV Irish Women's Writing and Traditions* (Cork, Cork University Press, 2002), p. 655.

4 The following account of the suffrage meeting is taken from a report in *Sligo Champion* (19 December 1896), p. 9.

5 *Vanity Fair* (December, 1896) from the Lissadell Collection.

6 By the 1860s over 806,000 Irish people were living in England and of this number almost half were to be found in Lancashire and Cheshire. From 1851 to 1901 the number of people living in central Manchester doubled and the Irish population continued to grow well into the 1920s.

7 For more on Eva Gore-Booth's political work: Sonja Tiernan, *Eva Gore-Booth: An Image of Such Politics* (Manchester, Manchester University Press, 2012).

8   For further information see Patrick Quigley, *The Polish Irishman: The Life and Times of Count Casimir Markievicz* (Dublin, Liffey Press, 2012).

9   Sonja Tiernan (ed.), *The Political Writings of Eva Gore-Booth* (Manchester, Manchester University Press, 2015), pp 65–75.

10   Stanislaw Dunin Markiewicz, 'Life of Constance Markievicz', National Library of Ireland, MS 44,619.

11   'Midnight Electioneering', *Manchester Guardian* (23 April 1908), p. 10.

12   'The Barmaid Cause', *Manchester Guardian* (24 April 1908), p. 8.

13   The final results were: William Joynson-Hicks (Conservative) 5,417, Winston Churchill (Liberal) 4,988 and Dan Irving (Socialist) 276.

14   Sebastian Haffner, *Churchill* (London: Haus Publishing, 2002), p. 35.

15   'Working Women in Trafalgar Square', *The Times* (15 June 1908), p. 9.

16   'House of Commons', *Manchester Guardian* (3 November 1908), p. 10.

17   Mary Jones, *Those Obstreperous Lassies: A History of the Irish Women's Workers' Union* (Dublin, Gill & Macmillan, 1988), p. 1.

18   'Irish Women's Workers' Union call for members', September 1911, National Library of Ireland, LOP 113/123.

19   Esther Roper (ed.), *Prison Letters of Countess Markievicz* (1934: London, Virago, 1987), p. 24.

20   *Ibid.*

21   *Ibid*, p. 26.

22   *Ibid.*

23   Eva Gore-Booth, *The Three Resurrections and the Triumph of Maeve* (London, Longmans, 1905).

24   Eva Gore-Booth, *The Death of Fionavar from the Triumph of Maeve* (London, Erskine Macdonald, 1916).

25   The one who died for peace can be identified as her friend, Francis Sheehy Skeffington. Skeffington was a devoted pacifist who was illegally shot along with two other unarmed men during Easter week 1916, under the orders of Captain J.C. Bowen Colthurst.

26   Amanda Sebestyen (ed.), *Prison Letters of Countess Markievicz* (London, Virago Press, 1987), p. xxxii.

27   'New Books', *Manchester Guardian* (9 October 1916), p. 3.

28   'Irish Rebel Illustrates Nonresistance Play', *New York Times* (10 September 1916), p. 2.

29   *Ibid.*

30   *Poems of Eva Gore-Booth*, pp 39–40.

31   Speech and notes for a radio talk on Eva Gore-Booth by Hanna Sheehy Skeffington, undated, National Library of Ireland, MS 41,189/5M.

32   'Strange Times in the House', *Manchester Guardian* (21 June 1917), p. 4.

33   'Arrival at Kingstown', *Irish Independent* (22 June 1917), p. 3.

34   As cited in 'Miss Eva Gore-Booth and Sinn Féin', *Irish Independent* (24 June 1917), p. 3.

35   *Ibid.*

36   'The Ruin Preparing in Ireland', *Manchester Guardian* (26 April 1918), p. 8.

37   Letter from Constance Markievicz to Eva Gore-Booth, 14 February 1919, in Roper (ed.), *Prison Letters*, p. 195.

38   The first woman to take her seat as an MP in the House of Commons was placed there partially under the influence of her husband. Nancy Astor was elected as an MP at the 1919 Plymouth by-election when her husband, Waldorf Astor, succeeded to the peerage and a seat in the House of Lords vacating his seat in the House of Commons.

39   *Bread and Roses: The Story of the Irish Women Workers' Union*, documentary (Breslin Benevolent Fund, 2009).

40   As cited in Anne Haverty, *Constance Markievicz*, p. 229.

41   Stanislaw Dunin Markiewicz, 'Life of Constance Markievicz', National Library of Ireland, MS 44,619, p. 136.

CONSTANCE MARKIEVICZ
SOCIAL AND PERSONAL

Pauline Conroy

Constance Gore-Booth, like other prominent women of the late nineteenth century, was born into a prosperous landowning Protestant family from the area of Lissadill in County Sligo in 1868.[1] Her father was an adventurer who undertook risky expeditions into the Arctic and far afield, returning with stories and gifts from his travels. Sligo at the time was desolate and experiencing severe emigration of 900–1,000 persons a year. The overwhelming majority of people were in lowly-paid domestic, industrial or agricultural work.[2] The Gore-Booth mansion-style 72-room house was surrounded by poor peasant dwellings housing tenants of the family and other landowners. The children of these tenants were the company chosen by Constance to visit and play with. When Seán Ó Faoláin interviewed those who knew her as a child for his 1934 biography they were all in agreement that she was quite wild and unusually good as a horsewoman.[3] This chapter attempts to explore some of the influences on her life before she became known as a political activist.

Constance Gore-Booth had no formal school education. As was the custom among the aristocracy she was educated at home by a governess. She was interested in literature and was able to read in French, German and Italian. From an early age she was constantly sketching and drawing. One of her favourite activities was horse riding. She rode a pony from the age of six or seven, quickly abandoning the grooms charged with leading her by the reins or accompanying her on a horse. As she got older she became a very accomplished and daring rider and hunter. She seemed fearless in jumping her horse over tall hedges and fences and had a strong affinity with horses. She was competitive in hunting. She loved acting, dressing up and playing tricks on others. At the age of 17 she spent six months in Florence, Italy in the company of her governess, Miss Noel, studying drawing. It is not clear with whom these studies were undertaken.

Of her four brothers and sisters, Constance was closest throughout her life to her sister Eva who was just two years younger. Eva was an extraordinary woman in her own right, she had a strong interest in literature and in social justice for women. Lady Gore-Booth was unable to persuade Eva take on the life of a debutante and marry. Following illness in 1896 she went to Italy to the artists' village of Bordighera near the French border. There she met the love of her life, Esther Roper. The two became inseparable and lived together in England, in Manchester and London, for the rest of their lives.[4] Esther was a women's rights activist among women trade unionists, women in the franchise leagues and among the labour movement in Manchester. Eva joined her in these movements, became a renowned poet and supported Constance throughout her life, being one of her closest confidantes. The more militant section of the suffragette movement, the Women's Social and Political Union and the North of England Society for Women's Suffrage, were the points of influence where Eva and Christabel Pankhurst were active – she had been a protege of Eva in the latter.[5]

Constance, like her younger sister, showed no interest in marrying following her 'coming out' debutante season in London when she was presented to Queen Victoria. She attended all the parties available, wore beautiful dresses, danced and was much admired. After three seasons her mother abandoned hope of marrying off Constance and had to turn her attention to others supposedly waiting for their turn. During the 1892 season in London when she was 24 years old Constance was already showing signs of moving to an independent life as an artist. She was working up to four hours a day at the Bolton studios of Swedish oil painter Anna Kristina Nordgren (1847–1916) who painted her portrait. Anna would later accompany her on a visit to Lissadell. Anna had studied for five years at the Royal Swedish Academy of Arts, then at the Académie Julian in Paris where she stayed for eight years in all, before moving to London around 1882. Anna was a radical and independent artist promoting women's rights as citizens and artists. She had founded the '91 Club for Women Artists and the Women's International Art Club in 1900.[6] The '91 Art Club had about 100 members and was established in 1891 to promote the interaction of women artists and to give exhibitions of members' works.[7]

In 1893 her parents agreed that Constance could enrol in the new Slade School of Art at University College London. A register of the period 1895–96 shows her enrolled for 1893–1894 as Constance G. Booth of Sligo.[8] This radical institution had been founded in 1868 and the first buildings completed in 1871.[9] At the time the Slade was associated with the Parisian artist Professor Alphonse Legros of the Realist art perspective. Constance arrived at a most exciting time in the art world. Among the students at the Slade in the 1890s who were to become notable in their fields were writer G.K. Chesterton (1892), illustrator Edna Clark Hall (1895), Albert Rutherston (1898, aged 16), Augustus John (1894) and his sister Gwen and fellow Irish woman and renowned furniture designer and architect Eileen Grey (1898). William Orpen studied there in 1897 as did Irish woman Grace Gifford in 1907, who later married Joseph Plunkett on the eve of his execution in 1916. The Slade was unique in offering women art education on equal terms with men and providing them with a stepping stone into decision-making society.[10] Constance and her bicycle were immersed in an emerging world of art student life. This was her first experience of formal study and she was 25 years old.

Her arrival at Slade was a planned event on Constance's part. She was guided in the Slade direction not only by Anna Nordgren but also by the famous Irish portraitist and stained glass painter Sarah Purser[11] who had, like Anna, studied art in Paris at the Académie Julian. Sarah had been commissioned by Lady Gore-Booth to paint Constance and Eva as young girls in 1880 and this portrait was significant in Sarah's career. During her visit to their home in Lissadell she had observed with approval Constance's drawings and sketches. Lady Gore-Booth later commissioned Sarah Purser in 1907 to design a stained glass window in the Church of Ireland chapel at Lissadell.

While in London, as well as the Slade she continued her studies at the Bolton Studios. These had been opened up in 1883 in a poor part of the city on the Fulham Road in Little Chelsea, hidden away at an intersection of Redcliffe Road and Gilson Road. The studios were established on a small scale, probably by the sculptor Charles Bacon, and by 1890, just before Constance arrived, there were 27 studios connected by a corridor.[12] In this sense the studios were more a collective artistic space than the individualised studios of today. In London at the Slade she met with the Waterford-born poet and illustrator Althea Gyles. After four years in London, during the initial part of which she resided at the Alexandra House Hostel for Girl Art Students in South Kensington, Constance moved to France for further studies in 1898.[13] Paris was a ferment of artistic and cultural activity. Poetry, architecture, painting, photography – all were the subject of new departures, thinking overturned and upturned genres. Impressionism in painting had taken hold not only in concept but was possible due to the technical development of paint delivered in little metal tubes which could be carried into the streets and outdoor landscapes.[14] There had been a challenge in 1863 to the official aesthetic manifested in national exhibitions or salons of art by the opening of an alternative 'Salon des Refusés', an exhibition of rejected works of art.

Constance enrolled in the then amazing radical private Académie Julian at 31 rue du Dragon in Paris.[15] This was a school she would have known about from former students Sarah Purser and Anna Nordgren. The school had been established by the painter Rodolphe Julian as a studio in 1868 and then as an art academy in 1873. It rapidly grew to over 100 students, attracting major figures from the French art milieu and leading academic centres. Specialising in drawing and sculpture, the Académie was a cosmopolitan mix of French, American, English and Irish students amongst others. A significant number of the students were Polish.[16] The school studios expanded into as many as six different studio locations across Paris and offered women in particular an opportunity for professional and formal training in art leading to independent careers.[17]

It was a highly competitive atmosphere with many students eager to gain entry to the State-run École des Beaux-Arts. There, foreign students were discouraged from registering by the admission requirement of a French language test designed to keep them out. There were lots of competitions among the students for the best work of art at Julian and these were judged by a range of established artists and lecturers to whose gaze the students' works of art were exposed as often as weekly.

Women and men generally studied separately after attempts at joint study were criticised by both women's families and other schools. Women apparently endured very overcrowded studios and workshops for which they were charged almost twice the fees (700 FF) compared with men (400 FF).[18] The separate study arrangements were to prevent women seeing nude male bodies in life classes. The Académie Julian attracted several notable Irish artists such as John Lavery (1880s), Eileen Grey (1902–1905), Paul Henry (in 1898) and Sarah Purser (c. 1879).[19]

In Paris Constance lived at an English pension in the fashionable rue de Rivoli where Violet Hunt (1862–1942), English feminist writer and supporter of the 'New Woman' movement', was staying. Violet was frequently visited by her friend Daisy Forbes-Robinson, actress and militant suffragette who was imprisoned in 1913 for her views.[20] It was Daisy's brother, Eric, who accompanied Constance to a fateful dance in Paris where she was to meet her husband-to-be, Casimir de Markievicz, a professional landscape and portrait painter who had also been at the Académie Julian.[21] He was of Polish nationality from a landowning family around the village of Zywotowka in central Ukraine, which was then under Russian occupation. A qualified lawyer, he was establishing himself as a painter and had exhibited with success at the Paris Salon in 1900.[22] He spoke no English so the relationship developed in French which was the language of Russian nobility. He was a Catholic, already married with a wife and two sons back in the Ukraine and was six years younger than Constance. His wife and youngest child died in 1899 in the Ukraine. Constance and Casimir determined to marry in 1900. He was 26, she was 32. The wedding, by the standard of the times, was small. They married at least twice in London, under English and Russian law.

After their honeymoon cycling – a then new fashion – in Normandy, Constance and Casimir established themselves in Paris in an apartment large enough for both of them to paint. Unsurprisingly they gravitated to the artists' district on the left bank of the Seine around Montparnasse in the 14th district. Their apartment at number 17 rue Campagne-Première was also the address of French photographer Eugene Atget (1857–1927).[23] He is best known for having photographed the entirety of the buildings of old Paris. The street was a magnet for artists of the avant garde. It later became home or studio to Tristan Tzara (1919), Man Ray (1920s) and to Louis Aragon (1929). In 1901 they spent the summer in Sligo awaiting the birth of their first child.

These years of London and Paris at the turn of the 20th century exposed Constance, the young woman, to radical ideas, perspectives and opinions and formed the floor of more militant ideas she was to develop in Ireland. She had experienced radical and progressive women in the arts who had taken steps to make an independent life of their own and to organise movements around their ideas.

Maeve Alys de Markievicz was born on 13 November 1901.[24] By that time, her sisters Mabel and Eva had left the family home along with their brother Mordaunt. There remained Lady Gore-Booth and Constance's unmarried brother Josslyn, the Baronet, along with thirteen servants.[25]

Some months later the couple returned to Paris leaving Maeve in the care of her grandmother.[26] The year 1902 found the couple in Ukraine in Casimir's home estate where they spent several months painting. They subsequently returned to Lissadell for Christmas and then back to the Ukraine (1903) where they collected Casimir's six-year-old son Stanislaw[27] from his deceased mother's family and returned to settle in Dublin, in Rathgar,[28] in the same neighbourhood as Maud Gonne MacBride and George Russell (AE).

For a short five year period the family was reunited with Casimir, Constance, 'Stasko' and Maeve. It was apparently quite chaotic with the children running happily wild and 'Con' and 'Casi' engaged in a round of parties and receptions. Casimir not only obtained some portrait commissions but took to writing plays in which Constance sometimes acted.[29] Together with George Russell, Lady Gregory, W.B. Yeats and other artists, they formed the United Arts Club in 1907 which was immensely successful in this period of national cultural revival. At the end of this short period, Maeve was sent back to Sligo to live with her widowed grandmother – she never again lived with her mother. Stasko was sent to a controversial Benedictine boarding school in Gorey, County Wexford.[30]

While much is made of her aristocratic and landowning background, a significant number of figures from the period were from highly educated backgrounds: Roger Casement had been a diplomat, Joseph Plunkett, a philosopher, poet and dramatist; Padraig Pearse had qualified as a barrister; Thomas MacDonagh, a lecturer; Arthur Griffith, a journalist and Erskine Childers, a novelist. Many of the principal leaders had been born (de Valera) or educated outside of Ireland (Maud Gonne), had lived (James Connolly, Joseph Plunkett, Arthur Griffith) or been imprisoned (Tom Clarke) abroad, or were returned emigrants (Michael Collins).[31] A short eight year period between 1908 and 1916 saw Constance make the transition from more personal political statements to a deep commitment to organised political opposition and broadly socialist ideas. She joined Drumcondra Sinn Féin which was where playwright Sean O'Casey belonged. He developed a deep antagonism towards her and later left the Irish Citizen Army on account of her. The young Helena Molony recruited her to Inghinidhe na hÉireann where she became close to its leader Maud Gonne MacBride.

In 1909 she founded a nationalist boy scout movement, Na Fianna Éireann. This was a big step from joining already existing organisations to forming an entirely new one. Baden-Powell's scouting movement had taken off with his book *Scouting for Boys* in 1908 and Constance had spotted this. She had the brilliant idea of forming a nationalist form of scouts in Ireland, a notion which she developed with her friend Bulmer Hobson. So while the 2nd patrol of the Irish Baden Scouts was meeting at 5 Upper Camden Street from 1908, Constance took rooms for the Fianna at 34 Lower Camden Street. She wanted her scouts to have specific skills. So besides learning to drill, camp and survive, Constance wanted her boys to handle real weapons and to learn to shoot. The Fianna came from working class or very poor households. It was many of these same boys – later teenagers and young men – who were to join in the uprising in 1916. An approach by James Connolly to Inghinidhe na hÉireann to start providing school meals brought Constance into direct contact again with children and poor families. She also tried, unsuccessfully, to establish a commune at Belcamp Park in Raheny on the model of the earlier rural Ralahine. Like Ralahine it ended in spectacular failure with chaos and debts.

During the 1913 lockout the employers determined to starve the workers back to their jobs if they would not agree to give up membership of the Irish Transport and General Workers Union. In fact the workers and their families did begin to starve. The union decided to allow a soup kitchen to be opened in the basement of Liberty Hall on Beresford Place which had once been the Northumberland Hotel in the 1830s and had kitchens and storage rooms in the basement.[32] Constance, Hanna Sheehy Skeffington and many from the franchise movement wearing franchise emblems involved themselves in the food kitchen. Vegetables were scrounged from here and there in the mornings, peeled and chopped for hours and converted into cauldrons of steamy soup or stew.[33] Constance was in the thick of it, according to Louie Bennett:

> Madame Markievicz [was] in a big overall, with sleeves rolled up, presiding over a cauldron of stew, surrounded by a crowd of gaunt women and children carrying bowls and cans.[34]

One can also add: with her hair falling down and a cigarette in her mouth. In front of her was 'a procession of countless gaunt and despondent faces'.[35] The painter William Orpen came to the basement to make sketches of the scenes. He described it:

> The air was pungent with the smell of the cauldrons of soup from the basement, and of the Dubliners who came with their bottles, tin cans, or any kind of utensil that would hold this hot, life giving stuff. All day long lines of starving people waiting for their turn, very quiet and silent, no rough words or jostling: they were too weak for such thing.[36]

James Connolly's daughter Nora commented:

> There were big tubs on the floor; around these girls were peeling potatoes and preparing vegetables; others were busy cutting up meat; others were tending the boilers; all under the supervision of Madame Markievicz. She was in charge of the

kitchens, and from early morning till late at night was to be found there. Never sparing herself – her only thought that the hungry should be fed.[37]

Sean O'Casey, who supported the kitchens, saw her as an aristocrat, while Maud Gonne in contrast had the following perception, 'for Madame had a personal and real sympathy with the poor that removed all taint of the Lady Bountiful and made her a comrade among comrades'.[38]

There were other food relief operations at the time.[39] Some were organised by the newly-formed Irish Women Workers' Union, and by the suffragettes. Others were an expanded version of the penny dinners already provided by charitable bodies and religious institutions. Yet more were initiatives of the Society of St Vincent de Paul or supported by the Ladies Relief Committee under the Lady Mayoress of Dublin. Liberty Hall was the biggest in scale and lasted in different forms for most of the seven months of the lockout. Admission was by a 'ticket' for trade union members and their families.

The British Trade Union Congress shipped over eleven large food consignments between 1913 and 1914. Part was delivered directly to workers in the form of food parcels and the remainder cooked, taking account of the cost and availability of fuel supplies. A ship arriving on 4 October 1913 carried 20,000 packages of groceries and 20,000 packages of potatoes. At one point, when food was running low, a plan was developed to send some of the strikers' children to hospitable labour-minded families in England. This led to an almighty row between the unions and the Catholic Church and had to be abandoned.[40]

In 1913 the Irish Citizen Army was born as a preventive measure against the attacks on workers during the strike. The lockout ended in defeat in 1914.[41] There are many anecdotal references to Arnotts having supplied the uniforms of the Irish Citizen Army. However this is not confirmed in Arnotts' own history of itself.[42]

Constance and Casimir's lives were heading in different directions. During 1913, Casimir left his wife and children and left Ireland altogether. She did not hear from him again for six or seven years. Maeve was already in Sligo and Stasko was sent to England, to the family of Constance's married sister, Mabel Foster.

In 1916, Constance was second officer in command in St Stephen's Green. Under bombardment from the Shelbourne Hotel side her unit took over the College of Surgeons and held siege there for almost a week. A field hospital was established in the basement. She was the only woman officer during the Rising. When word came that the rebels were to surrender on Sunday 30 April 1916, she was not at all demoralised:

> The Countess walked out of the building at their head. She was dressed entirely in green ... She walked up to the officer and, saluting, took out her revolver, which she kissed affectionately, and then handed it up.[43]

She refused the offer of a lift to prison and preferred to walk with dignity through the city. She was imprisoned and condemned to death by court martial, later commuted to penal servitude for life. She was removed to England to Aylesbury prison.

Markievicz was the first woman to be elected to the British Parliament at Westminster in 1918 and the first woman Cabinet member in Western Europe. She did not take her seat but did visit the House of Commons and saw her name above the coat peg reserved for her. She was not, however, the first woman to enter a parliament. That honour goes to Alexandra Kollontai who was named Commissar of Social Welfare immediately after the Bolshevik Revolution which overturned the Russian Tsar in October 1917.[44] She represented the St Patrick's constituency in 1918 and the Dublin South City constituency in 1921.

As Minister for Labour Markievicz was part of the Cabinet of the first Dáil Eireann. Delia Larkin had founded the Irish Women Workers' Union in 1911, and James Larkin, Hanna Sheehy Skeffington and Constance spoke at the launch. There are some differences in historical interpretation of this event as to whether the main driving force was a labour movement initiative, or a separatist-feminist orientation.[45] By 1916 Constance had been elected Honorary President, with Helena Molony as General Secretary from 1915. She recalled the following resolution of a labour dispute:

> The conference had droned on for hours. Miss Bennett was eloquent, the employer was adamant, and no appreciable advance had been made. Then Madame Markievicz strode in, pulled out her gun, pointed it at the terrified employer – 'ten minutes to settle, after that, I shoot!' The employer settled after seven minutes.[46]

Markievicz played an important role in the disaffection and desertion of Royal Irish Constabulary (RIC) members from the police force during the War of Independence. An order was issued to all Sinn Féin clubs that 'these men should be given every opportunity to live as good Irish citizens in their native districts'[47] and be provided with hardship funds if needed and employment. Former RIC officer Jeremiah Mee, who had led a mutiny against a British officer in Listowel, County Kerry, was eventually placed in her offices with a view to implementing this policy.[48]

By 1921 employers and workers were increasingly seeking the settling of disputes via the new parallel government with Constance as Minister for Labour. Her office dealt with farms, mills, quarries, road workers, dairies, hospitals and clerical workers.[49] This was not to be rewarded. In the new Cabinet of 1921 the labour portfolio was placed outside the Cabinet – perhaps an omen of what was to come.

She herself had argued in 1913 that there were three great national movements developing concurrently – 'the national movement, the women's movement and the industrial movement'.[50] Efforts were made to organically connect them so that labouring women's working conditions were not ignored by some of the better educated women in franchise groups. *The Irish Citizen* urged the appointment of additional factory inspectors, and suffrage women who joined in supporting the lockout in 1913 wore their suffrage badges.[51] The theme emerges repeatedly as she spoke in 1915:

> ... The two brilliant classes of women who follow this higher ideal are Suffragettes and the Trades Union or Labour women. In them lies the hope of the future. But for them, women are everywhere today in a position of inferiority.[52]

Despite the tendency for memberships to maintain strict lines of contact, there was considerable overlap in fact. Between 1908 and 1916 Constance managed to keep friendships and lines of contact open between the main political and national tendencies, with the exception of the Irish Republican Brotherhood (IRB) which was extremely secretive but centrally, both politically and operationally, significant in the 1916 Rising.

In aligning herself openly and clearly with the movement of labour, Constance knew what she was doing and was conscious of James Connolly's analysis of socialism as involving the reconquest of Ireland, meaning the social as well as the political independence from servitude for every man, woman and child.[53]

Following the War of Independence she refused with other elected women to recognise the Treaty which in her opinion provided for dominion status to Ireland.[54] She argued, 'It is the capitalist interests in England and Ireland that are pushing the Treaty to block the march of the working people in England and Ireland'.[55] Margaret Mac Curtain, examining the debates of the time, found that the Republican women in the treaty debates expressed a political ideology that had not moved with the times. 'Had they been more constitutionally agile in the Treaty Debate they might well have held the balance of power between the two sides', she argues.[56]

Jason Knirck too proposes that the role of the six anti-Treaty women in the debate left a lasting mark on the subsequent second class treatment of women by political parties. Several of their arguments did not apply to Constance but she did not de-legitimise them.[57] Many of the women argued that they were speaking for or on behalf of their now dead family members, or were speaking directly as their dead kin would have wanted them to speak. They stressed the suffering of those left behind as widows, sisters, mothers. Markievicz did not need to justify her presence as a family member of a martyr – she had fought herself, had risked death and been condemned to death and then life in prison.

In the immediate year and later years after the Rising, Constance was repeatedly arrested, imprisoned, tried or interned in both Ireland and England. She spent over 14 months in prison in Aylesbury, England (1916–1917); she endured time in Kilmainham (1916), in Holloway, London (1918), in Cork (1919), in Mountjoy (1920) and in the North Dublin Union (1923). Her sister Eva and her companion Esther supported her physically, socially and psychologically during these imprisonments. Her spirits were cheered by a successful two month speaking tour of America in 1922 at the request of de Valera[58] and by a period in Scotland writing, editing and printing. She was a clever speaker in addressing American audiences. Here is what she said in Seattle:

> America in 1776 would not have accepted from England what England offers Ireland today. The United States would not have consented to a Governor General with a power greater than a king. She would not have allowed England naval supervision of all her ports. Ireland wants her independence just as badly as did America in 1776.[59]

Constance regularly drove out to Roebuck House around 1926 and met up with a crowd which included Maud Gonne MacBride and Charlotte Despard, writers R.M. Fox and Patricia Lynch, Roddy Connolly (son of James), Helena Molony and Peadar O'Donnell.[60]

Those long stretches in prison, sometimes in solitary confinement, in the cold and with disgusting food eventually took their toll. Her appearance and health deteriorated. She seemed depressed and worn out. In 1926 Eva, her beloved sister, life-long friend and confidante, died. The following year Constance too died following an operation for appendicitis at the age of 59 in a public ward in Sir Patrick Dun's hospital in the presence of Casimir,[61] Maeve,[62] Stasko,[63] Esther Roper, Helena Molony, Mrs Coghlan and Hanna Sheehy Skeffington. She left no house, she had no home, no estate, few belongings. She left £329 to Maeve.

Her funeral was as controversial as her life. She died two days after the funeral of Minister of Justice Kevin O'Higgins who had been assassinated. The Mansion House was refused as a place for her to lie – Kevin O'Higgins had lain there. Eventually she was placed in the Rotunda where 100,000 came to mourn her passing.[64] She was brought in a slow and solemn walk to Glasnevin Cemetery followed by miles of mourners.[65] Eight lorries of flowers followed her. An estimated 300,000 lined the streets of Dublin to mark her last passing. At the graveside, where de Valera spoke the oration, police hovered menacingly to prevent shots being fired over her grave.

Constance Markievicz was cosmopolitan, bohemian, independent, instinctive and spontaneous, artistic, unconventional, driven, exasperating, financially hopeless, but above all a fearless woman.

ACKNOWLEDGEMENTS
I am grateful to Brendan Rooney, Curator of Irish Art at the National Gallery of Ireland and to Robert Winckworth at the Archives of the Slade School held at University College London. Colin Conroy clarified a number of facts concerning Stanislaw's education and the role of Arnotts Department Store in Henry Street. Patricia Kinane of the Royal College of Surgeons in Ireland and Joe Sherlock, Chief Porter, facilitated an interesting visit to the points of interest concerning 1916 in the building.

SOURCES
1   Lisadill was the spelling of the townland in the Census which we now call Lissadell.
2   *Census of the Population of Ireland*, 1871. Table XLI, Online Historical Population, University of Essex.
3   Seán Ó Faoláin, *Constance Markievicz* (London, Sphere Books, 1967).
4   Sonja Tiernan, *Eva Gore-Booth: An image of such politics* (Manchester, Manchester University Press, 2012).
5   Rosemary Cullen Owens, *A Social History of Women in Ireland 1870–1970* (Dublin, Gill and Macmillan, 2005), p. 40.
6   Anders Lindkvist, 'Anna Nordgren – A cosmopolite on the art scene at the turn of the century'. Thesis at Master level (in Swedish), Department of Art History, Uppsala University, Sweden, 2011.
7   See woodward entry in www.1890s.ca.
8   Courtesy of the archives of University College London, 2013, holder of the Slade archives.
9   www.ucl.ac.uk/slade/about/history.
10 Negley Harte and John North, *The World of UCL 1828–2004* (London, UCL Press, 2004), pp 135–40.

11   Sarah Purser (1848–1943) was a portraitist and founder of 'An Túr Gloine' (The Glass Tower) movement to resurrect and restore stained glass art in Ireland. Some images of her work and commentaries can be viewed online at the National Gallery of Ireland at www.nationalgallery.ie.

12   Chelsea in Kensington, *Survey of London*, vol. 4.1, pp 162–194, at www.british-history.ac.uk.

13   Anne Haverty, *Constance Markievicz: Irish Revolutionary* (London, Pandora, 1988), p. 34; and Anne Marreco, *The Rebel Countess: The Life and Times of Constance Markievicz* (New York, Chilton Books, 1967), p. 56.

14   Patented by Winsor Newton company in 1840. see: www. winsornewton.com.

15   This address is today occupied by the ESAG Penninghen School of Art and Architecture and was visited by the author in February 2013. ESAG Penninghen, *Livret de l'Étudiant 2012–2013* (Paris, 2012).

16   Marek Zgórniak, 'Polish students at the Académie Julian until 1919', *RIHA Journal*, 0050, 10 August 2012. Originally published in Polish, http://www.riha-journal.org/articles/2012-jul-sep/zgorniak-polish-students; accessed 7.2.2013.

17   Gabriel P. Weisberg and Jane R. Becker, *Overcoming all obstacles: the women of Académie Julian* (New Jersey, Rutgers University, 1999).

18   Catherine Fehrer, 'Women at the Académie Julian in Paris', *The Burlington Magazine*, Vol. 136, No. 1100, November 1994, pp 752–757.

19   See www.irishmeninparis.org/Artists.

20   *New York Times*, 25 November 1913, p. 4. Her daughter Beatrice Forbes Robertson Hale went on to write a book entitled *What Women Want* published in 1914.

21   Kazimierz Dunin Markiewicz in the more Polish spelling.

22   Wanda Ryan-Smolin, 'Casimir Dunin Markievicz: Painter and Playwright', *Irish Arts Review*, 1995, Vol. 11. pp 180–184.

23   Atget is believed to have influenced the work of Matisse and Picasso.

24   *De Markievicz* is the birth registration name of Maeve.

25   See census at www.nationalarchives.ie 1901 online for occupants of houses in Lissadill, County Sligo.

26   Clive Scoular, *Maeve de Markievicz: Daughter of Constance* (author, 2006).

27 Known as Stasko for short, c. 1896–c.1972.
28 'St Marys', Frankfort Avenue. See 'Countess Markievicz: The Rebel Countess', essay of Irish Labour History Society, Dublin.
29 A full-length portrait of Constance painted by Casimir is in the possession of the National Gallery of Ireland.
30 Opened by Fr Sweetman it was never fully approved of by the Benedictines and was later closed down.
31 Dorothy Macardle, *The Irish Republic* (Dublin, The Irish Press, 1951).
32 Jacqueline Van Voris, *Constance de Markievicz in the Cause of Ireland* (University of Massachusetts Press, 1967), p. 111.
33 An extensive account of the relief operations is provided by Ann Mathews in 'Poverty paraded the streets, 1913: the mothers and children' in Francis Devine (ed.), *A Capital in Conflict: Dublin City and the 1913 Lockout* (Dublin City Council, 2013).
34 R.M. Fox, *Rebel Irishwomen*, (Dublin, Progress House, 1967).
35 Haverty, *op cit*, p. 22.
36 William Orpen, 'Larkin at Liberty Hall' in Donal Nevin (ed.), *James Larkin: Lion of the Fold* (Dublin, Gill and Macmillan, 1998), p. 204.
37 Nora Connolly O'Brien, *Portrait of a Rebel Father* (Dublin, Talbot Press, 1935), p. 152.
38 Haverty, *op cit*, p. 110.
39 Mary Jones, *Those Obstreperous Lassies: A History of the Irish Women Workers' Union* (Dublin, Gill and Macmillan, 1998), p. 11.
40 Fergus D'Arcy, 'Larkin and the Dublin Lock-out', in Donal Nevin (ed.), *op cit*, p. 44.
41 Margaret Mac Curtain, 'Women, the Vote and Revolution', in Margaret Mac Curtain and Donncha Ó Corrain (eds), *Women in Irish Society: The Historical Dimension* (Dublin, Arlen House, 1978), p. 53.
42 R. Nesbitt, *At Arnotts of Dublin 1843–1993* (Dublin, Farmar, 1993).
43 *Irish Times*, 2 May 1916, p. 3.
44 Alix Holt (ed.), *Selected Writings of Alexandra Kollontai* (London, Allison and Busby, 1977), p. 3.
45 Jones, *op cit*, p. 25; Therese Moriarty in Donal Nevin (ed.), *op cit*, p. 95.
46 Jones, *op cit*, p. 43.
47 Van Voris, *op cit*, p. 285.

48 J.A. Gaughan (ed.), *Memoirs of Constable Jeremiah Mee* (Cork, Mercier Press, 2012).

49 Macardle, *op cit*, p. 388.

50 Cullen Owens, *op cit*, p. 93.

51 A very detailed analysis of this period is provided in Cullen Owens, *op cit*, chapters 4–6.

52 Rosemary Cullen Owens, *Smashing Times: A History of the Irish Women's Suffrage Movement 1889–1922* (Dublin, Attic Press, 1984), p. 93.

53 Cited from J. Connolly in R.M. Fox, *op cit*, p. 17.

54 Of interest among a multitude of publications on this topic are those of Dorothy Macardle, *op cit*; Jason Knirck, *Women of the Dáil: Gender, Republicanism and the Anglo-Irish Treaty* (Dublin, Irish Academic Press, 2006); Margaret Ward, *Unmanageable Revolutionaries: Women and Irish Nationalism* (London, Pluto Press, 1995).

55 Macardle, *op cit*, p. 630.

56 Mac Curtain, *op cit*, p. 55.

57 Knirck, *op cit*.

58 Joanne Mooney Eichacker, *Irish Republican Women in America: Lecture Tours 1916–1925* (Dublin, Irish Academic Press, 2003), pp 138–155.

59 *Ibid*, p. 149.

60 Margaret Mulvihill, *Charlotte Despard: A Biography* (London, Pandora, 1989), p. 150.

61 Casimir died in Warsaw, Poland in 1932.

62 Maeve died in Hampstead, North London on 8 June 1962 and left £2,592.8s.8d. Her address was 30 Parliament Hill, London NW3.

63 Stasko eventually returned to Ireland where he wrote a series of articles about his family in the *Irish Times* in late 1937 and early 1938. He later moved to London and from there to the US where he died around 1972.

64 Esther Roper (ed.), *Prison Letters of Countess Markievicz* (London, Longmans Green and Co., 1934), p. 110.

65 Macardle, *op cit*, p. 117.

IRELAND'S MAGDALENE LAUNDRIES: CONFRONTING A HISTORY NOT YET IN THE PAST

Maeve O'Rourke and James M. Smith[1]

... In the laundries themselves some women spent weeks, others months, more of them years, but the thread that ran through their many stories was a palpable sense of suffocation, not just physical in that they were incarcerated but psychological, spiritual and social.[2]

... Nowhere in any of this did the word or concept of citizenship, personal rights and personal freedoms appear ... This was an Ireland where justice and morality were conflated so that there was much in the way of morality but little in the way of justice, and justice was not done for these women.[3]

Statements of An Taoiseach, Enda Kenny, TD
and An Tánaiste, Eamon Gilmore, TD
Dáil Éireann, 19 February 2013

INTRODUCTION

On 19 February 2013, the Taoiseach and Tánaiste offered an emotional apology to women who had survived Ireland's Magdalene Laundries – the infamous convents where over 10,000 girls and women were imprisoned and forced into unpaid labour between 1922 and 1996.[4]

The apology was the result of a hard-fought campaign by several groups, including Justice for Magdalenes (supported by the National Women's Council of Ireland, Labour Women, the Irish Council for Civil Liberties, Amnesty International Ireland and others), Magdalene Survivors Together, the Irish Women Survivors Support Network (UK), and individual survivors. We know of one survivor who wrote to successive Presidents, Taoisigh and Ministers for Justice over numerous decades recounting her experience and asserting the State's responsibility. It was also the product of the late Mary Raftery's tenacious investigative journalism regarding the exhumation and cremation in 1993 of Magdalene women who had been buried in the grounds of the Magdalene Laundry at High Park, Drumcondra. Those exhumations led to the establishment of the Magdalen Memorial Committee (MMC), comprised primarily of relatives and friends of the High Park women, which successfully lobbied the Office of Public Works for a national memorial – the bench and commemorative plaque in Dublin's St Stephen's Green. In 2003, Raftery revealed that the Sisters of Our Lady of Charity had received exhumation licences from the State in 1993 for 155 bodies without producing death certificates for 80 women or the full names of 46 women.[5] This prompted Mari Steed, Claire McGettrick and Angela Murphy to join with some of the original members of the MMC to establish Justice for Magdalenes (JFM), with the aim of achieving a State apology and redress for all survivors.[6]

This chapter describes what is known about the treatment of girls and women in Ireland's Magdalene Laundries and the State's involvement in the institutions' operation, while knowingly failing to regulate them to prevent arbitrary detention, slavery or servitude, forced labour, psychological or physical torture or ill-treatment, denial of education to children, and many other forms of abuse. It outlines the advocacy campaign to bring about a State apology, including JFM's use of domestic and international human rights avenues. The chapter then discusses the redress measures which have been offered to survivors and highlights major shortcomings in the reparation afforded so far. Ultimately, the chapter concludes, more needs to be done to demonstrate that the Irish State (including Irish society) now respects and understands its obligations to protect these women's and others' fundamental human rights.

Although this chapter does not address Ireland's Mother and Baby Homes, it speaks to the need for civil society organisations and members of the public to be fully engaged and critically informed as the State's 'Commission of Investigation into Mother and Baby Homes and Certain Related Matters' conducts its work and reports its findings on abuses in institutions that, while distinct and separate, operated on similar lines and impacted women in similar ways as did the Magdalene Laundries.[7]

EVIDENCE OF GROSS AND SYSTEMATIC HUMAN RIGHTS ABUSE IN IRELAND'S MAGDALENE LAUNDRIES

Women who spent time in Magdalene Laundries have spoken out about their experiences, from about the 1940s to the late 1970s, by recording oral histories,[8] providing testimony to the United Nations,[9] giving written and oral testimony to the government's Inter-departmental Committee to establish the facts of State involvement with the Magdalene Laundries,[10] engaging with the Magdalen Commission,[11] speaking out in the media and in writing.[12]

Justice for Magdalenes Research has deposited approximately 3,700 pages of archival material on the

Magdalene Laundries to the University College Dublin archives,[13] and the group's website[14] and several academic studies[15] are further sources of information.

In 2011, the Fine Gael/Labour government established an Inter-departmental Committee to establish the facts of State involvement with the Magdalene Laundries (IDC), the State having maintained in defence of calls for a Magdalene apology over the preceding decade that the institutions were privately owned and operated and that the number of referrals facilitated by the State was insignificant. Although this inquiry drew no conclusions regarding the State's responsibility for abuse or failures to prevent it and was not an independent, thorough investigation into the abuse itself, the Committee's 1,212-page report revealed significant new information regarding the State's interactions with the institutions. It also provided some statistics about the number of girls and women who entered the Laundries, and their ages and routes of entry and exit – although these were hampered by gaps in the nuns' records, and the original data was not made available for examination outside the Committee.

The sources referred to in the above paragraphs, combined, tell us the following:

Ten Magdalene Laundries operated in Ireland from 1922 until the last remaining institution, at Sean McDermott Street in Dublin, closed in 1996. They were attached to convents in towns and cities around the country and were run by four religious congregations of Catholic nuns: the Sisters of Mercy (Galway and Dún Laoghaire), Good Shepherd Sisters (Cork, Limerick, Waterford and New Ross), Religious Sisters of Charity (Donnybrook and Cork) and Sisters of Our Lady of Charity (Drumcondra and Sean McDermott Street, Dublin).[16]

In the Magdalene Laundries, girls as young as nine and women were locked away and forced into penal servitude for a wide variety of reasons. Some had grown up in the care of the nuns, in residential schools funded and regulated by the State, and were deemed unsuited for independence and/or still in need of 'protection' upon reaching the age of release (typically 16 for Industrial Schools and 18 for Reformatory Schools). Some had been sexually abused, by a family member or other person, and the Magdalene served the purposes of 'containing' the problem and avoiding shame in a society that prioritised respectability. Confining the female victim in the Magdalene also protected the perpetrator of the crime. Some girls and women who had given birth to a child outside marriage, often at a Mother and Baby Home or County Home, and had been separated from their child, were then placed in a Magdalene to prevent the same thing happening again and/or because, cast out by her family, she had nowhere else to go.

The State used Magdalene Laundries as alternatives to prison (and in the absence of a female borstal), paying for the detention of girls and women following conviction, on probation and on remand. The State also used these institutions as places to detain girls and women in need of care, under the Health Acts. Priests and family members arranged for women to be confined for many reasons (eg, land and inheritance disputes, remarriage by a widower, etc), and a number of girls and women appear to have self-referred because of their need for shelter. The IDC reported that 26.5% of referrals to Magdalene Laundries were made or facilitated by the State. This statistic is called into question by the fact that the Committee treated transfers from other Magdalene Laundries (the second most common known route of entry) as non-State referrals,[17] and treated Legion of Mary and NSPCC referrals as neither State nor non-State because they included State and non-State referrals 'in unknown proportions'.[18]

According to the IDC, just over 10,000 girls and women were detained in Magdalene Laundries between 1922 and 1996. This is a significant under-estimate. The Sisters of Mercy could not produce records for the Dun Laoghaire laundry and produced only limited records for the Galway institution and the Committee excluded girls and women who entered before 1922 and remained thereafter – referring to such women as 'legacy' cases. JFM brought numerous examples to the IDC's attention of women listed on the 1901 and 1911 censuses who died in Magdalene Laundries post-1922, some as late as 1961, 1967 and even 1985 (in the care of the nuns after the closure of the Limerick institution). It has also emerged that many girls detained in 'voluntary' (unregulated but funded by the State) residential children's and teenage institutions known as 'Training Centres', sometimes on the same grounds as Magdalene Laundries, were forced by the nuns to enter and work in the Laundries for some or all of their days.[19]

Once inside the convents, girls and women were imprisoned behind locked doors, barred or unreachable windows and high walls (often with broken glass cemented at the apex). They were usually given no information as to when or whether they would be released. Upon entry, their names were often changed and they were given an identification number. Many women recall being instructed not to speak about their homeplace or family. Their hair was cut and their clothes were taken away and replaced with a drab uniform. A rule of silence was imposed at almost all times in Magdalene Laundries and, in many women's experiences, friendships were forbidden. Correspondence with the outside world was often intercepted or forbidden. Visits by friends or family were not encouraged and were often monitored when they did occur.

The girls and women were forced to work from morning until evening – washing, ironing or packing laundry, and sewing, embroidering or doing other manual labour. These Laundries were run on a commercial, for-profit basis, but the girls and women received no pay. No contributions ('stamps') were paid on their behalf to statutory pension schemes. The laundry they washed came not only from members of the public, local businesses and religious institutions, but also from numerous government departments, the defence forces, public hospitals, public schools, prisons and other State entities such as Leinster House, the Chief State Solicitor's Office, the Office of Public Works, the Land Commission, CIE and Áras an Uachtaráin (to name but a few).

Punishments for refusal to work included deprivation of meals, solitary confinement, physical abuse, forced kneeling for long periods or humiliation rituals, including shaving of hair. Survivors speak of constantly being under surveillance, being verbally insulted, feeling cold, having a poor diet and enduring humiliating and inadequate hygiene conditions. None of the girls received an education, and survivors dwell on this fact as determining their 'loss of opportunity' in later life.

It was common for the girls and women to believe that they would die inside. Many did: comparison of electoral registers against grave records at the Donnybrook location shows that over half of the women on electoral registers between 1954 and 1964 died in that institution.[20] If girls or women escaped – perhaps in the back of a laundry van, out an open door at delivery or collection time, or by scaling the wall – they were often captured and returned by the local Gardaí. The nuns punished escapees, in many cases, by transferring them to a different Magdalene Laundry. If and when a girl or woman was released, it was invariably without warning, without money and with only the clothes she was wearing. Some girls and women were given jobs in other institutions run by nuns; many fled abroad as soon as possible.

The State never regulated the Magdalene Laundries, despite its use of the institutions as places both of detention and care, its commercial dealings with them, its knowledge of the detention of young girls of school-going age, and its awareness that the girls and women were working for no pay.[21] The IDC noted that the commercial laundry premises were subject to the Factories Acts, and that Factories Inspectors visited the Laundries from 1957 onwards. According to the IDC's report, however, the inspectors were concerned with machinery and factory premises only. They did not question the age of the girls or the conditions under which the girls and women worked and lived.

THE CAMPAIGN FOR AN APOLOGY AND REDRESS
In the early 2000s, the then government refused to include the Magdalene Laundries in the investigation or compensation scheme concerning child abuse in State-funded, Church-managed residential institutions (in other words, the Commission to Inquire into Child Abuse[22] or the Residential Institutions Redress Board).[23] Speaking in Dáil Éireann on 12 February 2002, Dr Michael Woods, TD, then Minister for Education, explained why:

> The laundries differ substantially from the institutions now covered by the Bill in that the residents concerned were for the most part adults and the laundries were entirely private institutions, in respect of which public bodies had no function.

In 2009, following the publication of the Commission's report – commonly referred to as the Ryan Report – there were renewed calls to investigate abuses in the Laundries and provide redress to survivors as the media spotlight again fell on 'historic' Church-related institutional abuse.

The government's position remained the same. A new Minister for Education, Batt O'Keeffe, TD, insisted that the Laundries 'were not subject to State regulation or supervision' and that the 'State did not refer individuals to Magdalen Laundries nor was it complicit in referring individuals to them'.[24]

Dr James Smith of Boston College, a JFM advisory committee member, had at this point gathered significant evidence from State archives demonstrating that, in fact, the State had used Magdalene Laundries as alternatives to prisons, and that it was aware of transfers of girls between State-regulated Industrial and Reformatory Schools and Magdalene Laundries at least from the 1970s and similarly aware of transfers between Mother and Baby Homes and the Laundries. There was also evidence to suggest that government departments held service contracts with the Laundries. Having first circulated draft language towards a distinct Redress Scheme for Magdalene survivors in July 2009,[25] JFM began to gather the support of backbench government and opposition TDs, and throughout 2009 and 2010 met with several government departments, saw the formation of a cross-party *ad hoc* Oireachtas committee of TDs and Senators dedicated to the issue, gained the formal support of Labour Women and the National Women's Council of Ireland for a distinct redress scheme, and ensured the submission of numerous parliamentary questions on the issue.[26] JFM also wrote, on numerous occasions, to the four religious congregations directly involved, as well as meeting the Cardinal and Primate of all Ireland and the Archbishop of Dublin.[27]

In June 2010, and in light of the government's continuing refusal to accept State responsibility for the Magdalene Laundries, JFM submitted a detailed application to the Irish Human Rights Commission (IHRC) seeking an inquiry into the State's failure to protect the human rights of girls and women detained in the institutions between 1922 and 1996.[28] In it we argued that, far from absolving the State of responsibility for abuse, the refusal to regulate and supervise the Laundries while the State used these institutions for various purposes and was aware of their functions amounted to a gross failure to protect women and young girls from slavery, servitude or forced labour, in violation of numerous domestic, European and international legal obligations applicable at the time of the abuse.

Later the same year, in November, the IHRC responded by publishing a 27-page *Assessment* of potential human rights violations by the State and issuing a recommendation to government to immediately institute a statutory investigation into all allegations of abuse and to ensure compensation as appropriate.[29] The IHRC's intervention led to an adjournment debate in the Dáil, where backbench government and opposition TDs called for an apology and redress for survivors. It also helped generate widespread media coverage, which in turn resulted in significant public and political support for JFM's campaign.

By April 2011, the government (now changed, from Fianna Fáil-led to a Fine Gael/Labour coalition) had yet to respond to the IHRC's recommendation. Maeve O'Rourke, in support of JFM's campaign objectives, made a submission to the United Nations Committee against Torture (CAT) in advance of the CAT's first examination of Ireland's compliance with the UN Convention Against Torture.[30] Four women, survivors of the Laundries living in the United Kingdom, gave their testimony to JFM and, with their informed consent and having anonymised their testimonies, O'Rourke argued to the CAT (in writing and orally in Geneva) that the treatment they recounted amounted to torture or cruel, inhuman or degrading treatment or punishment. The CAT's proceedings, for the first time, were streamed online and JFM was able to share the footage with the women who had provided their testimony.

Although the last Magdalene Laundry had closed before Ireland ratified the Convention Against Torture in 2002, the CAT accepted O'Rourke's argument that the State held continuing obligations under the Convention, since ratification, to investigate allegations of and ensure redress for past torture or ill-treatment which was having significant continuing effects on survivors.[31] The CAT responded in June 2011, and like the IHRC, issued a recommendation to the Irish government to immediately establish an independent investigation into all allegations of abuse in the Laundries and to ensure redress. The CAT also recommended the prosecution of perpetrators. Moreover, the CAT deemed the issue of such urgency, especially considering the age profile of many survivors, that it earmarked this recommendation as one of four for which the State was given a year to demonstrate direct action. These recommendations were covered by news agencies worldwide, and they galvanised further public support at home and abroad – including through email petitions – for JFM's campaign.[32]

Just over one week after the CAT's recommendations, the Minister for Justice, Alan Shatter TD, announced the creation of an Inter-departmental Committee to establish the facts of State interaction with the Magdalene Laundries (IDC).[33] Although the Committee had an Independent Chair, in then Senator Martin McAleese, its other members were senior civil servants from six government departments which, it turned out, were responsible for referring women to and/or doing business with the Laundries in the past. This is one of the reasons why the UN has never accepted that Ireland has ensured an independent and thorough investigation, as required by international law. The Committee's mandate was narrow: it did not extend to investigating allegations of abuse or to making recommendations on the basis of its findings regarding State involvement. There were no published terms of reference for the investigation,[34] there was no public invitation to submit evidence, and the Committee had no statutory powers to compel evidence. At the outset, the Committee agreed with the four religious orders which operated the Magdalene Laundries that it would destroy all copies and return all evidence received from them at the conclusion of its work.[35]

The IDC carried out its inquiries over 18 months, during which time it met with a number of Magdalene survivors, approximately half of whom were still living in the care of the nuns at a variety of convent and nursing home locations. Over those 18 months, JFM gathered 3,700 pages of documentary evidence and almost 800 pages of testimony from survivors and other witnesses regarding State involvement with abuse.[36] We submitted this evidence, along with a 150-page narrative, or Principal Submission,[37] to the Committee in August 2012.[38]

While the IDC was proceeding, RTÉ broadcast a number of *Prime Time* documentaries on the Magdalene Laundries – the first documentaries to air on RTÉ television despite a number having been made over the decades[39] – and national and international newspapers and broadcasters continued to report on the issue.[40] JFM designed a revised set of reparation proposals[41] which we submitted to the Department of Justice at the Minister's invitation in October 2011. The UN Committee against Torture re-visited its Magdalene recommendation as part of the one-year Follow-Up procedure in May 2012, by which time JFM had also raised the Magdalene Laundries at the UN Human Rights Council's Universal Periodic Review of

Ireland in late 2011. In July 2012, Dr Geoffrey Shannon, Special Rapporteur on Child Protection in Ireland, called for redress for Magdalene survivors and recommended a full investigation 'with a view to criminal prosecutions where appropriate'.[42]

Finally, the IDC released its report (commonly referred to as the McAleese Report) on 5 February 2013. But, despite much anticipation, the expected apology was not immediately forthcoming. In his comments on the floor of Dáil Éireann that afternoon, the Taoiseach, Enda Kenny, TD, noted the State's involvement in 26% of placements in the Laundries but failed to comment on other forms of official support of their operation, or the State's abject failure to regulate and supervise them. The Taoiseach did not acknowledge any of the exploitation that had taken place, drawing the Dáil's attention instead to the fact that the report displayed 'no evidence of sexual abuse in the Magdalene Laundries'. As Dr Katherine O'Donnell, JFM advisory committee member, noted at the time, 'it was as if the *only* abuse of women worth noting by Kenny was sexual abuse'. The Taoiseach stated that he regretted 'the stigma attached to those who worked in Magdalen laundries and stayed in the accommodation there'. He then noted the Committee's statistics on duration of stay before calling for members of the Dáil to avoid 'jumping to conclusions' in advance of a planned debate on the report two weeks later.[43]

The manner in which the IDC chose to present the evidence it had gathered clearly enabled and was reflected in the Taoiseach's own response on 5 February 2013. Essentially, the Committee's report and Taoiseach's statement implied that, despite the undeniable extent of State involvement with the Magdalene Laundries, the girls and women were not treated as badly as children in Industrial and Reformatory Schools and, in any case, they did not stay confined for very long. Neither of these suggestions withstands scrutiny, not only because of the inappropriateness of the implied 'hierarchy' of abuse or the suggestion that several months or years of arbitrary detention is 'not as bad' as several decades, but also because of the existing evidence to the contrary.

The Committee chose to go outside its remit to include a chapter (the second last in its report) on 'Living and Working Conditions', in which it failed to investigate whether or not the girls and women had been locked into the Magdalene Laundries and whether or not they had been forced to work for no pay. It further failed to inquire into whether or not girls had been denied an education. Chapter 19 begins by stating that:

> [i]t is likely that assumptions have been made regarding these institutions based on the evidence of the grievous abuse suffered by male and female children in Industrial and Reformatory Schools in Ireland throughout the twentieth century.[44]

It then discusses sexual abuse, of which the Committee reports one allegation only (although the Committee notes that a number of women suffered sexual abuse before being placed in a Magdalene institution).

Regarding physical abuse, Chapter 19 states that '[a] large majority of the women who shared their stories with the Committee stated that they had neither experienced nor seen other girls or women suffer physical abuse', despite Chapter 19 containing paragraph after paragraph of testimony describing constant forced labour as well as some women's evidence of being shaken, 'dug' at with implements and slapped. Chapter 19 classifies as 'non-physical punishment' being forcibly returned to a Laundry by the Gardaí, being forced into solitary confinement, being forced to kneel for two hours and having soiled bedsheets pinned to one's back, and does not classify as punishment at all the hair cutting girls and women were subjected to upon entry. Although Chapter 19 includes a section entitled 'Lack of information and a real fear of remaining there until death', it fails to analyse this as evidence of psychological torture or cruel, inhuman or degrading treatment, or abuse at all. The IDC did not include in Chapter 19 (or elsewhere in its Report) one line from the almost-800 pages of testimony submitted by JFM, despite assuring us that our offer to have the testimony sworn was unnecessary.

Regarding duration of stay, the IDC's Executive Summary fails to note several major limitations to its statistical findings. In the Dáil on 5 February 2013, the Taoiseach highlighted the IDC's finding that 61% of girls and women stayed in a Magdalene Laundry for less than one year. When 288 survivors spoke to Mr Justice John Quirke's 'Magdalene Commission' later in 2013, only 9% reported being detained for less than 12 months.[45] According to the IDC (although not noted in its Executive Summary), the average duration of stay was 3.22 years. The body of the IDC's report makes clear, however, that its findings were based on only 42% of entry records because duration of stay was recorded in only 6,151 cases (of 14,607 entries, including repeat entries, for which there are records). Furthermore, the Committee treated each transfer between Laundries as beginning a new duration of stay, and the Committee disregarded entirely for these statistics the continued detention, post-1922, of women who had entered before independence.[46] The Committee's statistics on deaths in the Laundries exclude all women who remained in the institutions after their closure and later died in nursing homes while still in the nuns' care. Its statistics on duration of stay also exclude the continued institutionalisation of these women following the Laundries' closure.

For two weeks following the publication of the IDC's report, JFM and other groups campaigned tirelessly for the government to apologise to the women and ensure reparation. The Taoiseach and a number of Ministers met with women at Leinster House and at the Irish embassy in London, where the women repeated what they had told the Committee about the conditions they had endured and the ongoing impact on their and their families' lives. JFM worked with a number of TDs, from government and opposition parties, to read anonymised survivor testimony from the group's Principal Submission to the IDC into the Dáil record during a Private Members' debate on 12 February 2013. Again, the testimony spoke to the women's lived experience during and after their time in the Laundries and several deputies took the opportunity to assert, 'I believe the women'. Finally, on 19 February 2013, the day of the much-anticipated State apology, and working alongside Amnesty International-Ireland and the Irish Council for Civil Liberties, JFM conducted a briefing on the IDC Report for all members of the Oireachtas at Leinster House.

APOLOGY AND 'EX GRATIA' REDRESS: HAVE WE DONE ENOUGH?
The State apology to Magdalene survivors on 19 February was hugely significant. It lifted the silence that shrouded the experiences of girls and women in these institutions since the foundation of the State. It was an attempt – the Taoiseach's words made clear – to relieve the women of the burden of stigma and shame which Irish society had imposed on them in its effort to rationalise its appalling abuse as acceptable.

On the evening of the apology, the Taoiseach tasked the President of the Irish Law Reform Commission, Mr Justice John Quirke, with devising an *ex gratia* redress scheme for the surviving women. Mr Justice Quirke's 'Magdalen

Commission' spoke with 337 women about their needs, and also with the religious congregations who had 117 women still living in their care. Of 288 survivors living independently who gave information about their duration of stay in Magdalene Laundries, 68% had been detained for between one and five years and 22% for over five years. 90% of the women had received only primary level education. 66% reported serious health issues, and approximately one third lived alone. According to the Commission's report, one quarter of the women said that their living conditions were not warm and comfortable and 'a number of women spoke of having no hot water and no central heating'.[47]

In June 2013, the Minister for Justice announced Mr Justice Quirke's recommendations and stated that the government would accept them 'in full'.[48] The Department of Justice arranged for hundreds of women who had made contact with it and the Magdalen Commission to receive a copy of Judge Quirke's detailed recommendations. The recommendations included a medical card equivalent to the HAA Card provided to State-infected Hepatitis C patients in the 1990s (allowing for wide-ranging private and public health and community care provision), and equal provision of entitlements for women abroad, full contributory State pension payments (although only from August 2013, not backdated to retirement age), lump sum payments from €11,500 to €50,000 (with additional small weekly instalments for women detained for longer than 3½ years), and a Dedicated Unit to provide assistance to the women in meeting each other and the nuns if desired, advice regarding educational and housing benefits, a helpline accessible daily and a process to establish a memorial.

Bearing in mind the Constitutional rights violations, trauma and loss of opportunity suffered, the redress recommended was minimal. The government's characterisation of the scheme as *ex gratia* was significant: the measures on offer were 'as a gift', rather than as of right or as compensation for wrongdoing by the State. Yet, the women's position – their age, health and lack of access to legal aid, funds or evidence with which to bring court action if they wished – meant that they would readily accept.

Mr Justice Quirke recommended, and the Department of Justice implemented, a requirement that the women sign away all of their legal rights against the State upon accepting the initial financial benefits under the scheme. It is highly questionable whether this waiver is compatible with international human rights law or, indeed, the Constitution. The rights to freedom from slavery, servitude, forced labour, torture and ill-treatment are absolute, and therefore are arguably incapable of being signed away in this manner and under acute financial pressure. The scheme never purported to offer full redress, commensurate with the gravity of the harm suffered by each woman. The barrier the waiver presents to litigation is all the more concerning in light of the State's total failure to ensure accountability for the Magdalene abuses, either through an independent, thorough, statutory investigation with the power to make findings and recommendations or the prosecution of perpetrators. Relatives of Magdalene women who have died were not included in the *ex gratia* scheme. Their rights – as well as the rights of surviving women and their families – to the truth, accountability, access to records, information about the fate and whereabouts of their loved ones, guarantees of non-repetition and other forms of reparation have not been satisfied by the measures provided to date.

In 2013, the UN Committee against Torture wrote to the government asking whether and when it would establish the independent, thorough investigation recommended in 2011, and the UN Human Rights Committee and UN Committee on Economic, Social and Cultural Rights have since repeated the CAT's 2011 recommendation. In response, the government has refused to consider any further investigation, stating that the IDC carried out a 'comprehensive and objective' investigation into 'the factual position' regarding the Magdalene Laundries.[49] The government has asserted that the Committee found 'no factual evidence to support allegations of systematic torture or ill treatment of a criminal nature in these institutions'[50] and that '[t]he facts uncovered by the [Inter-departmental] Committee did not support the allegations that women were systematically detained unlawfully in these institutions or kept for long periods against their will'.[51]

Writing in 2016, the centenary year of the Easter Rising and the Proclamation of the Republic of Ireland, we find ourselves in a situation where the State, having apologised to the women in 2013, is once again distorting and refusing to acknowledge the reality of the Magdalene Laundries abuse because of the obligations which doing so would entail. As a result, numerous women who died in Magdalene Laundries still lie in unmarked or wrongly marked graves around Ireland. A detailed publication by Claire McGettrick, JFM's co-founder,[52] explains the failure of the IDC to establish the whereabouts and identities of many women who died in the institutions pre- and post-1922. The religious congregations still refuse to open their records to the public and, to date, they have not apologised or offered any form of reparation.[53] There have been no measures of accountability, and there has been no official attempt to root out and overturn the beliefs, behaviours, policies and structures which allowed the Magdalene Laundries abuse to happen and continue with impunity. The government's current stance in correspondence with the UN suggests that it still does not recognise the gravity of what occurred and, therefore, cannot guarantee that it will not happen to others or in similar ways again.

There have been numerous problems with the administration of the *ex gratia* scheme. As of July 2015, over 500 women had received lump sum payments from the scheme and presumably are now also benefitting from receipt of pension payments.[54] However, three years on from the apology, the women still have not received several other elements of the promised *ex gratia* redress, and the healthcare provided to women in Ireland is a vastly reduced version of what Mr Justice Quirke recommended.[55] Survivors living abroad were promised that they would receive equivalent health and community care benefits to those enjoyed by women resident in Ireland, yet to date the matter of healthcare for women abroad is still under review and many continue to suffer deteriorating health (and a number of women known to JFM have passed away since 2013). The Dedicated Unit, which was supposed to provide services and devise a memorial, has not yet materialised. Survivors of An Grianán 'training centre', who were forced by the nuns to work in the High Park laundry despite being registered as residing elsewhere, are deemed ineligible by the *ex gratia* scheme. Finally, JFM has always been concerned that survivors still living in the care of the religious congregations should have access to independent advocates; despite our repeated requests to government, however, independent advocacy services are not part of the scheme.

It stands to reason that if it took more than nine decades after independence for State policy regarding the Magdalene Laundries to be reversed, proper reparation will take sustained effort and commitment into the future. In a 'Follow-Up Report on State Involvement with the

Magdalen Laundries', published in June 2013, the IHRC recommended numerous policy and legislative reforms – alongside effective redress and independent, statutory investigations into allegations of torture or ill-treatment – to counteract the Magdalene legacy. The recommended reforms concern societal attitudes to women and girls; equality legislation; protection from forced labour and servitude; the rights of persons with disabilities; protective frameworks where the State outsources its functions; community based delivery of mental health services; tracing rights for adopted persons; and oversight of exhumations and cremations.[56]

It is the least we owe to the women who survived, and those who have died, to continue to question whether we are doing enough to make amends to the extent possible, and whether we have really transformed into the society we want to be – a society that guarantees no repetition of the past in the present or the future. As things stand, we have a long way to go to ensure that the Magdalene women are heard and that their rights, and the rights of all in Irish society, are respected today.

SOURCES

1   The authors wish to acknowledge Claire McGettrick, Mari Steed and Dr Katherine O'Donnell (University College Dublin) as their collaborators and partners in all work by JFM and JFM Research referred to in this essay and thank them for their comments on earlier drafts of this essay.

2   Remarks of the Taoiseach, Enda Kenny TD, Dáil Éireann, Magdalen Laundries Report: Statements (19 February 2013), https://www.kildarestreet.com/debate/?id=2013-02-19a.389; See also https://www.youtube.com/watch?v=hOQyl7ZpoH8

3   Remarks of the Tánaiste, Eamonn Gilmore TD, Dáil Éireann, Magdalen Laundries Report: Statements (19 February 2013), https://www.kildarestreet.com/debate/?id=2013-02-19a.391

4   For the history of these institutions prior to 1922, see Maria Luddy's *Women and Philanthropy in Nineteenth-Century Ireland*

(Cambridge, Cambridge University Press, 1995), Frances Finnegan's *Do Penance or Perish: A Study of Magdalen Asylums in Ireland* (Oxford, Oxford University Press, 2004), and James M. Smith's *Ireland's Magdalen Laundries and the Nation's Architecture of Containment* (South Bend, IN, University of Notre Dame Press, 2007). Luddy documents some 10,000 plus women entering these institutions prior to 1900, but cautions that the religious archives she had access to were incomplete and thus the final number is likely higher. See Luddy 125–29 and Smith 190.

5   See Mary Raftery, 'Restoring Dignity to Magdalenes', *The Irish Times*, 21 August 2003, 14. As Raftery explains, the initial exhumation license listed only 133 names, but the discovery of an additional 22 humans remains required an amended license be issued to the nuns, which it was immediately and without any investigation at the time.

6   JFM recognised survivors living in society, in Ireland and also as part of the Irish Diaspora worldwide, survivors still living in the 'care' of the religious congregation, the children born to some of these women and subsequently adopted or raised in residential institutions and blocked as adults from obtaining information about their birth-identities, and, in a special way, the women who died in the Laundries and whose final resting place remained shrouded in doubt and uncertainty.

7   See Commission of Investigation into Mother and Baby Homes and certain related matters, http://www.mbhcoi.ie/MBH.nsf/page/index-en

8   See Evelyn Glynn, *Breaking the Rule of Silence*, http://www.magdalenelaundrylimerick.com, University College Dublin, *Magdalene Institutions: Recording an Oral and Archival History*, http://www.magdaleneoralhistory.com

9   See Justice for Magdalenes, Submission to the United Nations Committee against Torture (May 2011), http://tbinternet.ohchr.org/Treaties/CAT/Shared%20Documents/IRL/INT_CAT_NGO_IRL_46_9041_E.pdf, pp 22-42.

10   See Justice for Magdalenes, Principal submissions to the Inter-departmental Committee to establish the facts of State involvement with the Magdalene Laundries (18 September 2012), http://www.magdalenelaundries.com/State_Involvement_in_the_Magdalene_Laundries_public.pdf; Report of the Inter-departmental Committee to establish the facts of State

involvement with the Magdalen laundries (February 2013) (hereafter 'IDC Report'), http://www.justice.ie/en/JELR/Pages/ MagdalenRpt2013, Introduction (paras 9, 10, 14, 18), Chapter 19.

11   See Report of the Magdalen Commission (May 2013), http://www.justice.ie/en/JELR/Pages/PB13000255

12   Among others: Julian Vignoles, 'Magdalene Laundry Institute for Outcast Women', RTÉ Radio 1, Ireland – Documentary on One (14 November 1992), http://www.rte.ie/radio1/doconone/ 2013/0207/647346-radio-documentary-magdalene-laundry-gal way/; *Washing Away the Stain*. 1993. Directed by Sarah Barclay and Andrea Miller. BBC2 Scotland (16 August); *Witness: Sex in a Cold Climate* (1998). Produced by Steve Humphries. Testimony Films for Channel 4, Great Britain. (16 March), https://www.yo utube.com/watch?v=FtxOePGgXPs; *Les Blanchisseuses De Magda len*. 1998. Une Film du Nicolas Glimois et Christophe Weber. Produced by Arnaud Hanelin. France 3/Sunset Preste; 'The Magdalen Laundries'. 1999. Narr. Steve Croft, prod. L. Franklin Devine. *60 Minutes*, CBS News, New York (3 January 1999); Mary Norris in Angela Lambert, 'A very Irish sort of hell', *Sunday Telegraph* (2 March 2003); RTÉ Radio 1, 'Liveline' (28, 29 September 2009); TG4, *The Forgotten Maggies* (July 2011); RTÉ Prime Time, 'The experiences of some of the Magdalene Laund ry women' (25 September 2012), http://www.rte.ie/news/player /2013/0205/3401239-the-experiences-of-some-of-the-magdalene- laundry-women/; Costello N, Legg K, Croghan D, Slattery M, Gambold M, *Whispering Hope* (Orion, 2016).

13   This archive replicates the evidence submitted by JFM to the IDC.

14   See www.magdalenelaundries.com

15   See note 4 above. A number of women also spoke to print journalists in the years running up to the State apology and ensuing months.

16   In the nineteenth-century, Ireland had as many as thirty of these institutions, both Catholic and Protestant, see Luddy, note 4 above. And, after 1922, a number of Magdalene institutions continued to operate in Northern Ireland, again both Catholic and Protestant.

17   See IDC Report, note 10 above, Chapter 8, p. 162.

18   See IDC Report, note 10 above, Chapter 8, p. 163.

19   On the evening of the apology, the government decided to include two such 'training centres', Stanhope Street and St

Mary's Wexford, in Mr Justice Quirke's terms of reference for the design of an *ex gratia* redress scheme, but excluded others such as 'An Grianán' in High Park, Drumcondra.

20 See Claire McGettrick, 'Death, Institutionalisation and Duration of Stay: A Critique of Chapter 16 of the Report of the Inter-departmental Committee to establish the Facts of State involvement with the Magdalen Laundries', www.magdalene laundries.com/JFMR_Critique_190215.pdf, pp 59–60.

21 The 1936 Conditions of Employment Act exempted the nuns operating Magdalene Laundries from the requirement to pay wages.

22 See www.childabusecommission.ie/

23 See www.rirb.ie

24 Letter from Batt O'Keeffe, Minister for Education and Science to Tom Kitt, TD, (4 September 2009), reproduced in Justice for Magdalenes, Information Booklet, http://www.magdalene laundries.com/jfm_booklet.pdf , p.6.

25 See http://www.magdalenelaundries.com/press/JFM%20PR% 2006-07-09.pdf

26 Press Releases documenting these, and other campaign activities are archived by date at, http://www.magdalenelaund ries.com/press_releases.htm

27 Despite productive meetings with Archbishop Diarmaid Martin and Cardinal Sean Brady, who encouraged JFM to petition the Congregation of Religious of Ireland (CORI) to facilitate a meeting with the four congregations, CORI announced on 1 October 2010 that the nuns would not meet with JFM.

28 See complete IHRC submission at 'Justice for Magdalenes Key Documents', http://www.magdalenelaundries.com/

29 See Irish Human Rights Commission, *Assessment of the Human Rights Issues Arising in relation to the 'Magdalen Laundries'*, November 2010, http://www.ihrec.ie/download/pdf/ihrc_asses sment_of_the_human_rights_issues_arising_in_relation_to_the _magdalen_laundries_nov_2010.pdf.

30 See complete UNCAT submission at 'Justice for Magdalenes Key Documents', http://www.magdalenelaundries.com/

31 These effects include psychological and physical trauma, social isolation, poverty (not just due to trauma and the denial of wages or pension contributions while incarcerated, but also – significantly – due to the loss of educational opportunity), and

a deeply ingrained sense of stigmatisation and shame. O'Rourke's submission also highlighted identification difficulties for family members seeking to trace women who had died in Magdalene Laundries.

32   See, for example, Patsy McGarry's Opinion-Editorial in *The Irish Times*, http://www.irishtimes.com/opinion/state-must-con front-magdalene-tragedy-1.590166; *The Irish Examiner*, Editorial http://www.irishexaminer.com/viewpoints/ourview/magdalen e-scandal-a-just-and-swift-remedy-is-required-156994.html and Mary Raftery's *Guardian* Opinion-Editorial, http://www.the guardian.com/commentisfree/2011/jun/08/irealnd-magdalene-laundries-scandal-un. JFMR has archived all media coverage from the time at, http://www.magdalenelaundries.com/news_ 2011.htm.

33   Department of Justice and Equality, Statement on the Magdalene Laundries, 14 June 2011, http://www.justice.ie/en/ JELR/Pages/PR11000082. See the website of the Inter-departmental Committee at http://www.justice.ie/en/JELR/ Pages/PB11000256

34 . JFM called for published terms of reference on numerous occasions, see https://www.kildarestreet.com/wrans/?id=2011-07-19.1888.0&s=magdalen+mcaleese+terms+reference#g1890.0.r

35   See Inter-departmental Committee to establish the facts of State involvement with the Magdalen Laundries, Interim Progress Report, 20 October 2011, http://www.justice.ie/en/JELR/App endix%201.pdf/Files/Appendix%201.pdf, para 35.

36   Again, this testimony was collected after obtaining informed consent and working in accordance with ethical, human-subject criteria.

37   See 'Principal Submission' at 'Justice for Magdalenes Key Documents', http://www.magdalenelaundries.com/

38   JFM also met with Senator McAleese on three occasions to discuss submitted evidence and to prompt the Committee to consider various aspects of our findings. Likewise, we twice arranged for the Senator and his assistant to meet with groups of survivors at Leinster House – women who had spent time in the institutions themselves and family members searching for information about their relatives. At all times, JFM pursued a policy of openness and full engagement with the work of the Committee, sharing all information – human and archival – that came our way.

39 See, note 12 above for list of TV documentaries.

40 JFM was repeatedly approached by these journalists and producers to facilitate access to survivors (something we agreed to rarely, only if we were aware of a survivor's desire to speak out in public, and only after ensuring the survivor's consent was informed and her conditions respected), to share archival resources and to help shape and fact-check the ensuing story.

41 See http://www.magdalenelaundries.com/JFM%20Reparations%2014%20October.pdf

42 See http://www.dcya.gov.ie/documents/publications/5Rapport eurRepChildProtection.pdf and http://www.Magdalenelaundr ies.com/press/JFM%20PR%2007-25-12.pdf

43 https://www.kildarestreet.com/debate/?id=2013-02-05a.192

44 See IDC Report, note 10 above, Chapter 19.

45 See Report of the Magdalen Commission (May 2013), http://www.justice.ie/en/JELR/Pages/PB13000255, p42.

46 See IDC Report, note 10 above. Chapter 8, at pp 194–196, identifies 762 of these women (although this is based on records from eight of the ten Magdalene Laundries only) and notes that, from the 46% of records where duration of stay is known, 62.7% of women spent more than 10 years in a Magdalene Laundry. The route of exit for 55% is noted as 'unknown, and stayed in Laundry'.

47 See Report of the Magdalen Commission, note 15 above, p. 8.

48 See https://www.kildarestreet.com/debates/?id=2013-06-27a.38 4&s=Shatter+Quirke+commission#g386.

49 United Nations Human Rights Committee, Replies of Ireland to the list of issues, UN Doc CCPR/C/IRL/Q/4/Add.1 (5 May 2014), para 52; Permanent Mission of Ireland to the United Nations, Follow-up material to the Concluding Observations of the UN Human Rights Committee on the Fourth Periodic Review of Ireland under the International Covenant on Civil and Political Rights, 20 July 2015, p. 2.

50 United Nations Human Rights Committee, Replies of Ireland to the list of issues, UN Doc CCPR/C/IRL/Q/4/Add.1 (5 May 2014), para 53; Permanent Mission of Ireland to the United Nations, Follow-up material to the Concluding Observations of the UN Human Rights Committee on the Fourth Periodic Review of Ireland under the International Covenant on Civil and Political Rights, 20 July 2015, p. 2.

51 United Nations Human Rights Committee, Replies of Ireland to the list of issues, UN Doc CCPR/C/IRL/Q/4/Add.1 (5 May 2014), para 54.

52 See Claire McGettrick, 'Death, Institutionalisation and Duration of Stay: A Critique of Chapter 16 of the Report of the Inter-departmental Committee to Establish the Facts of State Involvement with the Magdalen Laundries', www.magdalenel aundries.com/JFMR_Critique_190215.pdf.

53 See http://www.irishtimes.com/news/social-affairs/religion-an d-beliefs/inquiry-needed-to-compel-congregations-to-reveal-tr uth-about-treatment-of-magdalenes-1.1473458.

54 See https://www.kildarestreet.com/debate/?id=2015-07-14a.346

55 See Justice for Magdalenes Research, NGO Submission to the United Nations Committee on the Elimination of Discrimination Against Women (2015), http://tbinternet.ohchr. org/layouts/treatybodyexternal/Download.aspx?symbolno=IN T%2fCEDAW%2fNGO%2fIRL%2f21860&Lang=en.

56 See Irish Human Rights Commission, *Follow-Up Report on State Involvement with Magdalen Laundries*, June 2013, http://www. ihrec.ie/publications/list/ihrc-followup-report-on-state-involve ment-with-mag/, pp 6–8.

THE IMPACT OF THE CONSTITUTION ON WOMEN'S RIGHTS

Ivana Bacik

INTRODUCTION

Bunreacht na hEireann, the 1937 Constitution, takes precedence as a superior source of law over legislation and judges' decisions in Ireland.[1] Yet, despite many instances of laws or policies which have discriminated on gender grounds, the guarantee of equality contained in Article 40.1 of the Constitution has been used by women in relatively few legal cases. Indeed, the text of the Constitution actually reinforces gender discrimination by providing in Article 41.2, the family rights guarantee, that women and mothers (but not men or fathers) have 'duties in the home'. Article 40.3.3 of the Constitution, inserted by way of amendment in 1983, also copperfastens gender discrimination, by equating the right to life of a pregnant woman with that of the foetus she carries.

In this chapter, it is proposed to review the impact that the Constitution has had upon the recognition and development of women's rights in Irish law, with particular reference to these expressly gendered provisions.[2] It will be argued that these provisions, particularly the application of Article 40.3.3, have contributed to an undermining of the equality guarantee, and a devaluing of the concept of gender equality as a human right. It is argued that European human rights law, while not directly binding within our legal system, offers greater potential than the Constitution for the strengthening of equality on gender grounds in Ireland, particularly with reference to reproductive health rights.

Before considering the impact of the 1937 Constitution for women's rights, a brief overview of the context for its introduction will be provided.[3]

COMMON LAW

The Irish legal system is based on common law, the framework of laws spread gradually throughout the country to replace the indigenous Brehon Law system following the Norman conquest in the twelfth century, as documented by scholars such as Kelly[4] and Binchy.[5] At common law, women were regarded as legally incompetent, along with criminals, minors and the 'insane'. Moreover, until the late eighteenth century, the common law gave women no right to hold property nor to guardianship of their own children.

At common law, women also had a duty to submit to sex with their husbands; intercourse had to be 'unlawful' as well as non-consensual to constitute rape, and 'unlawful' was defined as meaning outside of the marital relationship. Thus, according to Hale's infamous statement:

> A husband cannot be guilty of rape upon his wife for by their mutual matrimonial consent and contract the wife hath given

up herself in this kind to her husband, which she cannot retract.[6]

Although discriminatory laws were challenged by individual women,[7] it was not until the Married Women's Property Act 1882 that women were permitted to keep their own property on marriage, in both Ireland and England, since after the Act of Union of 1800, the Westminster Parliament passed laws for Ireland. This situation persisted throughout the nineteenth century, until the emergence of an independence movement resulted in the creation of the Irish Free State.

In the late nineteenth and early twentieth century, an influential women's liberation and suffrage movement developed alongside the emerging campaign for Irish independence, although there existed a certain tension between those espousing the causes of feminism and of nationalism. Feminist organisations like the Irish Women's Franchise League, led by Hanna Sheehy Skeffington, campaigned for women's suffrage;[8] while many women were active in the struggle for independence, particularly through the Cumann na mBan organisation, with which Constance Markievicz was strongly associated.

The suffrage campaigns in Britain and Ireland culminated in the passage of the Representation of the People Act 1918, which granted the right to vote to women over 30, subject to certain property restrictions.[9] In the general election of December 1918, Markievicz was elected as the first woman MP to the House of Commons; she chose not to take her seat there but rather to sit as a TD in the first Dáil.

After the Easter Rising of 1916, and during the War of Independence that followed, women remained prominent in the nationalist movement.[10] For a brief period between

1920–1924, both before the creation of the Irish Free State and during the Civil War that followed independence, women played a particularly formal role in the Dáil Courts, a grassroots courts structure set up as a part of the independence movement. In Kotsonouris' definitive history of these courts, she mentions a number of women who played an important part; as secretaries, registrars and even judges.[11]

WOMEN IN THE IRISH FREE STATE

After 1922, many of the women who had been prominent in the independence movement and during the birth of the new State faded from public view; few women were involved at a policy-making level in the new State. For many years there was no sign of any organised women's movement, although women continued to be politically active through grassroots organisations such as the Irish Countrywomen's Association and the Irish Housewives' Association.[12]

Progress on women's suffrage was made with the adoption of the Constitution of the Irish Free State in 1922, Article 3 of which provided that every person:

> without distinction of sex ... is a citizen of the Irish Free State (Saorstát Éireann) and shall ... enjoy the privileges and be subject to the obligations of such citizenship.

The franchise was extended by Article 14 of the Constitution, on an equal basis, to all women and men over 21. A cynical commentator, however, might describe this as the last example of progressive law-making for women in Ireland for over 50 years.

THE IRISH CONSTITUTION 1937

The present Irish Constitution, or *Bunreacht na hEireann*, was introduced in 1937, in order to make a clear break with the arrangements demanded by the British

Government, which had been embodied in the Irish Free State Constitution.[13] The drafting of a new Constitution was largely attributed to the then Taoiseach Eamon de Valera, and was passed by the people through referendum.[14] Articles 40 to 44 of the Constitution represent the 'Fundamental Rights' section of the Constitution, the equivalent of a bill of rights.[15] The equality guarantee contained in Article 40.1 of the 1937 Constitution provides:

> All citizens shall, as human persons, be held equal before the law. This shall not be held to mean that the State shall not in its enactments have due regard to differences of capacity, physical and moral, and of social function.

This general guarantee of equality is framed in highly qualified language, and this framing has undoubtedly contributed to the limited nature of its practical impact.[16] It must also be read alongside two other Articles from the fundamental rights section of the Constitution, mentioned earlier. First, Article 41.2 of the Constitution (which guarantees the rights of the family) refers specifically to women having a 'life within the home' and declares that the State shall endeavour to ensure 'mothers' are not forced into the workforce 'to the neglect of their duties in the home'. This Article has been widely criticised, but despite numerous calls for its removal from the Constitution, it remains in place.[17] Secondly, Article 40.3.3 of the Constitution provides that life of 'the unborn' shall be protected as equal with that of 'the mother'; again this has been widely criticised from a feminist perspective, and has given rise to immense political and legal controversy, discussed further below.[18]

The inclusion of fundamental rights provisions in the 1937 document marked a change from the 1922 Constitution which did not guarantee enforceable personal rights. However, the provisions in the 1937 Articles generated little case law until some decades after their introduction, perhaps because neither the judiciary nor the citizens of the new State had any experience of the concept of personal constitutional rights.[19] It took over 20 years for a change in legal culture, but Articles 40 to 44 now form the basis of many significant judicial decisions, and are regularly invoked before the courts.[20] This change is particularly evident from the late 1960s on, and may be attributed in particular to the appointment of a new generation of judges to the superior courts. However, while Irish constitutional jurisprudence on individual liberties has developed relatively liberally in many respects, the equality guarantee has always been interpreted in a conservative manner by the courts.

As Mullally writes, 'the Irish judiciary has displayed a marked reluctance to apply Article 40.1, preferring to rely on other substantive constitutional rights where possible'.[21] This pattern has been evident from a series of cases, where although the applicant may have based their legal arguments upon the equality guarantee, any court decision in their favour was made on alternative grounds; for example, the unenumerated personal right to earn a livelihood in *Murtagh Properties v Cleary*; the rights of the marital family in *Murphy v Attorney General*; or a number of different grounds as well as the equality ground in *de Burca*.[22]

A number of reasons may be identified for this restrictive judicial approach. First, as noted above, the language of the Article is itself limited, guaranteeing as it does only the narrow concept of equality 'before the law', or 'formal' equality, meaning a view of equality limited to prohibiting discrimination, rather than the broader concept of substantive equality, which goes further by recognising the need to address pre-existing inequalities. Second, while the guarantee clearly applies to vertical discrimination (between the State and the individual), it does not explicitly apply to horizontal discrimination (i.e. between two private actors). Nor does it include any reference to specific prohibited grounds of discrimination, unlike the South African Constitution, for example.[23]

The guarantee has also been limited through restrictive judicial interpretation. First, the Article allows the State to provide for discrimination, having regard to differences, including differences of 'social function'. This proviso was used, for example, to justify the failure of the State to treat deserted husbands in the same way as deserted wives for the purpose of social welfare payments.[24] When read in conjunction with Article 41, the family rights provision, which has been held to provide protection only to the family based upon marriage, this proviso has also been applied by the courts so as to justify discrimination against unmarried persons.[25] Most recently, in 2012 the Supreme Court relied on the proviso in upholding the constitutionality of a law that penalised boys who engaged in sexual intercourse with girls under 17 but provided no such sanction for girls, on the basis that the Oireachtas was entitled to take into account biological difference and risk of pregnancy in enacting such legislation.[26]

The courts have also used the phrase 'as human persons' contained in the Article to limit the guarantee further, through development of a 'human personality' doctrine, based on the idea that the right to equality may only be claimed in respect of some 'essential attribute' of human personality. Thus, in the *Murtagh Properties* case, the owners of a pub claimed that a picket by trade unionists to object at the hiring of female bar staff was a breach of the rights of the potential women employees to earn their livelihood without gender discrimination. The pub owners won on the basis that the women had the right to earn a livelihood, rather than on any equality argument;

the judge stating that the equality guarantee related to human personality, rather than to trading activities or conditions of employment.[27] Although a more flexible approach has been developed by the courts in subsequent years, and the human personality doctrine is being slowly undermined,[28] it has nonetheless, as Mullally writes, 'served within the Irish jurisdiction to restrict unduly the effectiveness of equality protection'.[29]

However, the equality guarantee has been relied upon successfully in a number of gender discrimination cases, for example to allow equal selection of men and women for jury in 1976;[30] to declare the common law defence of 'marital coercion' unconstitutional in 1981;[31] or in 1992 to extend the common law right of action for loss of consortium, which traditionally applied only to a husband, to enable a wife whose husband had been injured to make such a claim.[32] But in some of these cases, a principle of equality of spouses within marriage implicit in Articles 41 and 42 of the Constitution was also relied upon by the courts to bolster the equality argument.[33]

EUROPEAN COMMUNITY LAW

In 1973, Ireland became a member of the EEC, a watershed for the development of gender equality in Ireland. The original 1957 Treaty of Rome contained a guarantee of equal pay for equal work for men and women.[34] Since then, largely through feminist legal and political activism,[35] a strong gender equality policy has emerged at EU level, albeit generally confined to the economic sphere.[36] Thus, when Ireland joined the EEC, it was required to change many overtly discriminatory laws and practices. As Fennell and Lynch wrote:

> [Irish equality legislation] was introduced, it should be noted, not as a result of the benevolence of the Irish government ...

but due to our membership of the European Community, and the necessity to comply with EC Directives.[37]

Irish membership of the EEC necessitated the passing of the Anti-Discrimination (Pay) Act 1974, and the Employment Equality Act 1977, both prohibiting discrimination on gender grounds in employment.[38] In addition, over the same period, the civil service 'marriage bar' was abolished; the Civil Service (Employment of Married Women) Act 1973 removed this ban on married women working in the public service. The same year a ban on married air hostesses was lifted in Aer Lingus following union negotiations.[39] In 1981 the Maternity (Protection of Employees) Act gave women the right to paid maternity leave, and the right to return to work following such leave.[40] In 1998, the Parental Leave Act was introduced to implement another Directive, giving both parents the right to time off work to care for a young child.[41]

PROGRESSIVE LEGAL CHANGE ON WOMEN'S RIGHTS
Although EC law provided a significant impetus for much of this legislative change, the decades following 1970 also represented a period of strong feminist activism. The Irish Women's Liberation Movement was formed in 1970, and this, together with the establishment of other, broadly speaking, feminist organisations, marked an increase in political campaigning by women. In 1985, Ireland ratified the United Nations Convention on the Elimination of all Forms of Discrimination Against Women ('CEDAW'), and this development also ensured an international dimension to equality campaigns.

The period also saw a significant increase in litigation around equality issues, often led by women lawyers. Mary Robinson, in particular, acted in a number of cases in which challenges were made to discriminatory laws, and which led to legal change.[42] But as Robinson writes, particular credit for using law as an instrument of social change must go to 'those individual women who were prepared to use the courts to challenge the existing system': women like Mary McGee who challenged the law banning the import or sale of contraceptives, leading to a lengthy legalisation process for contraception rights; Máirín de Burca, whose case changed the law on jury selection; and Josie Airey, whose case before the European Court of Human Rights established the right to civil legal aid.[43]

During the 1990s, also, apart from the litigation taken to challenge discrimination or strengthen protection for women's rights, there were also significant advances made through the enactment of equality legislation. In particular, the Employment Equality Act 1998 and the Equal Status Act 2000 provided for the creation of an Equality Authority,[44] and for new procedures and mechanisms to challenge discrimination both in the workplace and in the provision of goods and services on a range of nine grounds, including that of gender.[45]

These Acts, which have subsequently been amended by a series of other Acts,[46] have now provided a more effective and accessible means of challenging gender discrimination than that afforded by the Constitution. The most high-profile gender equality claims made in recent years have been taken under this legislation rather than under the Constitution. Many such claims have been successful, and some have generated immense public debate generally, for example the 2014 Equality Tribunal decision finding the promotion practices in NUI Galway to be discriminatory against women.[47]

Not all such claims have succeeded, however. In perhaps the biggest gender equality case of recent years, in 2010, a challenge taken by the Equality Authority to the men-only membership policy of a well-known golf club failed on the basis of a very restrictive interpretation of the Equal Status legislation.[48] The Supreme Court by a 3:2 majority ruled that it was not a requirement under the Act, in order to justify discrimination, that the club had to show a logical connection between the principal purpose of the club (ie golf) and the category of person to which membership was limited (ie men). Thus the club was entitled to discriminate by not allowing women into full membership. This case demonstrates the limitations of the equality legislation, and the restrictive approach taken by the courts to interpretation of equality law.

REPRODUCTIVE RIGHTS AND THE EIGHTH AMENDMENT

Despite such setbacks, great progress for women's legal rights was undoubtedly made over the decades following the assertion of a feminist movement in Ireland.[49] However, during this time a powerful backlash was also evident in the area of reproductive rights. Indeed, it is in this area that the provisions of the Constitution have been most clearly detrimental to any advancement of women's rights. Ironically, the McGee case proved to be a catalyst for constitutional retrenchment. In McGee v Attorney General, the Supreme Court had held that a right to marital privacy was implicit in the Constitution, thereby enabling a married couple to import contraceptives for their own use.[50] However, the privacy concept upheld in the McGee decision was seen by anti-choice campaigners as opening a door to the prospect of a judgment similar to that of the US Supreme Court the same year in Roe v Wade.[51] In Roe, the US court had recognised the existence of a constitutional right to abortion, based on earlier case law around the right to privacy and contraception.[52] The Irish anti-choice campaign feared a similar judicial development would lead to the legalisation of abortion in Ireland. Their intensive lobbying of the Government to stop this happening resulted in the passing of the Eighth Amendment in September 1983; the bitter campaign on this referendum marked a particularly bleak moment in the history of the Irish women's movement.[53] The amendment inserted a new Article 40.3.3 into the Constitution, providing that:

> The State acknowledges the right to life of the unborn and, with due regard to the equal right to life of the mother, guarantees in its laws to respect, and, as far as practicable, by its laws to defend and vindicate that right.[54]

The text of the Article clearly devalues the lives of pregnant women, rendering them equal only to foetal life. This devaluing was far from symbolic; the practical effect of the text became swiftly evident. Shortly after the passage of the Amendment, the Society for the Protection of Unborn Children (SPUC) began to use the new provision as the basis for a series of cases taken against counsellors and students' unions, for providing women with information on abortion clinics in Britain.[55] In 1986, the High Court accepted their argument that the provision of such information interfered with the 'fundamental right' to life of the unborn.[56]

This decision, upheld by the Supreme Court, established that the provision of information on abortion was unlawful under the Constitution. The agencies, however, appealed to the European Court of Human Rights (ECtHR), which in October 1992[57] ruled that the Irish Government's ban on abortion information was in breach of the freedom of expression guarantee in Article 10 of the European Convention on Human Rights (ECHR).[58]

In the case taken by SPUC against students' unions, the High Court referred the issue to the European Court of Justice (ECJ), as it concerned a service available legally in another EU Member State.[59] The ECJ concluded that because there was no commercial connection between the students' unions and the British clinics, the information ban could not be regarded as a restriction under EC law.

THE X CASE AND 1990S DEVELOPMENTS

Before the students' union case had returned to the Irish courts, a dramatic legal development took place, in a case concerning a 14-year-old girl, 'X', who had been raped and had become pregnant. She wished to terminate the pregnancy and her parents took her to England for that purpose. The Attorney-General then obtained a court injunction to stop the girl from travelling out of Ireland for the abortion. There was outrage at the notion that X might be forced to proceed with an unwanted pregnancy.

In the face of mounting public pressure, an appeal was heard within a matter of weeks, and the Supreme Court allowed the girl to travel, ruling that because the girl was suicidal, the continuation of the pregnancy would have threatened her right to life. In such situations, the court ruled that where there is 'a real and substantial risk to the life, as distinct from the health, of the mother, which can only be avoided by the termination of her pregnancy', then such termination was permissible.[60]

Following this case, three amendments to Art.40.3.3° of the Constitution were put before the people in November 1992. The aim of the first was to rule out suicide as a threat to the life of a pregnant woman – this was defeated. However, the other two amendments were passed, guaranteeing the freedom to travel abroad, and allowing the provision of information on services lawfully available in other states.[61]

Following these amendments, the Regulation of Information (Services Outside the State for Termination of Pregnancies) Act 1995 came into force, providing for the conditions under which information on abortion may be provided.[62]

In 1997, another case similar to that of X came before the High Court.[63] The previous year, an expert Constitution Review Group had recommended that legislation be enacted to clarify the application of the X case test. In 1999, the Government published a Green Paper on abortion.[64] This was referred to the All-Party Oireachtas Committee on the Constitution (APOCC), which presented three options in its report, one of which was to amend the Constitution to rule out suicide risk as a ground for threat to life.[65]

The Government was again persuaded by the anti-choice movement's intensive lobbying, and in March 2002, another referendum was put to the people to reverse the decision in the X case by ruling out suicide risk as a ground for abortion. However, the referendum was ultimately defeated – for a second time, the Irish people had voted to uphold the X case test.

THE EUROPEAN COURT OF HUMAN RIGHTS (ECtHR)
Following the defeat of the 2002 referendum, abortion slipped off the political agenda for several years.[66] A case was then taken before the ECtHR against Ireland by a woman, 'D', whose pregnancy had resulted in a diagnosis of fatal foetal abnormality. She had to go to England to terminate the pregnancy and argued that this breached her rights under the ECHR. In its decision, however, the ECtHR found the application inadmissible because the applicant should have taken her case in Ireland first and exhausted domestic remedies.[67] The D case was followed by the more substantive decision of the ECtHR in A, B & C v Ireland.[68] Three women, all of whom had been living in Ireland when they had become pregnant and had been obliged to travel to England to terminate their pregnancies, argued that Ireland had breached their human rights under the ECHR. The ECtHR unanimously ruled that

Ireland's failure to implement the existing constitutional right to a lawful abortion in Ireland when a woman's life is at risk, as the applicant C's had been, had violated her rights under Article 8 of the ECHR, which guarantees the right to privacy.[69]

THE PROTECTION OF LIFE DURING PREGNANCY ACT 2013

In November 2012, an expert group appointed by the Government set out the framework for legislation to clarify the criteria under which abortions might be carried out in order to save a woman's life.[70] Tragically, just before the publication of the report, in October 2012, a young woman called Savita Halappanavar died while undergoing a miscarriage at Galway University Hospital. Her death generated immense public outrage at reports that she and her husband had requested, but been denied, a potentially life-saving termination of pregnancy. The lack of legal clarity as to when life-saving abortion could be carried out clearly contributed to the failures in her medical treatment.[71]

In the aftermath of this tragedy, the Government announced an intention to legislate for the X case test, in order to comply with the A, B & C judgment. Extensive hearings on the proposed legislation were held by the Oireachtas Health Committee in January 2013.[72] The legislation was eventually passed through the Oireachtas, during often heated debates, by the end of July 2013 to become the Protection of Life During Pregnancy Act 2013 (the '2013 Act').[73] This Act provides for the procedure to be followed whereby a termination of pregnancy may be carried out by doctors to save a pregnant woman's life, and requires that two doctors must certify that a real and substantial risk to life exists; three doctors where the risk is of suicide.

POST-2013 ACT DEVELOPMENTS

The provisions of the 2013 Act came into political focus in August 2014. It was revealed in the media that a young asylum-seeker with a crisis pregnancy had been denied an abortion despite having been found suicidal in accordance with the 2013 Act. It appears that by the time the Act was invoked, the pregnancy was too advanced for an abortion to be performed; instead the baby was delivered at about 25 weeks' gestation by Caesarean section.[74]

In December 2014, another tragic case came to light, with the report that a young pregnant woman, despite having been pronounced dead, was being kept alive by a hospital against her family's wishes because of concerns to preserve the right to life of the 15-week old foetus that she carried.[75]

While the High Court ultimately ruled in favour of the family's wish to terminate life support, the judgment was based on the consideration of the best interests of the 'unborn child', and the clear medical evidence that its prospects for survival even if the woman were kept on life-support were 'virtually non-existent'. Thus, it may be surmised that had the foetus been at a more advanced gestation, the decision would have been different and the rights of the woman's family, and indeed her own right to dignity, would have been overridden.

Most recently, and more promisingly, the much less restrictive abortion law framework in Northern Ireland was ruled to be in breach of Article 8 of the ECHR; the High Court in Belfast held that the failure to allow abortion in cases of fatal foetal abnormality and rape constitutes a gross interference with the personal autonomy of pregnant women.[76] While the judgment may be appealed, it clearly has implications for Irish law, which because of the Eighth Amendment is much more restrictive than in Northern Ireland.

After so many tragic cases, and with such a significant recent judgment in Belfast, political momentum is growing, both nationally and internationally, for a referendum to repeal the Eighth Amendment. More than 21 years after the X case, there is now clear public support for legislation allowing abortion on a wider range of grounds than the very restrictive cases permitted by the Eighth Amendment.[77]

CONCLUSION

As previously argued, the provisions of the 1937 Constitution have not proved especially helpful for any great advancement of women's rights. In particular, the equality guarantee has provided little support for challenges to gender discrimination; both due to the restrictive language of the text itself, and the conservative approach to its interpretation. In addition, the gendered language in Article 41 emphasising women's domestic role confirms this approach.

Feminist campaigning has brought about much progressive legal change in recent years. Equality legislation providing an accessible framework to protect against discrimination has also proven to be effective in vindicating women's rights in certain cases on employment and access to goods and services. European human rights law offers another potential route to redress for women experiencing discrimination in Ireland.

However, Article 40.3.3 of the Constitution, with its explicit devaluing of the lives of women, has proved particularly hostile to the advancement of women's rights to reproductive choice. While some progress has been made in this area through recourse to the European Court of Human Rights, undoubtedly the only way to achieve the enactment of legislation allowing women access to legal abortion on grounds beyond risk to life is through repeal of the Eighth Amendment. Removal of Article 40.3.3, and of the gendered language relating to women's domestic role in Article 41, would enable more effective protection for women's rights through the structures of the Constitution – and might at last breathe new life into the text of the equality guarantee.

SOURCES

1   Article 29 of the Constitution provides however that EC or EU law may override the Constitution.

2   For a general overview of the impact of the Constitution on women's rights, see Yvonne Scannell, 'The Constitution and the Role of Women' in Brian Farrell (ed), *De Valera's Constitution and Ours* (Dublin, Gill & MacMillan, 1988), chapter 9.

3   This chapter draws upon previous publications, in particular Ivana Bacik, Cathryn Costello and Eileen Drew, *Gender InJustice: Feminising the Legal Professions?* (Trinity College Dublin Law School, 2003), chapter 1.

4   Fergus Kelly, *A Guide to Early Law* (Dublin, Institute for Advanced Studies, 1988).

5   Donald Binchy, in Rudolf Thurneyson, *Studies in Early Irish Law* (Dublin, Hodges Figgis for the Royal Irish Academy, 1936).

6   'History of the Pleas of the Crown', 629. This rule was abolished in 1990, after a long campaign by the Rape Crisis Centres, with the enactment of section 5 of the Criminal Law (Rape)(Amendment) Act, 1990.

7   See Carrie Menkel-Meadow, 'Feminization of the legal profession: The Comparative Sociology of Women Lawyers' in Richard Abel and Philip Lewis, *Lawyers in Society: An Overview* (Berkeley, University of California Press, 1995), 221, 226.

8   See further Linda Connolly, *The Irish Women's Movement: From Revolution to Devolution* (Dublin, Lilliput Press, 2003), 59–71.

9   The same legislation abolished most property qualification requirements for men, who could vote at the age of 21.

10   For a detailed account of the history of this period, see Margaret Ward, *Unmanageable Revolutionaries: Women and Irish Nationalism* (London, Pluto Press, 1995).

11   Mary Kotsonouris, *Retreat from Revolution: The Dail Courts, 1920–1924* (Dublin, Irish Academic Press, 1994), 38; 45; 126. These courts were dismantled under the Courts of Justice Act 1924, and replaced with a system much closer to that of the English model. It was to be almost forty years (in 1963) before the first woman, Eileen Kennedy, was appointed a District Justice within the new post-1924 constitutional court system.

12   See Carol Coulter, *The Hidden Tradition: Feminism, Women and Nationalism in Ireland* (Cork, Cork University Press, 1993).

13   Basil Chubb, *The Constitution and Constitutional Change in Ireland* (Dublin, IPA, 1978), 7.

14   For a definitive account of the drafting of the 1937 Constitution, see Gerard Hogan, *The Origins of the Irish Constitution 1928–1941* (Dublin, Royal Irish Academy, 2012).

15   Discrimination on specific grounds and in specific areas is dealt with in a number of other Articles, such as Article 9.1.3, which prohibits discrimination on the ground of sex in relation to nationality and citizenship, and Article 40.6.2, which forbids discrimination on the grounds of political opinion, religion and class in any laws regulating the exercise of the freedoms of assembly and of association.

16   There are other constitutional Articles relevant to gender equality; Article 9.1.3 which provides that no-one may be excluded from Irish citizenship by reason of gender; Article 16.1 which prohibits discrimination on the grounds of gender in relation to voting rights and membership of the Dáil; and Article 45.2, which refers to the right of men and women equally to an adequate means of livelihood.

17   See for example the *Report of the Constitution Review Group* (Dublin, Government Publications, 1996), 333; this expert group recommended the replacement of this Article with a revised gender-neutral provision recognising the importance of persons who perform a caring function within the home. More recently, see the recommendation of the Constitutional Convention that these provisions be replaced; Constitutional Convention, *Second Report*, May 2013, at https://www.constitut ion.ie/AttachmentDownload.ashx?mid=268d9308-c9b7-e211-a5 a0-005056a32ee4. See also international commentary, notably the UN Human Rights Committee, *Concluding Observations on Ireland and the International Covenant on Civil and Political Rights*

of 24 July 2014, paragraph 7, recommending the amendment of Article 41.2 of the Constitution to render it gender neutral.

18   See for example, James Kingston and Anthony Whelan with Ivana Bacik, *Abortion and the Law* (Dublin, Round Hall Sweet & Maxwell, 1997); Jennifer Schweppe (ed), *The Unborn Child, Article 40.3.3 and Abortion in Ireland: Twenty Five Years of Protection?* (Dublin, The Liffey Press, 2008); Aideen Quilty, Sinead Kennedy and Catherine Conlon (eds), *The Abortion Papers Ireland: Volume II* (Cork University Press, 2015).

19   Ronan Keane, 'Fundamental rights in Irish Law; a note on the historical background', in James O'Reilly (ed), *Human Rights and Constitutional Law* (Dublin, Round Hall Press, 1992), 25.

20   See for example, Gerard Hogan and Gerry Whyte in *The Irish Constitution* (Dublin, Tottel, 4th ed, 2003), section on 'Fundamental Rights'.

21   Siobhan Mullally, 'Equality Guarantees in Irish Constitutional Law – the Myth of Constitutionalism and the "Neutral" State' in Tim Murphy and Patrick Twomey (eds), *Ireland's Evolving Constitution 1937–1997* (Oxford, Hart, 1998).

22   [1972] IR 330; [1982] IR 241; [1976] IR 38.

23   Article 9(3).

24   *Dennehy v Minister for Social Welfare*, High Court, 26 July 1984.

25   For example, in *O'B v S* [1984] IR 316, the Supreme Court held that the exclusion of 'illegitimate' children from the right of succession upon a father's intestate death was justified by reference to the protection of the marital family under Article 41. This decision was overturned by legislation; and the State subsequently settled the plaintiff's application to the European Court of Human Rights in the same case.

26   *MD v. Ireland* [2012] 1 IR 697.

27   [1972] IR 330.

28   See for example, *Howard v Commissioners of Public Works in Ireland* [1993] ILRM 665; and *The Irish Constitution*, above, at 1348.

29   Mullally, above, at 154.

30   *De Burca v Attorney General* [1976] IR 38.

31   *State (DPP) v. Walsh & Conneely* [1981] IR 412; the common law rule meant that where a wife committed a crime in the presence of her husband, she was presumed to have been coerced by him into doing so.

32 *McKinley v. Minister for Defence* [1992] 2 IR 333 (Supreme Court). The plaintiff Finola McKinley won her case suing the State for damages for loss of consortium where her husband had been injured due to State negligence.

33 For example, to strike down the rule giving the father a permanent right to custody of a child in *Re Tilson, Infants* [1951] IR 1; and to declare unconstitutional the rule that a wife could not give evidence that her husband was not the father of her child, in *S v. S* [1983] IR 68.

34 See Catherine Barnard, 'The Economic Origins of Article 119 EEC' in Tamara Hervey and David O'Keeffe (eds), *Sex Equality Law in the European Union* (Chichester, Wiley, 1996), 321.

35 Catherine Hoskyns, *Integrating Gender – Women, Law and Politics in the European Union* (London, Verso, 1996).

36 Gillian More, 'Equality of Treatment in European Community Law: the limits of Market Equality' in Anne Bottomley (ed), *Feminist Perspectives on the Foundational Subjects of Law* (London, Cavendish, 1996) and 'The Principle of Equal Treatment: From Market Unifier to Fundamental Right' in Paul Craig and Grainne de Burca (eds), *The Evolution of EC Law* (Oxford, Oxford University Press, 1999).

37 Caroline Fennell and Irene Lynch, *Labour Law in Ireland* (Dublin, Gill and Macmillan, 1993), 58.

38 Now replaced by the Employment Equality Act, 1998, as amended (Equality Acts 1998–2015).

39 Irene Lynch, 'Labour Law' in Alpha Connelly (ed), *Gender and the Law in Ireland* (Dublin, Oak Tree Press, 1993), 53.

40 Now amended by the Maternity Protection Act, 1994 and Maternity Protection (Amendment) Act 2004.

41 Directive 96/34/EC of 3 June 1996 on Parental Leave.

42 For example, in *de Burca*, the voting rights case, where she acted as the plaintiff's junior counsel; and in *Airey v Ireland*, the case before the European Court of Human Rights establishing the right to civil legal aid; where she again acted for the plaintiff. In 1990, she was elected as Ireland's first woman President; a development heralded as marking significant advance for women's rights.

43 Mary Robinson, 'Women and the Law in Ireland' in Ailbhe Smyth (ed), *Irish Women's Studies Reader* (Dublin, Attic Press, 1993), 101. The cases she refers to are: *McGee v Attorney General* [1973] IR 284; *De Burca v Attorney General* [1976] IR 38; *Airey v*

Ireland, European Court of Human Rights, 9 October 1979, Series A, No. 32.

44 Now part of the Irish Human Rights and Equality Commission.

45 The original version of the legislation was struck down by the Supreme Court as unconstitutional, on grounds unrelated to gender equality, but including undue encroachment on property rights related to the discriminatory ground of disability, in *Re Article 26 and the Employment Equality Bill 1996* [1997] 2 IR 321.

46 Now referred to as the Equality Acts 1998–2015.

47 *Sheehy Skeffington v. NUI Galway*, DEC-E2014-078, 13 November 2014.

48 *Equality Authority v. Portmarnock Golf Club* [2010] 1 IR 671.

49 Evidenced by, for example, the introduction of a State allowance for single mothers in 1973, by progressive change on legalising contraception through a series of Acts passed following the judgment in the *McGee* case; the introduction of divorce by way of referendum in 1995; and reform of the laws on rape and domestic violence, for example.

50 [1974] I.R. 284.

51 William Binchy, 'Privacy and Family Law: A Reply to Mr. O'Reilly' (1977) *Studies* 330 at 330.

52 (1973) 410 U.S 113.

53 See, for example, Ailbhe Smyth (ed.), *The Abortion Papers Ireland* (Dublin, Attic Press, 1992); Aideen Quilty, Sinead Kennedy and Catherine Conlon (eds), *The Abortion Papers Ireland: Volume II* (Cork University Press, 2015); Sandra McEvoy, 'From Anti-Amendment Campaigns to Demanding Reproductive Justice: the Changing Lndscape of Abortion Rights Activism in Ireland 1983–2008' in Jennifer Schweppe (ed.), *The Unborn Child, Article 40.3.3 and Abortion in Ireland: Twenty-Five Years of Protection?* (Dublin, Liffey Press, 2008).

54 For further discussion see J. Kingston and A. Whelan with I. Bacik, *Abortion and the Law* (Dublin, Round Hall Sweet & Maxwell, 1997).

55 See, for example, Pauline Conroy Jackson, 'Women's Movement and Abortion: The Criminalisation of Irish Women' in D. Dahlerup (ed.), *The New Women's Movement: Feminism and Political Power in Europe and the US* (London, Sage, 1996).

56 *Attorney General (SPUC) v Open Door Counselling Ltd* [1987] I.L.R.M. 477.

57 *Open Door Counselling and Dublin Well Woman v Ireland* (1993) 15 E.H.R.R. 244.

58 (1993) 15 E.H.R.R. 244 at 265.

59 *SPUC v Grogan (No. 2)* (Case 159/90) [1991] 3 C.M.L.R. 849.

60 *Attorney General v X* [1992] 1 I.R. 1.

61 Brendan Kennelly and Éilís Ward, 'The Abortion Referendums' in Michael Gallagher and Michael Laver (eds), *How Ireland Voted 1992* (Dublin, PSAI Press and Folens, 1993), 115–134.

62 The first comprehensive study of women and crisis pregnancy in Ireland, conducted subsequently, found that information on both contraception and abortion was still difficult to obtain for many women and girls: E. Mahon, C. Conlon and L. Dillon, *Women and Crisis Pregnancy: A Report Presented to the Department of Health and Children* (Dublin, Stationery Office, 1998).

63 *A & B v Eastern Health Board and C* [1998] 1 I.L.R.M. 460. This case involved a 13-year-old girl who had been raped and become pregnant. Again, the Court found that the girl was suicidal, and that the continuation of her pregnancy would pose a 'real and substantial risk' to her life.

64 Interdepartmental Working Group, *Green Paper on Abortion* (Dublin, Stationery Office, 1999).

65 Report of the All-Party Committee on the Constitution, *Fifth Progress Report: Abortion* (Dublin, Stationery Office, 2000).

66 Although some cases continued to be heard on the issue, notably *D v District Judge Brennan, HSE and Ireland*, unreported, High Court, 9 May 2007; McKechnie J, in which a 17-year-old girl with an anencephalic pregnancy sought permission from the HSE to allow her to travel to obtain an abortion (she was in State care). The High Court ruled that she had a right to travel.

67 *D v Ireland*, Application No. 26499/02, ECtHR, para.103.

68 *A, B and C v Ireland* (2011) 53 E.H.R.R. 13.

69 At para.367 of the judgment.

70 *Report of the Expert Group on the Judgment in A, B and C v Ireland* (Department of Health and Children, 2012), available at: http://health.gov.ie/blog/publications/report-of-the-expert-group-on-the-judgment-in-a-b-and-c-v-ireland/ [last accessed 23 September 2014].

71   See, for example: http://www.irishtimes.com/news/politics/leg
      al-confusion-in-savita-case-shatter-1.1360821 [last accessed 23
      September 2014].

72   See *Report on Public Hearings on the Implementation of the
      Government decision following the publication of the Expert Group
      Report on A, B, & C v Ireland* (Joint Oireachtas Committee on
      Health   and   Children,   January   2013),   available   at:
      http://www.oireachtas.ie/parliament/oireachtasbusiness/comm
      ittees_list/health-and-children/ [last accessed 23 September
      2014].

73   See   http://www.irishstatutebook.ie/2013/en/act/pub/0035/inde
      x.html. For more discussion about the origins of this legislation
      and recent legal developments generally, see, for example,
      Ivana Bacik, 'Legislating for Article 40.3.3' (2013) 3(3) *Irish
      Journal of Legal Studies* 18; and Ivana Bacik, 'A History of
      Abortion Law in Ireland and Prospects for Change' (2014) 20(2)
      Medico-Legal Journal of Ireland 75.

74   See, for example: http://www.irishtimes.com/news/health/wo
      man-in-abortion-case-tells-of-suicide-attempt-1.1901256   [last
      accessed 23 September 2014].

75   *PP v. HSE* [2014] IEHC 622.

76   *Re Application of the Northern Ireland Human Rights Commission*
      [2015] NIQB 96. The law in Northern Ireland allows abortion
      where the continuance of a pregnancy would leave a woman
      or girl a 'physical or mental wreck', as per *R v. Bourne* [1938] 3
      All ER 615. However, abortion remains criminalised in
      Northern Ireland in all other circumstances under the 1861
      Offences Against the Person Act, as evidenced by the recent
      prosecution for 'procurement of miscarriage' taken against a
      young woman in Belfast in April 2016, resulting in the
      imposition of a suspended sentence on the individual woman;
      for reports of the case, see for example *Belfast Telegraph*, 7 April
      2016, accessible at http://www.belfasttelegraph.co.uk/news/no
      rthern-ireland/belfast-protest-against-prosecution-of-northern-
      ireland-woman-who-used-abortion-drugs-held-outside-public-
      prosecution-service-34607776.html.

77   For an overview of these polls, see *http://www.ifpa.ie/Hot-
      Topics/Abortion/Public-Opinion*. See for example the 2015 launch
      of a campaign challenging Irish abortion law by Amnesty
      International at https://www.amnesty.ie/sites/default/files/rep
      ort/2015/06/EUR2915982015%20AMENDEDFINAL4JUNE.PDF;

and the 2014 UN Human Rights Committee *Concluding Observations on Ireland and the International Covenant on Civil and Political Rights* of 24 July 2014, paragraph 9, recommending the revision of Irish law on abortion to provide for lawful abortion 'in cases of rape, incest, serious risks to the health of the mother, or fatal foetal abnormality'.

BODILY HARM

Marie O'Connor

It is not difficult to imagine how Countess Markievicz would have viewed the practice of symphysiotomy, a childbirth operation that effectively unhinges the pelvis. Performed without consent on three generations of women, the surgery was driven by religious ideology and medical ambition. Ireland was the only country in the industrialised world to practice symphysiotomy as an operation of first resort in preference to Caesarean section. Some symphysiotomies were performed in the aftermath of a C-section, while others, equally unprecedented, were carried out during late pregnancy, before labour began. Much more usual – and cruel in the extreme – were the symphysiotomies done during labour: women were still in labour after the surgery, carrying a baby they were required to birth post-operatively. An estimated 1,500 women and girls, some as young as 14, were subjected to symphysiotomy. Life long disability, chronic pain, mental suffering and family breakdown followed.

Operated upon in 1957 by Dr Sutton in St Finbarr's Hospital, Cork, on the birth of her first child, Kathleen, a former nurse, now sadly deceased, described how after the operation she thought she was paralysed:

> my legs were as dead as dead could be. I asked what was wrong, nobody told me ... After the second week, they put me walking in a corridor, I fainted with the pain, it was like walking on thorns ... The wound was discharging [*at home*], there was a terrible smell ... It was the winter, the pain in my back was so bad, it would be a fine thing to be dead, I thought ... I was shuffling for six months ... Arthritis set in straight after. My sister got married and I couldn't go to the wedding ... I had a friend who came in to help me with the baby ... The pelvis stayed [*making a rocking motion from side to side with her hands*], it was very hard to keep your balance ... It was so sore and painful, I was never right after it. It took the wind out of my sails ... Everything was thrown to one side, the doctor said ... I had a bad prolapse of the womb after ... I had to have a total hysterectomy, my bladder, everything, all gone ... My husband was a cross man. You're only half a woman, he said, after the hysterectomy.[1]

Symphysiotomy had long been shunned by mainstream obstetrics due to its documented dangers: the medical literature is replete with references to its risks.[2] Mothers frequently died from their genital wounds. Those who survived often suffered from walking difficulties and urinary incontinence, and many babies died. So dangerous was symphysiotomy in the eyes of the medical profession in Paris that the Society of Medicine decided, in 1799, that doctors had a duty to perform a Caesarean section instead, an operation then generally fatal to women. Outside France, doctors also refused to practice the surgery except as a last resort. Other solutions, such as forceps operations, were available to the problem of obstructed labour. Medical policy in Britain in 1855 favoured craniotomy, an operation that decapitated the fetus, because it had a lower maternal death rate than Caesarean section.[3] Symphysiotomy was never in contest.

The operation was the subject of a mass medical experiment at the National Maternity Hospital (NMH), Dublin, in 1944. Senior Catholic doctors disapproved of Caesarean section – the standard treatment for difficult births in Ireland since the 1930s – because of its association with birth control. Two years after Alex Spain, a former clerical student, was elected master (or chief executive officer) of NMH, he embarked on an experiment to see whether symphysiotomy, a discarded eighteenth century operation, could replace Caesarean section in certain cases. Childbearing without limitation was the goal: healthy women, pregnant with their first child, were targeted for the surgery where there was any doubt about the 'adequacy' of their pelves. Young women and girls who were economically or socially disadvantaged were particularly at risk of selection.

That Spain's experiment was impelled by religious, not medical, considerations is clear from his writings, which show him to be a devotee of the Natural Law. In his view:

> the obstetrician is the man who should stand by whilst nature is fulfilled per vias naturales. When he resorts to Caesarean section he has failed to stand by and how often also, outside Catholic communities, does he go further and destroy by mutilation [sterilisation] one of nature's most important functions.[4]

As Nuala, another casualty of the surgery, later explained: 'you were only allowed to have three Caesarean sections [for safety reasons], so you were curbing your family [if you resorted to birth control]'. This issue was ventilated in a successful action for damages taken against the Medical Missionaries of Mary arising out of a post Caesarean symphysiotomy in 1969 (Kearney v McQuillan):

> ... If doctors were to perform caesarean sections more or less as required, there would come a point at which they would

have to advise a woman that she not have any more children and that would lead to the consequence that she might be tempted to use artificial contraception or she might even look for sterilisation or some other means of preventing a pregnancy. This consideration or these thoughts were sufficient to justify the doctor's hostility to caesarean section. This led them to be favourable to symphysiotomy ...[5]

Medical ambition was also a factor. Symphysiotomy, which needed neither theatre nor electricity, was seen as *enormously useful* for trainees from Africa and India by doctors set on developing NMH as an international training hospital.[6]

Spain's successor, Dr Arthur Barry, was a leading member of the Guild of Saints Luke, Cosmas and Damian, a global medical organisation dedicated to putting Catholic teaching into clinical practice. Spain felt hindered by the experimental nature of the surgery:

that I have not employed it more frequently is due to the fact that it is an entirely new procedure to me and one that has to be faced against the weight of opinion of the entire English-speaking obstetrical world.[7]

Barry showed greater confidence. At an international Catholic medical congress in 1954, Barry acknowledged the safety of Caesarean section, exhorting his colleagues to cut the symphysis for religious – not medical – reasons:

every Catholic obstetrician should realise that Caesarean section is probably the chief cause for the practice by the profession of the unethical procedure of sterilisation and furthermore it is very frequently responsible for encouraging the laity in the improper prevention of pregnancy or in seeking its termination.[8]

Barry pushed the symphysiotomy experiment at NMH to its limits. Visiting professors from Britain condemned the surgery on the grounds that it led to death and brain damage in babies and skeletal and other injuries in women. The Master of the Rotunda (the only one of

Dublin's main maternity hospitals to be identified as Protestant) pleaded for Caesarean section to be used instead, but Barry was undeterred. Pregnant women continued to be used as guinea pigs at NMH. The surgery spread to other private Catholic institutions that provided maternity services on behalf of the State, such as the International Missionary Training Hospital, Drogheda, and the Coombe Lying-In Hospital, Dublin. The fact that these were teaching hospitals helped to disseminate the surgery geographically, while the hierarchy of the mastership system in the Dublin maternity hospitals ensured that symphysiotomy was carried out, *willy nilly*, under the direction and control of the masters.

Women have described how the consultant would sweep into the labour ward and order that the patient, who was rarely addressed, be prepared for surgery. The operation involved incising the joint of the symphysis pubis, one of the main joints of the pelvis, located in the clitoral area: the joint unites the hip bones, one of which is the pubic bone. The nature of the operation was never disclosed in advance, and women were often misled. Their medical records show the use of 'blanket' forms 'consenting' to any operation the surgeon deemed advisable. Women subjected to symphysiotomy from the 1950s to the 1980s have testified that, in signing these generic forms – often in the height of labour – they believed they were consenting to Caesarean section, the only childbirth operation they knew.

Most women were operated upon in advanced labour: medical opinion held that a cervical dilatation of five cms was required for the surgery.[9] In 1952, the NMH took the view that, because of the risks posed by general anaesthetic to the fetus, symphysiotomy should be performed under local anaesthetic.[10] However, private patients have testified that they were operated upon at the NMH under general anaesthetic in theatre, while public patients were subjected to the surgery, fully conscious, in the labour ward. Vera, operated upon in 1968 at the International Missionary Training Hospital, recalled how Dr Connolly:

> came in with a big entourage. It was very invasive, you were tied up, you had no control. There was a good crowd there, nurses, other people ... my feet were tied up in stirrups for the symphysiotomy. I had gas and air ... I was in terrible distress. What he did to me – you have no power, when your legs are caught up like that.[11]

Women have related how they were in labour for hours before being set upon by hospital staff, their legs splayed in stirrups, and operated upon, wide awake and often screaming. Those who resisted were physically restrained by midwives. Then, still in labour following surgery, with the baby's head acting as a battering ram, women were left for as long as it took, hours or days, before being required to push the baby out through the agony of an ever-unhinging pelvis.[12] Nuala, operated upon by Dr Michael Neary at the International Missionary Training Hospital in 1975, was having her fifth child:

> she was a brow presentation, stuck for hours on end, mid-cavity, they said. You still had to push after the symphysiotomy, she was born within ten minutes, the vein in my neck was swollen from pushing. We were all awake, you had to deliver the baby, you had to be awake for it, to push the baby into the world. It was a dreadful, dreadful experience.[13]

In a tacit admission that the outcome of symphysiotomy was uncertain for the index baby (who might die or suffer brain damage), Feeney asserted that 'the *real harvest* [emphasis added] of symphysiotomy is reaped in subsequent deliveries'.[14] He was referring to the vaginal delivery of future babies, as yet unconceived, nine or ten being seen by the proponents of symphysiotomy as the ideal family size. However, the medical belief that symphysiotomy invariably resulted in a permanent enlargement of the pelvis was mistaken, as the number of women who required a Caesarean section either in the index birth or in a subsequent delivery showed. Hospital clinical reports record that women unable to deliver vaginally post symphysiotomy were eventually delivered by Caesarean section (by doctors who had earlier withheld this operation from them). Dolores, now unfortunately deceased, had both operations at the Rotunda Hospital in 1961 on the birth of her first and only child:

> they brought me to the operating theatre, I thought I was going to have the baby, I was put out, I nearly suffocated with what they gave me ... When I woke up, I asked the nurse, is the baby alright. You didn't have it yet, the nurse said, you've had your pelvis broken ... The labour ward was cold, miserable ... I was left so long ... I was dying, it was freezing cold. The next morning ... they rushed me to the theatre, they didn't speak to me ... They broke the bone on Monday, and on Tuesday, at twelve, I had a [*Caesarean*] section ... I was very bad after the first operation, after the second, it was impossible ... I don't know how long I was in [*hospital*] for, I was knocked out ... The smell of it, the anaesthetic, I couldn't breathe. It was a miracle I was alive ... I didn't want to live.[15]

Feeney later recorded that one baby in ten died post symphysiotomy:[16] others were left with suspected brain damage[17] or were otherwise injured. The long-term consequences for women were left unexamined: locomotor difficulties, pelvic instability and chronic pain; bladder and bowel injuries, lifelong incontinence; organ prolapse; chronic wound infections; sexual problems, relationship and mental health issues.

A pall of silence surrounded the surgery. Most women left hospital unaware that their pelves had been broken. They made this discovery some decades later, following the exposure of the practice in 1999 in a national newspaper by Jacqueline Morrissey, a doctoral student at University

College Dublin. Her conclusion that symphysiotomy was religiously motivated elicited contradictory defences. While former NMH Master, Dr Peter Boylan, asserted in 1999 that symphysiotomy was done to avoid the dangers of repeat Caesarean section, the voice of the specialty in Ireland, the Institute of Obstetricians and Gynaecologists (IOG), suggested in 2001 that symphysiotomy was the norm for obstructed labour until it was replaced by the 'modern' Caesarean section 'from 1950 onwards'.[18] Successive Ministers for Health, Micheál Martin, Mary Harney, James Reilly and Leo Varadkar, stymied repeated demands from Survivors of Symphysiotomy for an independent inquiry into the practice. Several unsuccessful attempts were made by the authorities to commission 'reviews' from known proponents of symphysiotomy, such as Dr Kenneth Bjorklund, author of a defective literature review that was highly favourable to symphysiotomy,[19] (engaged by the Department of Health in 2003), and Dr Nynke van den Broek (approached by the IOG in 2010). In response to proposals for a Bristol-style inquiry[20] from Survivors of Symphysiotomy, the Department effectively redirected the group to the Institute,[21] whose membership included doctors who carried out these operations and others loyal to employer hospitals that were sites of symphysiotomy.

Instead of mounting a prompt and full inquiry into symphysiotomy in 1999, the State took twelve years to commission a narrow review, whose terms of reference (agreed with the Institute, apparently, and with the author), excluded survivor testimony and unpublished data, such as medical records, outruling consideration of the clinical circumstances under which these operations were performed.[22] Commissioned in 2011, the final version of the Walsh Report was withheld until 2014, when it was published by the Government in the run up to the review of Ireland's performance under the International Covenant on Civil and Political Rights by the UN Human Rights Committee.

An all-volunteer group, Survivors of Symphysiotomy, with an elected national executive made up almost exclusively of survivors, unfunded by the State and independent of government, appeared before the UN Human Rights Committee in Geneva in July 2014. Its presentation was made by the author. The group had grown six-fold since 2010 to become the national membership organisation for some 400 survivors of symphysiotomy and their families, with its campaign actively supported by human rights watchdogs, such as the Irish Council for Civil Liberties and women's coalitions, such as the National Women's Council of Ireland.[23] The UN Human Rights Committee found that, under Article 7 of the Covenant, the practice of symphysiotomy constituted torture, cruel, inhuman or degrading treatment, and involuntary medical experimentation. The Committee prescribed an independent and thorough inquiry, prosecution and punishment of the perpetrators, and fair and adequate compensation.[24] Far from accepting the UN Committee's judgement or implementing its prescriptions, Ireland has continued to maintain that the practice of symphysiotomy was acceptable, and has refused to implement any of the Committee's rulings.

The Walsh report was partial in its investigation of the practice of symphysiotomy:

(i) the exclusion of unpublished data from the terms of reference meant, in effect, that 99% of hospital records were closed to external scrutiny, so the report's claim that these operations were justified is without foundation;

(ii) the exclusion of survivor testimony from the terms of reference prevented the first hand accounts of survivors from becoming part of what is known about the practice of symphysiotomy, further calling into question the veracity of this 'history' of symphysiotomy in Ireland;

(iii) the report ignored contemporaneous and later evidence showing conclusively that the introduction of symphysiotomy into clinical practice in Dublin in 1944 was a mass medical experiment aimed at replacing Caesarean section with symphysiotomy in certain cases;

(iv) the report also disregarded the evidence of the time, which showed conclusively that C-section was the treatment of choice in Ireland for difficult births in 1944, wrongly defending the practice of symphysiotomy on the basis that it was 'safer' than Caesarean section;[25]

(v) finally, the report ignored Ireland's 1937 Constitution and the decisions of its Supreme Court:[26] Walsh wrongly justified doctors' failure to seek patient consent by stating that informed consent to medical treatment was not a legal requirement in Ireland during the period under review (1944–1984).[27]

A further element in the State's strategy for dealing with abuse is to compensate – or appear to compensate – the victims while at the same time protecting the perpetrators. The publication of the Walsh Report was accompanied by the announcement of (financial) 'closure',[28] a tribute to Survivors of Symphysiotomy's long running campaign for truth and justice and a tactic designed to avert the litigation that so many members had embarked upon – in the form of a scheme that could be fashioned into a shield for wrongdoers. Such a scheme had been heralded by former judge Yvonne Murphy in a Government-commissioned report aimed at weighing up the balance of financial advantage to the State in allowing the court process to proceed versus setting up a payment scheme.[29]

Published in heavily redacted form in March 2014, the Murphy Report effectively anchored itself in the Walsh Report, and concluded, in effect, that an *ex gratia* scheme would save the State around €60m.[30] Women were given just 20 days in which to apply, making it difficult for claimants in Ireland and virtually impossible for those resident outside the jurisdiction to do so. This was in marked contrast to the Magdalen scheme, which is of unlimited duration,[31] and to the residential institutions redress[32] and Hepatitis C schemes,[33] whose gates remained open for three years. The symphysiotomy payment scheme gave a sole assessor unbridled discretion, outruled case-by-case assessment, provided no mechanism for hearing survivor testimony or accepting medical reports from independent doctors, gave 20 days in which to accept the scheme's offer, contained no right of appeal,[34] and paid 'compensation' averaging €65,000 per person or 20% of court awards for commensurate injuries.

Far from facilitating access to judicial remedies, as recommended by the UN, Ireland has repeatedly blocked all avenues that might offer survivors a determination of truth or a mechanism for justice, including accountability. Instead of prosecuting and punishing the perpetrators, including medical personnel, as prescribed by the UN Human Rights Committee, Ireland has done everything in its power to protect them. In 2013, invoking unspecified constitutional difficulties, the Government withdrew its support for a Private Members' Bill designed to facilitate survivors' access to the courts, thereby protecting doctors, hospitals – and the State itself – from civil suits for personal injuries. Survivors' access to judicial remedies is limited by the stringent law of limitations in Ireland, which affords no judicial discretion. The Bill aimed to set aside the Statute of Limitations for one year for survivors, as was done in 2002 for victims of abuse in residential institutions. The Government subsequently introduced its *ex gratia* payment scheme, headed by former judge Maureen Harding Clark, without any accompanying admission of liability. Under international human rights law, however, victims of human rights abuses are entitled to an effective remedy. The European Court of Human Rights has confirmed that *ex gratia* redress without an admission of State liability cannot be considered an effective remedy.[35] Symphysiotomy payments were, and remain, conditional on signing a waiver indemnifying and holding 'harmless' those responsible, directly or indirectly, for these acts of surgery.[36] It has been argued that this waiver made the scheme the functional equivalent of an amnesty law (which may be in breach of the Covenant).[37] Unlike the Madgalen scheme, the symphysiotomy waiver extended to private sector actors and entities, such as medical consultants, private hospitals and religious congregations.

Truth finding mechanisms are extremely limited. The Irish Human Rights Commission declined to conduct an inquiry into symphysiotomy in 2007. Changing its view in 2008, the Commission urged the Government to reconsider its refusal to review the practice. In April 2015, its successor, the Irish Human Rights and Equality Commission also declined to carry out an inquiry, asserting that the primary human rights obligation to do so, following the UN recommendation, fell to the State, not the Commission, and underlining the existence of an alternative mechanism to vindicate the (constitutional) rights concerned, namely the courts. However, the truth about the practice of symphysiotomy is unlikely to be established in personal injuries cases taken by individual litigants and the Supreme Court has ruled, in effect, that, because the doctors involved in these surgeries are largely deceased, the central issue of patient consent cannot be travelled.[38]

The need for an inquiry was highlighted by the unexpected 'discovery' of thousands of hospital records relating to symphysiotomy, following parliamentary questions from Dáil deputies in 2014. The newly disclosed records related to hospitals in Dublin, Cork and Waterford. For example, Airmount Hospital birth registers, labour ward books, theatre registers and obstetric notes spanning over half a century were 'found' to be in storage, held by an unidentified private records management facility in Dublin,[39] presumably for the owners of the former hospital, the Medical Missionaries of Mary. Such records, in some cases, may relate to women who remain unaware that they were subjected to the surgery.

The final strand in the government strategy emerged in early 2015 when it became apparent that the State was now bent on using its vast resources to defeat survivors who had the temerity to refuse the minimalistic compensation on offer and pursue their legal actions instead. It was open to the Government to instruct the State Claims Agency to settle survivors' legal actions: such an offer was made by their legal representatives in 2013 and rejected by the then Minister for Health, James Reilly. Three symphysiotomy cases have been heard to date: *Kearney v McQuillan*,[40] where the Supreme Court found in 2012 that symphysiotomy was not a generally accepted practice; *Anon v Ryan*, another post-Caesarean symphysiotomy case which settled after three days at hearing in February 2015, and *Farrell v Ryan*,[41] where the High Court found against the plaintiff in May 2015 in a symphysiotomy performed twelve days before the birth. At the time of writing, this case is on appeal to Ireland's Court of Appeal, and, with a significant number of personal injuries cases in the pipeline, the litigation battle is set to continue.

The removal of barriers to legal action has been recommended in other jurisdictions dealing with historical institutional abuse. The Australian Royal Commission into Institutional Responses to Child Sexual Abuse has advised that the law on limitations should not apply to personal injuries cases brought by victims of institutional sexual abuse.[42] Here in Ireland, the State is now employing an increasingly aggressive litigation strategy against survivors, and the Statute of Limitations has been invoked in every case to try to defeat litigants. In the most recent case (*Farrell v Ryan*), the State used its multi-million euro budget to employ medical consultants and other expert witnesses to contest all elements of the plaintiff's claims, including injury, with witnesses, such as Dr Peter Boylan and Professor Mary E. Daly, appearing for the defendant in a case that ran for fifteen days at hearing, in which many of the arguments of the 2014 Walsh Report were rerun by the defence, while the 2002 Bjorklund review was the mainstay of the hospital's contention, in 1963, that symphysiotomy was 'safer' than Caesarean section.

Performed without patient consent, as they were, these operations were illegal, breaching as they did women's constitutional and human rights, among others. Yet no person or agency has ever been held to account. The State continues to promulgate the view that the practice of symphysiotomy was appropriate, a view rooted in regulatory capture. It has been observed that:

> [the] absence of accountability fosters a climate in which wrongs gradually come to be regarded as acceptable, and in which society, over time, minimises its perception of the damage to victims. That leads to secondary victimisation ... a reckoning is essential.[43]

Under the Covenant, the State has a duty to investigate instances of torture, cruel, inhuman or degrading treatment. Survivors of Symphysiotomy will therefore continue to press its case for an independent inquiry. The issue is set to be examined in 2016 by the UN Human Rights Council and the UN Committee Against Torture will consider the matter in 2017.

Women's personal rights, the right to bodily integrity, the right to privacy, including self determination, and the right to refuse medical care or treatment during pregnancy and childbirth continued to be denied into the 1980s. While the symphysiotomy experiment ended officially in 1963 with the appointment of Dr Kieran O'Driscoll as master of NMH, survivor testimony and medical records show that the practice continued there into the 1970s, while it persisted at the International Missionary Training Hospital into the 1980s. Three decades later, blanket 'consent' forms are still in use in obstretrics in some Irish hospitals, and women's right to autonomy in pregnancy and childbirth has yet to be vindicated in the Irish courts. National consent policies deny pregnant women their personal rights and, until the time of birth, these rights may, and have been, overridden by the assertion of fetal rights under the Eighth Amendment to the Constitution.

As Markievicz would have observed, the practice of symphysiotomy was an exercise in male medical power over women's childbearing, a product of patriarchy overlaid with misogyny, of clericalism interleaved with colonialism, underpinned by western bio-medicine. She would have been disappointed to learn that women's participation at the highest level in the labour force has not brought about a more just society, one that respects human rights. Just as female judges and ministers for health have failed to tip the scales of justice for survivors of symphysiotomy, so female consultant obstetricians have done little to ensure women's right to autonomy in the labour ward. One hundred years after the 1916 Rising, women's lack of agency over where, how and with whom to give birth is greater than ever.

SOURCES
1   Kathleen, personal communication.

2   See, for example, Alexander Hamilton, *Outlines of the Theory and Practice of Midwifery* (Edinburgh, T Kay, 1803, 5th ed.), 333.

3   Colin Francombe *et al*, *Caesarean Birth in Britain* (London, Middlessex University Press, 1993), 25.

4   Royal Academy of Medicine in Ireland, 'Transactions', *Irish Journal of Medical Science* (1950), 859, in Jacqueline K. Morrissey, *An examination of the relationship between the Catholic Church and the medical profession in Ireland in the period 1922–1992, with particular emphasis on the impact of this relationship in the field of reproductive medicine.* Unpublished PhD thesis (University College Dublin, 2004), 161.

5   *Kearney v McQuillan & Anor* [2012] IEHC 127. Available at http://www.bailii.org/ie/cases/IEHC/2012/H127.html; for a discussion of Kearney v McQuillan, see Mairéad Enright, 'Kearney v McQuillan: Religion, Harm and History' (2012). Available at http://humanrights.ie/law-culture-and-religion/kearney-v-mcquillan-religion-harm-and-history/.

6   Tony Farmar, *Holles Street 1894–1994: The National Maternity Hospital: A Centenary History* (Dublin, A&A Farmar, 1994), 114.

7   National Maternity Hospital, 'National Maternity Hospital Report 1948', *Irish Journal of Medical Science* (1949), 456, in Jacqueline K. Morrissey (2004), *op cit*, 158.

8   Arthur Barry, 'Conservatism in Obstetrics', in John Fleetwood (ed), *Transactions of the 6th International Congress of Catholic Doctors* (Dublin, Guild of St Luke, SS Cosmas and Damian, 1954), 122–6, in *ibid*.

9   D. Crichton and E.K. Seedat, 'Symphysiotomy: technique, indications and limitations', *The Lancet*, 1 (1962), 554–59.

10   Jacqueline K. Morrissey, *op cit*, 171–2.

11   Vera, personal communication.

12   Survivors of Symphysiotomy. [Appendix to SoS Submission to UNHRC]. Submission to the United Nations Committee Against Torture (2014), 8–10. Available at http://tbinternet.ohch r.org/Treaties/CCPR/Share%20Documents/IRL/INT_CCPR_CS S_IRL_17504_E.pdf.

13   Nuala, personal communication.

14   Coombe Lying-In Hospital, 'Coombe Lying-In Hospital Report 1954', *Irish Journal of Medical Science* (1955), 51.

15   Dolores, personal communication.

16   Coombe Lying-In Hospital, 'Coombe Lying-In Hospital Report 1956', *Irish Journal of Medical Science* (1957), 452–4.

17 Royal Academy of Medicine in Ireland, 'Transactions', *Irish Journal of Medical Science* (1950), 860.

18 John Bonnar, then chairman of the Institute of Obstetricians and Gynaecologists, letter to Dr Jim Kiely, then chief medical officer, 4 May 2001.

19 Kenneth Björklund, 'Minimally invasive surgery for obstructed labour: a review of symphysiotomy during the twentieth century (including 5000 cases)', *British Journal of Obstetrics and Gynaecology* 109, 3 (2002), 236–48.

20 This inquiry was widely seen as exemplary. See Bristol Royal Infirmary Inquiry, 'The report of the public inquiry into children's heart surgery at the Bristol Royal Infirmary 1984–1995' (London, Department of Health, 2001).

21 Philip Crowley, then assistant chief medical officer, email to author, 25 August 2010.

22 Oonagh Walsh, 'Report on Symphysiotomy in Ireland 1944–1984' (Dublin, Department of Health, 2014). Available at http://health.gov.ie/wp-content/uploads/2014/07/Final-Final-walsh-Report-on-Symphysiotomy1.pdf, 9.

23 See http://symphysiotomyireland.com/; http://www.facebook.com/SoS-Survivors-of-Symphysiotomy-173631906029192/timeline/Twitter: @SoS_Ireland.

24 UN Human Rights Committee, 'Concluding observations on the fourth periodic report of Ireland' (2014), 4. Available at http://tbinternet.ohchr.org/_layouts/treatybodyexternal/Download.aspx?symbolno=CCPR%2fC%2fIRL%2fCO%2f4&Lang=en

25 Oonagh Walsh, *op cit*, 72.

26 *Daniels v Haskins* [1953] IR 73.

27 Oonagh Walsh, *op cit*, 67–71.

28 Noelle Higgins, 'Damages as Compensation for Human Rights Violations in Ireland', in Ewa Bagińska (ed), *Damages for Violations of Human Rights: A Comparative Study of Domestic Legal Systems* (Cham, Springer, 2016), 178.

29 Yvonne Murphy, 'Independent Review of Issues relating to Symphysiotomy' (Dublin, Department of Health, 2014), 1.

30 *Ibid*, 50.

31 Available at http://www.justice.ie/en/JELR/2.%20THE%20MAGDALEN%20COMMISSION%20REPORT.pdf/Files/2.%20THE%20MAGDALEN%20COMMISSION%20REPORT.pdf

32 Available at http://www.irishstatutebook.ie/2002/en/act/pub/0013/index.html.

33 Available at http://www.irishstatutebook.ie/1997/en/act/pub/00 34/.

34 http://www.payment-scheme.gov.ie/Symphyisotomy/Symphyi sotomy.nsf/page/Terms%20of%20the%20Scheme%20and%20A pplication%20Forms-en.

35 *O'Keeffe v Ireland* [2014] 35810/09 Available at http://hudoc.ec hr.coe.int/eng?i=001-140235#{%22itemid%22: [%22001-140235% 22]}.

36 The waiver covers 'all doctors, consultants, obstetricians, surgeons, medical staff, midwives, nursing staff, administrative staff, boards of management, associated with all hospitals or nursing homes, former hospitals or former nursing homes in the State whether public, private or otherwise and/or their insurers and the Medical Missionaries of Mary and/or any Religious Order involved in the running of any hospital and/or their insurers'. Deed of Waiver available at http://www. payment-scheme.gov.ie/Symphysiotomy/Symphysiotomy.nsf/ O/OAFC8447AC15B2D580257D89003FA7AE/SfileSCHEDULE1-DeedofWaiverandIndemnity.doc.

37 Mairéad Enright, 'What's Still Wrong with the Symphysiotomy Redress Scheme' (2014). Available at http://humanrights.ie/law-culture-and-religion/whats-still-wrong-with-the-symphysioto my-redress-scheme/.

38 *Kearney v McQuillan* [2010] IESC 6652 P. Available at http://www.bailii.org/ie/cases/IESC/2010/S6652.html.

39 Fiachra Ó Cionnaith, 'Unknown files on "barbaric" symphysiotomy op found', 10 December 2014. Available at http://www.irishexaminer.com/ireland/unknown-files-on-barb aric-symphysiotomy-op-found-301787.html.

40 *Kearney v McQuillan and North Eastern Health Board* [2012] IESC 43. Available at http://www.bailii.org/ie/cases/IESC/2012/S43. html.

41 *Farrell v Ryan* [2015] IEHC 275.

42 Royal Commission into Institutional Responses to Child Sexual Abuse, 'Redress and Civil Litigation Report' (2015), 76. Available at http://www.childabuseroyalcommission.gov.au/policy-and-research/redress/final-report-redress-and-civil-litigation.

43 Peter Cluskey, 'The Court's goal is not just worthwhile but admirable', 23 October 2015. Available at http://www.irishtime s.com/news/crime-and-law/the-court-s-goal-is-not-just-worth while-but-admirable-1.2400471.

JUSTICE, EQUALITY AND HUMAN RIGHTS

IRELAND AND GENDER INEQUALITY:
ECONOMIC, SOCIAL AND CULTURAL RIGHTS
UNDER THE INTERNATIONAL SPOTLIGHT

Jane O'Sullivan

Human rights and women's rights are not just aspirational ideals or optional extras to be benevolently bestowed when financial resources and public opinion allow. The Irish State has signed up to international treaties which create obligations. In 1966 the International Covenant on Civil and Political Rights and the International Covenant on Economic, Social and Cultural Rights (The Covenant) were created to give legal force to the promises of the Universal Declaration of Human Rights. While two separate treaties were created, all rights are of equal value and cannot be separated. In 1976, the Optional Protocol to the International Covenant on Civil and Political Rights came into force, creating a right of complaint for people (including people in Ireland) whose rights under the treaty, such as freedom from torture and the right to equal treatment before the law, have been violated. The same remedy did not exist for the

Covenant. Individual complaints on rights to food, housing, education, health, work etc, could not be examined by the UN Committee on Economic, Social and Cultural Rights. This changed in September 2009 when the Optional Protocol to the Covenant opened for signature. The Optional Protocol allows an individual who believes their social, economic or cultural rights are being violated by their own government to make an appeal to the UN. The Covenant has never been incorporated into Irish law, and the Irish Constitution is limited in its protection of these rights. For example, there is no right to housing in Irish law. Ireland signed the Optional Protocol to the Covenant in March 2012. It has not ratified it. People in Ireland can't use the Protocol to make complaints to the Committee on Economic, Social and Cultural Rights.

Access to justice is a huge barrier for women when it comes to the enforcement of rights. Without any real recourse in attempting to enforce their rights, people are left without an effective remedy. I am of the view that making economic, social and cultural rights legally enforceable is essential to tackling inequality and holding governments to account for policy decisions that disproportionately affect women. This is what Nelson Mandela was talking about when he said, in 1993, 'We do not want freedom without bread, nor do we want bread without freedom'.

The State's record in abiding by these international instruments is examined periodically by monitoring bodies, effectively shining a spotlight on the State's compliance. In 2014 and 2015, the Irish State faced examination by the UN Human Rights Committee and the UN Committee on Economic, Social and Cultural Rights respectively.

How Does an Examination Work?
The UN examination of a State's record under the Covenant is an important component in holding that State to account

in relation to its obligations under the treaty, which deals with the right to work, to social security, to the protection of the family, to housing, to an adequate standard of living, to health and education. I travelled to Geneva in June 2015 as part of a civil society delegation to the United Nations Committee on Economic Social and Cultural Rights (the UN Committee) on its third periodic report of Ireland's implementation of the International Covenant on Economic, Social and Cultural Rights. The UN Committee comprises a group of 18 independent international experts, who examine Ireland's progress in protecting, respecting and promoting the rights contained in the Covenant. The Government was asked to explain why the recession affected certain groups so disproportionately, overwhelmingly those who were already struggling in the fault lines at the margins of society, such as Travellers, people in direct provision and one-parent families living in poverty. The Troika bailout programme was implemented without any human rights or equality assessment.

Ireland had not been examined on its compliance with the Covenant since 2002. On 8 June 2015, the Irish Human Rights and Equality Commission, along with a group of Irish NGOs and civil society organisations, had an opportunity to highlight areas in which the State has failed in its implementation of these very fundamental rights. This all took place in the somewhat incongruously opulent Palais Wilson on the shores of Lake Geneva. Advocacy in this context can feel disconnected from the reality in some respects, but the range of organisations, from the well-established to the relatively new and often emerging from grassroots, does create a sense of empowerment. Besides the opportunity to formally address the Committee, informal meetings with individual members are facilitated. The members of the Committee were highly engaged with and well briefed on the issues raised by the civil society delegation, leading to a lively discussion in the informal session which took place after the formal morning session, at which the NGOs had an opportunity to speak for two minutes each to highlight their written submissions. There was a sense of quiet determination amongst the members of the delegation, as well as an emboldening feeling of solidarity. *Our Voice Our Rights*, a parallel report coordinated and submitted by FLAC in response to the State's report in advance of the examination, gives a detailed breakdown of the issues of some of the NGOs involved.[1] Submissions were also made by individual organisations including the Abortion Rights Campaign.

In the afternoon the spotlight was turned on the State's delegation, led by then Minister Sean Sherlock. The State delegation were seated at the top of a palatial yet airless long room, separated from the civil society delegation and observers by the Committee members, who sat at a large rectangular conference table and put their questions to the State representatives, sometimes through interpreters. The Minister outlined Ireland's performance from the State delegation's point of view, emphasising developments in human rights and in particular the then recent marriage equality referendum. It was then the turn of the Committee to ask questions of the State, based on the list of issues prepared in advance. The State delegation was made up of officials from various government departments. The detailed and often technical questions posed by the Committee at the informal session earlier in the afternoon to civil society organisations on their written submissions turned out to be an excellent indicator of the timbre of its examination of the State. They asked specific, searching, good quality questions and pushed for answers.

The Committee was particularly interested on the effect of austerity on the implementation of economic, social and cultural rights, and keen to emphasise the obligation on States to ensure that any austerity measures must be temporary, proportionate and only implemented where strictly necessary. The members focused on vulnerable and marginalised groups and also questioned the State on the failure to give these rights domestic legal effect. One cannot, for example, claim before an Irish court that your right to adequate housing has been violated. Article 11(1) of the Covenant recognises 'the right of everyone to an adequate standard of living for himself and his family, including adequate food, clothing and housing, and to the continuous improvement of living conditions'. The State's emphasis on a lack of financial resources failed to address what was driven home in the civil society submissions – that the vulnerable and the marginalised had not been prioritised either in times of economic buoyancy or austerity. The reliance on outdated figures and statistics was a source of frustration and served to highlight the concerns expressed by civil society about the shortcomings of the institutions of the State in gathering meaningful data. There were no revelations nor, it seemed, any real attempt to openly confront the difficult issues raised. This was no surprise in light of the State's response to the list of issues and to be fair, the format of the examination lends itself more to the State being put through the wringer than an opportunity for collaborative, honest and open consultation.

CONCERN OVER PERVASIVE GENDER INEQUALITY

The UN Committee on Economic, Social and Cultural Rights expressed concern in its Concluding Observations at:

> the pervasive gender inequality in the State party, in particular the under-representation of women in decision-making positions across all sectors in the society and the widening gender pay gap, as well as the strong gender role stereotypes in the family and society (art. 3).[2]

This over-riding concern at the persisting gender inequality in Irish society was borne out in the UN

Committees' detailed examination of particular issues brought to the attention of members. For example, both examinations have been characterised by scathing criticism of the state of women's reproductive rights in Ireland. During the UN Committee's examination in June 2015, just as in the UN Human Rights Committee 2014 examination, the issue of women and girls in Ireland who seek access to abortion services free from stigma and discrimination was brought to the attention of the Committee. The Irish Family Planning Association (IFPA) delivered an oral statement on behalf of 11 other pro-choice groups. The Committee asked the State how it reconciles the right to life of the foetus with the life and health of female citizens. In July 2014 the UN Human Rights Committee had condemned the state's restrictive abortion regime. Nigel Rodley, the former UN Special Rapporteur on Torture and Human Rights Committee member, articulated the experience of being a pregnant woman in Ireland in his closing remarks, stating that Ireland's abortion laws treat a pregnant woman 'as a vessel, nothing more'.

In turn, the UN Committee on Economic Social Rights in June 2015 expressed its concern at:

the State party's highly restrictive legislation on abortion and its strict interpretation thereof. It is particularly concerned at the criminalisation of abortion, including in the cases of rape and incest and of risk to the health of a pregnant woman; the lack of legal and procedural clarity on what constitutes a real substantive risk to the life, as opposed to the health, of the pregnant woman; and the discriminatory impact on women who cannot afford to obtain an abortion abroad or access to the necessary information. It is also concerned at the limited access to information on sexual and reproductive health (art. 12). The Committee recommends that the State party take all the steps necessary, including a referendum on abortion, to revise its legislation on abortion, including the Constitution and the Protection of Life During Pregnancy Act 2013, in line with international human rights standards; adopt guidelines to clarify what constitutes a real substantive risk to the life of a pregnant woman; publicize information on crisis pregnancy options through effective channels of communication; and ensure the accessibility and availability of information on sexual and reproductive health.[3]

The Committee, again in its Concluding Observations, expressed regret that article 41 (2) of the 1937 Constitution, which specifically delineates the role and status of women in Irish society, remains unchanged and it recommended that it be amended to reflect gender equality. It also recommended that the State party take effective measures to increase women's representation in decision-making positions in all areas, to close the gender pay gap and to eliminate strong gender role stereotypes.

Irish social policy has been highly gendered throughout its development. Article 41 provides that 'a woman, by her life within the home', supports the State for the 'common good' and that 'mothers shall not be obliged by economic necessity to engage in labour to the neglect of their duties in the home'. At this very fundamental legal level, the traditional stereotyping of women and men persists. This translates into stark differences in the way men's and women's contribution to society is valued. It is estimated, for example, that women provide two thirds of all care hours in Ireland,[4] increasing to approximately seven in ten from age 50.[5] By and large, Irish society does not acknowledge this care as work. The contribution to the economy of unpaid care-givers and the economic and societal pressure their work alleviates is under-valued. This is reflected in the expense of childcare and in the cuts to carers' allowances, particularly during the years of austerity. The strong gender stereotypes that stubbornly linger, therefore, result in practical difficulties in the lives of women.

Many of the issues that are explored in this book, such as symphysiotomy, reproductive rights, institutional abuse of women and children and its modern incarnation, direct provision, have been exposed and skilfully analysed by groups and individuals before both Committees. The Committees have been strident in their condemnation of the treatment of women by the institutions of our State. This international exposure has been an important tool in advocating for the rights of these women and in forging a space for them to advocate for themselves in the political and diplomatic world that many of them are so alienated from.

SOURCES

1   *Our Voice, Our Rights:* A Parallel Report in response to Ireland's Third Report under the International Covenant on Economic, Social and Cultural Rights submitted by FLAC to the UN Committee on Economic, Social and Cultural Rights (November 2014).

2   Committee on Economic, Social and Cultural Rights Concluding Observations on the third periodic report of Ireland, 8 July 2015 (para. 15).

3   Committee on Economic, Social and Cultural Rights Concluding Observations on the third periodic report of Ireland, 8 July 2015 (para. 30).

4   Central Statistics Office, Census 2011 – Profile 8 – Our Bill of Health (Dublin, Stationery Office, 2012).

5   Yumiko, K. *et al*, 'Profile of Community Dwelling Older People with Disability and their Caregivers in Ireland', *Irish Longitudinal Study on Ageing* (Dublin, Trinity College Dublin, 2012).

Abortion Over a Dáil Term

Clare Daly

When the Minister for Justice, Equality and Defence can stand up in the Dáil and say:

> This is a Republic in which we proclaim the equality of all citizens but it is a reality that some citizens are more equal than others.[1]

and then propose to do nothing to rectify that inequality, you know there is a problem. Yet this is exactly what was said by former Minister for Justice, Equality and Defence Alan Shatter in his contribution to our moving of the Medical Treatment (Termination of Pregnancy in Case of Risk to Life of Pregnant Woman)(No. 2) Bill on 27 November 2012, following the tragic death of Savita Halappanavar. He also stated:

> it can truly be said that the right of pregnant women to have their health protected is, under our constitutional framework, a qualified right, as is their right to bodily integrity ... It is also of course the position that a pregnancy that poses a serious risk to the health as opposed to the life of a woman, even

where such risk could result in permanent incapacity, does not provide a basis for affecting a termination in this State ... The reality of course is that there is no impediment to men seeking and obtaining any required medical intervention to protect not only their life but also their health and quality of life.[2]

Shocking as this statement is, that he acknowledged and truthfully spelt out the Constitutional situation for women in Ireland was in fact a major advance on the general denial of this issue in Irish society. He reflected frankly that: 'In the absence of Constitutional change there will continue to be a British solution to an Irish problem'.[3] And that is exactly what has continued to prevail.

While the government could find time to hold a referendum in 2015 on reducing the age of the President, no such action was taken to deliver said Constitutional change for women. No opportunity was given to the Irish people to repeal the 8th Amendment. This discriminatory provision, inserted into the Constitution in 1983, reads:

The State acknowledges the right to life of the unborn and, with due regard to the equal right to life of the mother, guarantees in its laws to respect, and, as far as practicable, by its laws to defend and vindicate that right.

It equates the life of a woman with that of the unborn, creates a wall between a woman's right to life and her right to health, and has no place in today's Ireland. Indeed it never had. This Article has been the justification for one of the most restrictive abortion provisions not only in Europe but throughout the world, with Ireland featuring in a 2015 Amnesty International Global Report alongside countries like Algeria, Tunisia, Morocco and El Salvador because of our gross violation of women's human rights in relation to our lack of abortion provision.

Political cowardice and abdication of responsibility on this issue have prevailed for decades. The manner in which the last government and the political establishment dealt with abortion over the lifetime of the 31st Dáil illustrates how everything is different yet stays the same. At the end of the Dáil term, the only change introduced was the Protection of Life During Pregnancy Act 2013 – a deeply flawed piece of legislation which continues to criminalise women who seek abortion, albeit with a penalty of 14 years imprisonment instead of the previous penal servitude for life! This Act essentially makes it impossible for any woman to access lawful abortion in Ireland when her life is in danger. Instead, with breathtaking hypocrisy, the reality is hidden, and vulnerable women coping with a crisis pregnancy are exported to Britain and beyond with all of the extra expense and emotional cost that such a situation brings.

And yet the Dáil saw numerous Bills being moved to try to legislate for abortion, multiple public outcries over the treatment of women because of Ireland's restrictive abortion legislation, and repeated criticisms of our abortion laws from the UN Committee Against Torture, the UN Committee on Economic, Social and Cultural Rights (UNCESCR), and the UN Human Rights Committee. As the UNCESCR pointed out in late June 2015,[4] in order to protect the lives and health of women the 2013 Act must be repealed, as must Article 40.3.3 of the Constitution (the 8th Amendment).

The UN special rapporteur for Ireland, Justice Ariranga Pillay, put it bluntly to the Irish delegation to the UN Committee on Economic, Social and Cultural Rights:

> According to your answers about why the abortion law cannot comply with the International Covenant standards, you said this is because of the Constitutional protection for the unborn foetus. If this is the case why have you not had a referendum? Why have you not answered this?[5]

Why, indeed? The need for a referendum is urgent, and has been urgent for many years. But the last government, in common with its predecessors, preferred to wring its hands and say it couldn't do anything to respond to this urgent need. The government talked about the will of the people, but seemed happy to ignore the reality that no woman of reproductive age in Ireland has ever had a vote on this issue.

While political cowardice and inaction on the need to repeal the 8th Amendment has too often prevailed inside the Dáil, public agreement on the need for legislative action has changed and grown. It is now increasingly clear that today's generation of young women, and indeed young men, are not willing to sit back and allow this situation to continue. The years from 2012 to 2016 have seen a huge groundswell of public opinion build around the need to deal with Ireland's abortion reality. This groundswell included and includes not just those of us who are pro-choice, but also those who support access to abortion on restricted grounds – be it in cases of rape or incest, fatal foetal abnormalities, and where a woman's health is in danger. However, legislative action that could give effect to broad public support for abortion is impossible without repeal of the 8th Amendment.

Upon election in 2011, myself and my colleagues, independent TD Mick Wallace and fellow United Left Alliance TD Joan Collins, decided we were not prepared to wait for the government to take action on this issue – or indeed to wait until another tragedy hit the headlines. Rather than letting it lie, and conscious of the approach of the 20th anniversary of the X case ruling, we began to prepare legislation to give effect to that ruling. The X case had shocked the nation in 1992 when a 14-year-old rape victim was prevented from travelling outside the country for an abortion. In the outcry that followed, the Supreme Court in 1992 ruled that the 8th Amendment allowed for abortion in Ireland where the life of a woman was at risk as a result of pregnancy – including a risk from suicide. A referendum followed that same year and ratified overwhelmingly the right to travel for an abortion, the right to abortion information, and upheld the Supreme Court's interpretation of the Constitution to allow for abortion when a woman's life was in danger. Notwithstanding this, ten years later in 2002, Fianna Fáil held another referendum to attempt to pull back the already limited abortion provision by removing the threat of suicide as a ground for legal abortion. This was rejected by the people of Ireland. Another 10 years passed and still nothing was done.

When, in 2010, the Grand Chamber of the European Court of Human Rights unanimously found Ireland to be in breach of Article 8 of the European Convention on Human Rights in the case of A, B, and C vs. Ireland, and declared that Ireland had an obligation to legislate for the 1992 Supreme Court decision in the X case, it was clear that international pressure was beginning to mount. In January 2012, the new government set up a so-called 'Expert Group'. Representatives from the legal and medical profession would examine the type of regulations or legislation necessary to give effect to a woman's right to abortion as outlined by the Supreme Court, and as the European Court of Human Rights ruling in the A, B, and C vs Ireland case in 2010 demanded.

Abortion was a subject that had sat on the backburner for a long time. Our proposed legislation, the Medical Treatment (Termination of Pregnancy in Case of Risk to Life of Pregnant Woman) Bill 2012 was the first pro-abortion legislation ever moved in the Dáil. In line with that, the moving of the Bill in Private Members' time on 18–19 April 2012 was the first time abortion was discussed proactively in the Dáil – without a tragedy to provoke it. We approached the Bill from the standpoint that it was an important health and human rights issue, and sought to have the debate on those terms. The Bill provided for abortion where necessary to save the life of a woman based on the medical opinion of two medical practitioners, one of whom must be a clinical psychologist or a consultant psychiatrist where the risk to life comes in the form of suicide. The Bill was defeated – 20 votes for and 111 votes against.

However, the large majority against the Bill masked the quality of the public debate that had swirled around its introduction and the subsequent open dialogue about abortion that took place across the airwaves and in the media. Four women came forward to tell their stories about having to make the journey to Britain for an abortion as their foetuses had fatal abnormalities incompatible with life. It was the first time that women openly identified themselves as women who had had terminations. The stories of mothers, daughters, sisters, wives and girlfriends were beginning to be told openly. With over 150,000 women travelling out of the State to access abortions for so many different reasons over the past three decades, it's clear that no family has been untouched by this issue, whether they know it or not.

While our Bill, because of the 8th Amendment, restricted the provision of abortion to the limited circumstances where a woman's life was in danger, we were unapologetic in making it clear that we favoured access to abortion in any circumstances that a woman sought it. Ironically, Labour deputies argued against our Bill on the basis that it did not go far enough, but later supported legislation that was far more restrictive.

The March for Choice on 29 September 2012 saw thousands confidently take to the streets of Dublin demanding abortion legislation. The mood of the participants and the response from shoppers and passersby clearly showed a new generation in the ascendancy who would not tolerate the ongoing hypocrisy of a situation in which Irish women have a legal right to an abortion, a right enshrined in the Constitution by her right to travel and right to information, but a right that cannot be exercised in the Irish State. Participants in the March for Choice asked whether we would have to wait for another tragedy, another X case, before legislation would be forthcoming.

Sadly that tragedy happened a month later on 28 October 2012, with the death of Savita Halappanavar in Galway University Hospital. Her death sparked an enormous outpouring of anger; anger that yet another woman had needlessly lost her life as a result of political inaction. Tens of thousands took to the streets to say 'Never Again'. The issue of whether her life would have been saved had our Bill been passed was openly discussed. We re-tabled that legislation on 27–28 November 2012. Again the vote was lost, by 27 votes to 101, with the same forces voting as before. This time, in an effort to cut across the growing momentum around the issue, the Expert Group's report into how Ireland should legislate for the X case decision was published the day the debate started. We were told action would be taken. Hearings were convened into the report at the Health Committee which came back early from the Christmas recess. Outside the Dáil, the anti-abortion lobby swung into force. In the end, the government's own abortion legislation was passed in July 2013. But the legislation introduced by the Fine Gael/Labour government, the Protection of Life During Pregnancy Act 2013, while symbolically important in that it legislated for abortion in Ireland for the first time, is, in practice, so restrictive as to make it effectively inaccessible to anyone.

Under the Act, even women experiencing inevitable miscarriage can still be denied an abortion because of the false dichotomy in the Act between a woman's 'life' and her 'health'. Prior to the 2013 Act, as Savita's sad death had shown, in a situation of inevitable miscarriage, in which the death of the foetus is certain, the presence of a foetal heartbeat legally restricts a doctor from offering to terminate the pregnancy.

This lack of legal clarity as to when a doctor can terminate a pregnancy to protect a woman's life has not been changed by the 2013 Act. In fact, the Act now gives legal protection to the so-called 'unborn' from the moment of implantation in the womb until delivery from the woman's body. This point was made by the consultant obstetrician who treated Savita. It informed the medical strategy of 'wait and see' that was adopted by her medical team. Yet waiting in that situation means that the woman is increasingly at risk of infection – the longer the delay in clearing the womb the greater the risk of sepsis. But doctors are legally obliged to wait until the foetus dies, or until a woman develops sepsis to the extent that her life is at risk, before they can clear the womb and thus remove the source of infection. This is an outrage, and it's a direct product of the Constitutional Chinese wall between a woman's right to life and her right to health; a Chinese wall the Act did nothing to tear down.

The 2013 Act also criminalises women who obtain abortions in Ireland outside the boundaries of the Act, and anyone who helps them. This means that women who use abortion pills they have bought over the internet can face up to 14 years in prison for using them – making it far less likely they will go for aftercare. And it denies women the right to choose when they wish to continue a pregnancy. An amendment to remove the criminalisation provision from the Bill, moved by myself and Deputy Joan Collins, was voted down 110 to 13.[6] The criminalisation provision has been the subject of repeated and trenchant criticism from a variety of human rights bodies since 2013. The denials of access to abortion in the Bill, along with the criminalisation of pregnant women, are why I and other pro-choice TDs voted against it. The 2013 Act is so restrictive that, as numerous people noted at the time, none but the most desperate, or those in State care, is likely to benefit from it, as women who have the means or the choice will travel abroad for terminations. The case of Ms Y, which came to public attention a year after the Act's passage, showed that for those desperate and in State care, the legislation was in fact violently harmful.

Ms Y had travelled to Ireland in early 2014 to seek asylum, having fled brutal persecution and rape in her home country. Shortly after arriving in Ireland, and having been placed in a Direct Provision Centre, she discovered that she was pregnant. She told the nurses and officials in the centre that her pregnancy was as a result of rape, that she was suicidal, and that she wished to have a termination. She was told that travel to the UK would be expensive, and obtaining a visa difficult. Eventually, in July 2014, Ms Y made it to the UK, but was arrested, detained and returned to Ireland as she was not legally allowed in the UK. Ms Y was transferred to a maternity unit where she continued to tell her healthcare team repeatedly that she was suicidal. She told them:

> I will kill myself if I cannot get rid of this baby … I don't want it inside me. I don't want to discuss it. I don't want to know about it. I want it out. I cannot continue with this pregnancy.[7]

She was not informed of her rights under the Protection of Life During Pregnancy Act 2013, but she was told, according to her medical records, that 'you cannot get an abortion in this country'. Eventually her doctors informed her that they would 'terminate' her pregnancy, but amidst legal wrangling termination was delayed and delayed. Ultimately, in August 2014, Ms Y delivered a baby by caesarean section. Her lawyer told Amnesty International: 'From what I have read, viability considerations and other legal implications were first and foremost in the minds of those involved'.[8]

The treatment of Ms Y demonstrates that the Protection of Life During Pregnancy Act 2013 is not fit for purpose, and that the scope for vulnerable and marginalised women to be denied terminations that the Act is supposed to permit is still wide.

Women who can travel, and who can afford to travel, will continue to do so, rather than suffer the indignity of having to 'prove' that they are suicidal in front of a panel of medical professionals; and rather than take the risk that they, like Ms Y, will be forced into continuing a pregnancy against their will, regardless of the threat to their mental or physical health. The Protection of Life During Pregnancy Act, and Article 40.3.3 of the Constitution that underpins it, forces women and their doctors into situations where women's lives are threatened. It also denies women abortions in cases of rape or incest, fatal foetal abnormality or risk of permanent damage to health. It is telling that in July 2014, after the passage of the Act, the UN's Human Rights Committee chair and former UN Special Rapporteur on Torture, Nigel Rodley, stated that the Irish law on abortion treats women 'as a vessel and nothing more'. Rodley also described the panel review system demanded by the Act for vulnerable women as a form of 'mental torture'.[9] Disgracefully, a Department of Health representative told the Human Rights Committee at that meeting that the State had 'no solution' to the problem of women who can't afford to travel for terminations.

On 16 December 2014 I moved a Bill to repeal the 8th Amendment of the Constitution, the Thirty-fourth

Amendment of the Constitution (Right to Personal Autonomy and Bodily Integrity) Bill. Minister for Health Leo Varadkar, speaking on the Bill on 16 December, told the Dáil that he believed the 8th Amendment to be 'too restrictive' and 'that it continues to exert a chilling effect on doctors'. Despite this, and despite the 31 years the 8th Amendment had been in place at that stage, and despite the Protection of Life During Pregnancy Act's manifest failures to really 'legislate for X', Varadkar cautioned that, 'This is not a decision that can be rushed', and that the government should 'not attempt a "rush job" referendum in the spring'. While a week is a long time in politics, decades, it seems, are not.

While the Bill was voted down, 110 votes to 13, there were signs in that debate that, even in the course of a year, attitudes had shifted very slightly in the House. Some Deputies who had supported the Protection of Life During Pregnancy Act the previous year placed on the record their view that provisions in it, such as the criminalisation of women and the need for scrutiny of a case by six medical practitioners, were wrong. Indeed, in the days immediately after that vote, another horrific case emerged to yet again give the lie to government protestations that the Protection of Life During Pregnancy Act would make things better for women in Ireland.

'PP' was a clinically dead pregnant woman who was kept on life support against her family's wishes. Her father was told by medical staff that for medical reasons 'they felt constrained to put [her] on life support because her unborn child still had a heart beat'.[10] The family took a case to the High Court, which ruled that life support should be withdrawn, on the grounds that the foetus had no chance of survival and therefore the maintenance of life support was 'a futile exercise', which 'would deprive [the pregnant woman] of dignity in death and subject her father, her partner and her young children to unimaginable distress'. The PP case, in which her family was denied the right to say goodbye, and had to suffer the unimaginable torture of fighting a High Court action to allow her to die a dignified death, put centre stage once again the failings of the Protection of Life During Pregnancy Act.

The signs of shifting attitudes were again revealed in poignant public discussions in 2015 around the need to provide for terminations where the foetus had a fatal abnormality. Some 50 Deputies are on record as saying something needs to be done to legislate for cases of fatal foetal abnormality. In 2012, an open letter written by Labour Party members, including three MEPs, three Senators and 14 Deputies, was circulated. The letter called on the government to introduce legislation to set out the criteria whereby terminations of pregnancy could be carried out in circumstances involving fatal foetal abnormalities. Simultaneous with this, a strong legal opinion emerged that it could be possible to legislate for abortion in cases of fatal foetal abnormality without a Constitutional referendum – as the right to life of the unborn, which has Constitutional protection, could not exist in cases where its condition was incompatible with life. Any notion that such a law would be unconstitutional could be tested by putting it to the Supreme Court.

In February 2015 I moved legislation that would provide for terminations in cases of fatal foetal abnormalities. The Protection of Life in Pregnancy (Amendment) (Fatal Foetal Abnormalities) Bill 2013: Second Stage (Private Members) aimed to put an end to the devastating situation where women and couples are given the news that a much-wanted child has no hope of surviving outside the womb. It aimed to put an end to couples being faced with the choice of carrying a baby with no chance of life outside the womb, being congratulated by friends and strangers alike, while they know that the foetus would not survive; or the choice of having to pack up and travel abroad, pushed out of their own country, away from family and supports, to obtain a termination.

Introducing the Bill, I read out a letter to the government from Amanda, one of the founders of the campaign group Termination for Medical Reasons. She wrote:

> Stop making excuses while women in this horrendous situation continue to contact us week after week, unsure of where to go or who to turn to; in shock at the extent to which they are abandoned and stigmatised in the wake of the Irish government's continuing excuse making. Enough is enough. You are the legislators. You are the law makers. You have signed up to these sensitive issues. It's your job. I'm tired of this sadness and the anger that comes with answering phone calls and emails from distressed expectant parents in the same situation that we were in two and a half years ago, and having so little to offer them other than emotional support. Change is beyond due. I would say to this government, it is finally time to recognise it and deal with this issue.

The government hid instead behind unpublished advice from the Attorney General that the Bill would be unconstitutional. This despite the fact that the previous Attorney General had argued, in the case of D v Ireland before the European Court of Human Rights in 2002, that it would be constitutional to legislate in circumstances where a foetus had no prospect of life outside the womb. Again, this appalling cruelty cannot be dealt with unless the 8th Amendment is repealed. If politicians really want to help people, as they consistently say they do, they have to support such a repeal.

Although Minister for Health Leo Varadkar, in speaking on the Bill, reiterated his earlier point that the 8th Amendment is 'too restrictive' and that 'this is legislation that had been overdue for more than 20 years', he simply went on to say that the Bill was 'well intended' and 'what I believe is required now is a considered and careful public debate to find a consensus'. As he did with the Bill to repeal the 8th Amendment, Minister Varadkar noted that a referendum would be necessary, and implicitly acknowledged the accusations of hypocrisy coming both from the Opposition and from much public commentary, saying: 'I am sure Deputies who support this proposal will question why I am not advocating the need for a referendum, if I truly believe that the eighth amendment is too restrictive'. You bet we are!

At least some of the prevarication from politicians is rooted in fear – it is notable that during the debates on the Protection of Life During Pregnancy Bill multiple Deputies made reference to emails and telephone calls from pro-life groups that were threatening or abusive. Many referred to the 'extreme' fringes of the debate. Much as UKIP has driven racist migration policies into the discourse of mainstream political parties in the UK, and as Le Front National has pushed the migration debate in the France far to the right, the 'extreme' fringe (and it is a fringe, and not at all reflective of mainstream views) of the pro-life movement in Ireland has successfully intimidated political parties into taking a position on abortion that is at odds with the one held by those who elected them.

It is clear that the prevarication around abortion legislation is not down to the general population, who have consistently demonstrated an understanding of the many varied and valid reasons why a woman might need an abortion. Rather, it is the political establishment who have lagged significantly behind the public, remaining timid about touching this issue for fear of stirring up a well-organised, vocal minority in the anti-abortion campaign along with the Roman Catholic Church.

While this might explain some of the gulf between mainstream opinion and the views oh-so-carefully expressed by politicians, it does not account for it all. Alongside this, there is a powerful sense that the mainstream political parties – particularly Fine Gael and Fianna Fáil – are out of touch with much of the populace. Again and again, as they lined up to speak on the Protection of Life During Pregnancy Bill, Deputies from these parties were eager to put on record that they were 'pro-life'; that they 'welcomed' the restatement in the Bill of the general prohibition on abortion in Ireland, but that they feared 'the opening of the floodgates' as mendacious, scheming womankind lied about feeling suicidal in order to get access to a termination. Again and again, the women who might be pregnant or have abortions were erased from the debate, quite literally, in a succession of subject-less sentences.

Taoiseach Enda Kenny led the charge with the following: '[The Bill] will cover existing Constitutional rights only, it will not create any new rights'. Kenny said that 'it will not create any new rights', but failed to say for *whom* those rights might be created. The women who might enjoy any new rights created are rendered invisible. Then Minister for Health James Reilly took the same approach, saying, '[The Bill] does not confer any new substantive rights to a termination of pregnancy'. Again, the women who might have such rights conferred on them are absent from the debate. On it goes. From Billy Kelleher of Fianna Fáil: 'It is the fundamental right of the unborn to be brought into this world' – the woman doing the bringing is absent.

Where women are present, they are radically disempowered, and entirely lacking in agency, as in this contribution from Micheál Martin: 'Provision is made for situations where it is presented that a termination may be required in order to prevent the loss of the mother's life through suicide'. In this construction, rather than an intervention resulting in a woman's life being saved, the intervention takes place to ensure that, as a 'mother' her loss is 'prevented'. Nowhere in this construction are the woman's wishes, feelings or basic humanity to be found, let alone her capacity or human right to choose what happens to her. She is to be subject to the State now that she is a 'mother' – her human rights, now that she is pregnant, no longer apply.

Such erasure is not accidental, and is entirely of a piece with the mentality that locked women behind the walls of Magdalene Laundries, or subjected them to the brutal practice of symphysiotomy. The thinking, feeling, voting women of Ireland always and forever have been the confounding problem for mainstream politicians in Ireland when it comes to talking about abortion. This is particularly the case in the last Dáil term, as it is no longer acceptable for men to say explicitly that they wish to deny women bodily autonomy or the right to choose. Far easier and politically safer to erase women from the debate altogether, and to talk in abstract terms about the 'right of the unborn to be brought into the world'. The 12 women a day who have terminations in British clinics were also rendered invisible by a debate that refused to come to grips with the fact that abortion is a reality in Ireland. The Oireachtas Health Committee hearings in the run-up to the legislation being moved did not hear from one woman who had had an abortion – despite approximately one in ten women of reproductive age being available to talk about theirs. As Deputies engaged in angels-on-a-pinhead arguments about suicidal ideation, the disconnect from that everyday reality was at times head-spinning.

That these politicians are out of step with public opinion is clear from a succession of opinion polls over the past four years showing broad support for abortion, particularly in cases of fatal foetal abnormality, incest, rape, or where the mother's health is at risk. The hundreds of women who have written to me to speak openly about their abortion experiences over the past five years show both the reality of abortion as something that many Irish women have experienced, and the broad support for it amongst the public.

As Fiona de Londras has pointed out:

> The key weakness in the Irish government's claim that the current constitutional position reflects a deep seated moral position on abortion held by the people of Ireland is that there has never been a referendum that offered the People the opportunity to truly liberalise abortion law in this jurisdiction ... Never once have we been asked, for example, to permit abortion in cases of rape or incest, not to mention to simply remove abortion from the Constitution and allow the political process to determine the limits of abortion availability as it does in so many other jurisdictions.[11]

While Irish women are in much the same position in 2016 as they were in 2012, in that their human rights continue to be denied when it comes to abortion, and they continue to travel abroad in their thousands every year to access it, there has been, as noted at the outset, a shift in public opinion, and a shift in the debate around abortion in Ireland. There has also been a degree of change within the Dáil. When I moved the Bill to repeal the 8th Amendment of the Constitution in November 2014, there was far more consensus on the need to hold a referendum (though no commitment to actually hold one) than there had been two-and-a-half years previously, on the introduction of our first abortion Bill in April 2012. Unrelenting international criticism and an ever more vocal public have begun to have an effect, and the Irish political establishment, timid as it has been in the face of this issue for too long, has finally begun to understand that taking action isn't a choice, it's a duty.

SOURCES

1   Speech delivered by Alan Shatter TD, Minister for Justice, Equality and Defence in Dáil Éireann during Private Members time, 27 November 2012.
2   *Ibid.*
3   *Ibid.*
4   http://tbinternet.ohchr.org/_layouts/treatybodyexternal/Download.aspx?symbolno=E%20C.12%20IRL%20CO%203&Lang=en
5   http://www.irishtimes.com/news/social-affairs/un-says-ireland-must-have-vote-on-abortion-1.2243406.
6   http://oireachtasdebates.oireachtas.ie/debates%20authoring/debateswebpack.nsf/takes/dail2013071100067?opendocument.
7   Amnesty International, 2015, *She is Not a Criminal: The Impact of Ireland's Abortion Law.*
8   *Ibid.*
9   http://www.irishexaminer.com/viewpoints/analysis/irish-abortion-laws-no-more-than-a-vessel-282582.html.
10   PP v. HSE [2014] IEHC 622, 26 December 2014.
11   http://humanrights.ie/constitution-of-ireland/a-modest-proposal-on-abortion-reform-in-ireland/.

Working Mothers, Childcare and the Gendered Order of Caring

Clare O'Hagan

Introduction

The legislation that prohibited married women working outside the home in Ireland was only removed as a precondition to Ireland's membership of the EU in 1973,[1] resulting in a dramatic increase in the proportion of married women, and specifically mothers, in the labour force thereafter. In 1971 only 8% of married women were in the labour force, however, by 2008, 69% of all married women aged between twenty-five and sixty-four were in the labour force.[2] Entering paid employment did not relieve women of their maternal responsibilities, however, and women entered the paid labour force only at the expense of taking on a second shift because they still retained responsibility for childcare and domestic duties.[3] Consequently, 40% of Irish women are prevented from achieving a desired balance between employment and care responsibilities.[4]

Perhaps one of the most significant aspects of the interface between family and work is the fact that the values and rationalities of each are diametrically opposed 'the assumption underlying all highly paid careers is that work will take priority over everything else'.[5] Commitment in the workplace is often judged by the number of hours employees are available to work, and sometimes by the availability of workers for out-of-work socialising. Jacobs and Gerson[6] argue that time itself has become a form of social inequality between women and men, parents and non-parents, while Gerson[7] finds that today's social and economic realities remain based on traditional distinctions between breadwinning and caretaking and the demands of balancing parenting and work are largely unresolved. There are very different gendered values attached to productive/work time and caring/process time.[8] As Smyth[9] argues, middle class and professional working mothers seem to be caught in a conflict between the need to constantly 'pass the test of manhood' at work, while at the same time engaging in intensively-devoted forms of maternal care-giving.[10] Given the realities of limited time, it is difficult to see how family and career commitments cannot come into conflict for women who continue to carry the major responsibility for family functioning.

When women become mothers, they experience inequalities in families because of their gender, undertaking the greater proportion of housework, childcare and household labour.[11] Where women participate in paid work, they experience inequalities in the workplace because of their gender, earning less and experiencing occupational segregation.[12] Where women with children engage in paid work, these inequalities are not added together, they mutate into new and complex forms of inequality.[13]

Childcare is central to women's ability to participate in paid work. Sourcing, arranging and paying for suitable, safe childcare is essential if women are to engage in paid work outside the home. However, the State does little to meet family's childcare needs which creates difficulties for 'working mothers'.

Childcare and the provision of childcare have received considerable attention in recent years. Landmark developments included the introduction of regulations of pre-schools in 1996, the appointment of the first ever Minister for Children in 1994, the first National Childcare Strategy in 1999 and the establishment of the National Children's Office in 2000. The Centre for Early Childhood Development and Education (CECDE) was founded in 2002, a Children's Ombudsman was appointed in 2003, a new Office of the Minister for Children was established in 2005, and in 2006 a new National Childcare Strategy (2006–2010) was launched, with a budget of €575 million.[14] The Irish National Action Plan for Social Inclusion (2007–2016) includes the long-term goal that 'Every family should be able to access childcare services which are appropriate to the circumstances and the needs of their children'.[15]

In 2006, *Síolta, the National Quality Framework for Early Childhood Education* was published to provide quality standards in pre-school childcare and applies to private, self-employed and community facilities as well as registered private childminders. Discourses of Children's Rights and Early Childhood Education have also informed policy and since 2010, the Early Childhood Care and Education Scheme (ECCE)[16] has provided limited free pre-school places in pre-school services who provide an appropriate educational programme which adheres to the principles of *Síolta*. Children aged between the ages of three years and two months and four years and seven months enrolled in pre-schools receive free pre-school education of three hours per day, five days each week for thirty-eight weeks. The pre-school receives €64.50 for each of the thirty-eight weeks, which equates to €4.30 per child per hour. It is proposed to double the provision to fifty-six weeks from September 2016.[17] In 2013, the Department of Children and Youth Affairs published *Right from the Start*, a report of the Expert Advisory Group on the Early Years Strategy.[18] The report makes fifty-four recommendations across ten themes. Thus far, only two recommendations are proposed to be introduced from September 2016: two weeks paid paternity leave and extending the provisions of the ECCE scheme.

In 2000, the government introduced The Equal Opportunities Child Care Programme (EOCP) to increase the supply and quality of childcare.[19] The EOCP provides funding for private, community and voluntary childcare sectors to establish and staff childcare centres, while grant assistance is given to community-based childcare facilities through thirty-three County and City Childcare Committees. The EOCP also funds these committees to organise training and information activities for small-scale childminders. However, small-scale childminders are specifically excluded from the notification process under the Child Care Act,[20] while the Childcare Regulations[21] make provision for the voluntary notification by childminders of their childcare service to the Health Services Executive (HSE). Under the Child Care Act (1991), a person minding more than three pre-school children from different families is obliged to notify the HSE,[22] however childminders who are relatives, or caring for children from only one family, or caring for three or less children from different families are exempt. At the end of 2011, the number of paid, non-relative, childminders registered with the HSE was 257.[23] Childminding Ireland provides training and support to small-scale childminders who register their services.

There is little data on the extent of private childminding in Ireland. One recent estimate based on 2007 data, suggests nearly 50,000 children in Ireland are cared for by private childminders,[24] while the OECD estimated that 75,000 children were placed with 37,900 childminders every working day in 2002.[25] The government is not directly involved in childcare provision, and is a facilitator of community and private childcare through provision of capital grants. Overall, in 2012, between day care, sessional and part-time services, there were just over 4,300 childcare facilities regulated by the HSE.[26] In an EU study of childcare, Ireland ranked lowest in terms of childcare supports and maternity leave,[27] and Ireland was ranked the worst of the original 15 member states in terms of public childcare provision. Childcare in Ireland is and has been uncoordinated, variable in quality and in short supply.[28] There have been some recent improvements in provision, though Ireland still has the highest net childcare costs as a proportion of average earnings in the OECD.[29] According to Fine Davis, the government is delegating provision to a plethora of private sector, public sector and community groups, while it provides capital grants. 'It is basically saying to the marketplace and community: "You do it". It is saying to parents: "You find your own childcare, you pay for it"'.[30] The lack of State support and childcare provision in Ireland has created a situation whereby childcare has been positioned as a private issue for families to resolve themselves.[31] This is what the OECD has termed a 'maximum private responsibility'[32] model of childcare, 'in which the joint problems of childcare, family life and labour force participation are entirely private concerns which are left to the individual to solve'.[33] In practice, 'the individual referred to here is usually the mother'.[34]

METHODOLOGY

A case study was conducted in a suburb of an Irish provincial city which is identified as predominantly middle class. In Ireland, the 11 category Socio Economic Grouping (SEG) classification system brings together people with broadly similar economic and social status and people are assigned to a particular SEG on the basis of their occupational and employment status.[35] The 7 category Social Class Groups classification aims to bring together persons with similar social and economic statuses on the basis of the level of skill or educational attainment required. The Social Class Group was first used in the 1996 Census and is based on the UK Standard Occupational Classification,[36] with modifications to reflect Irish labour market conditions. In determining social class, occupations are ranked by the level of skill required on a social class scale ranging from 1 (highest) to 7 (lowest).

Table 1: Irish classification system

Socio-economic groups	Social Class Groups
A Employers and managers	1 Professional workers
B Higher professional	2 Managerial and technical
C Lower professional	
D Non-manual	3 Non-manual
E Manual skilled	4 Skilled manual
F Semi-skilled	5 Semi-skilled
G Unskilled	6 Unskilled
H Own account workers	
I Farmers	
J Agricultural workers	
Z All others gainfully occupied and unknown	7 All others gainfully occupied and unknown

Women with children who engage in paid work of any kind were identified as research participants. Mothers of primary school-going children (aged 5 to 13 years) were targeted, allowing for the possibility that these women might also have older and younger children. In the area of the local study there are four primary schools, two boys' schools and two girls' schools with a school-going population between them of 1,800 children.

The schools sent participant invitation letters home in the schoolbags of those children currently living with their mothers, and thirty women self-selected to participate in the study. Women were almost equally divided between the 4 schools, with half of the women working full time, and half working reduced hours, part-time or job sharing. Women are almost evenly divided between public and private sector organisations. All participants in the study, according to the Irish Classification System are ranked in the top 5 socio-economic groupings [A-E] and the top 5 social class groups [1–5], reflecting their middle class status.

Focus groups were held with these women to explore women's experiences of being a 'working mother' and to reveal the range of diversity and difference within the group. Discussions of between five and seven women lasted on average two hours and were lively with women being interested in the ways other women combined motherhood with paid work. In order to explore the ways the social relations of mother and worker intersect with the institutions of workplace, family and society, and how they were experienced by individual women, these issues were explored with women in semi-structured, one-to-one interviews, which were conducted with the same women a year later. Focus groups and interviews were recorded and transcribed. All respondents selected pseudonyms, signed consent forms and approved focus group and interview transcripts. Interviews lasted on average more than an hour, with women claiming to have found focus group discussions informative regarding the ways other women combine motherhood with paid work.

Table 2: Women's socio-economic grouping and social class

Participant	Socio-economic Group	Social Class Group
Faye	A	1
Jasmine	A	2
Jane	A	2
Collette	A	2
Amanda	A	2
Audrey	A	2
Gina	A	3
Jean	B	1
Freya	B	1
Grace	B	1
Kate	B	1
Eithne	B	2
Amelia	C	2
Anita	C	2
June	C	2
Amy	C	2
Florence	C	2
Avril	C	2
Aisling	C	2
Agatha	C	3
Tamsin	C	3
Joy	D	3
Angela	D	3
Sabine	D	3
Anna	D	3
Cindy	D	3
Colleen	D	3
Yolanda	D	3
Anastasia	D	5
Brona	E	4

Women spend considerable effort on making childcare choices, because certain forms of caring, namely 'love labour'[37] cannot be provided on a hire and fire basis.[38] Because private childminders are not regulated, choosing childcare is one of the most difficult and important decisions a 'working mother' has to make. Amanda spoke about the stress involved in finding a childminder who would work in Amanda's home from seven in the morning and she noted the responsibility for arranging childcare in her family is gendered:

> That was a huge stress for me trying to hold onto a babysitter who would come in – in the morning, at seven. It was impossible to get and the fear of losing them, because, I felt it was my responsibility. My husband would not be involved in getting the new childminder ... it was always me. Me who would put the ad in the paper, [me] who would ask around (Amanda, focus group).

Care work is gendered. In families it is the woman who finds and engages childminders, and in all cases, childminders are women. All women were responsible for managing and organising caring, even if they do not do all the day-to-day hands on caring work.[39] Women spoke of the stress involved in finding childminders, particularly women who were not from the local area and did not have family support nearby:

> I had to find a childminder. I remember I came back here and there was no sort of [available register]. And I wasn't from [the local area] and my husband wasn't from [the local area] and it was the most stressful two years of my life, almost to the stage where I would, very, I almost gave up work, and it was a real struggle (Amy, focus group).

In Amy's account, the lack of state provision of childcare had a direct negative impact on her participation in paid work. Amy holds the lack of quality childcare directly responsible for her decision to reduce her hours in paid work following her return to the area of the study. However, the issue of childcare has not actually prevented women from entering the workforce. 'Irish women, and in particular Irish mothers, are entering the workforce in increasing numbers without the help of formal childcare'.[40] In families, childcare is the responsibility of individual women. Collette described the most common situation, whereby men are interested, but women have the responsibility for arranging care:

> I'd say my husband would be very interested in making sure we have the right person ... Yea, he would get involved, but yea, at the end of the day, I think it is utterly I think the mother's responsibility (Colette, focus group).

It has been argued that this inequitable burden has been found to cause women significant physical and emotional distress[41] and Amy, Amanda and Collette demonstrate the gendered inequalities they experience because they have responsibility for sourcing and arranging childcare. Women are concerned with the quality of the care children receive, both the 'love labour'[42] carers perform as well as the material tasks and work involved in caring so that children's physical, social and emotional wellbeing is not compromised when women leave their children in the care of others. The discourse of familialism strongly influenced middle class families' childcare choices, it:

> asserts that one to one care by the mother in the home is the best form of care, and if this is not available, it should be mimicked in other forms of care.[43]

However women are also concerned about availability when selecting childcare. Crèche and pre-schools are open every week of the year but will not accept children when they are sick, as opposed to childminders who may not be available every week of the year but generally will care for children if they are sick.

There is an unfounded assumption that crèche care is impersonal and formal with children not receiving the individual attention they would in a home environment, because it is regarded as commoditised caring on an industrial scale. There was widespread condemnation of crèche care by women who made other arrangements:

> And this business of children being in crèches from eight o'clock in the morning, till eight o'clock at night, five days a week, and (...) I don't think that's right. You know. I mean a child didn't ask to be brought into the world, and it most certainly didn't ask to be dumped into a crèche for forty-something hours a week you know (Grace, interview).

Grace engaged a childminder, and even though she was not entirely satisfied with her own childminding arrangements, she nevertheless felt they were superior to women who engaged crèche care. There is a gendered inequality in the way women experience public criticism for using crèche care, even though crèche care is regulated and arguably safer. Women who used crèche care generally explained their choice with reference to its availability every week of the year, which is the only form of childcare to guarantee this.

There is an interesting paradox surrounding crèche care. Popular views regularly link 'dumped' with crèche, and crèche care is commonly seen as inferior to childminder care. 'It goes against the whole thing about having a child if they're going to be sitting in a crèche from nine to six all day long' (Gina, interview). Yet, the government regards provision of childcare places through capital grants for crèche providers and crèche places for disadvantaged children as all that is necessary to facilitate women's employment. However, it became apparent in 2013, in a television documentary by the national broadcaster RTÉ, that government regulation of crèche facilities is 'light touch' and falls short of guaranteeing quality care for children.[44] Therefore women's concerns regarding crèche care are not without foundation. This media report into several facilities revealed that the childcare system is 'poorly regulated, deeply flawed and occasionally dangerous'.[45] The Government response was to establish a Child and Family Agency in 2014.

Women retain responsibility for the choice of childcare and for making the best choice within extremely limited options. Both Freya and Eithne combine crèche care with other forms of care. These are the only two women in the study who use crèche facilities despite crèches being the focus of state intervention. Freya has her older two children minded by an au-pair, while the baby attends a crèche. Eithne combines family care with crèche care, whenever her husband is available, and Eithne's girls attend a crèche, one for the full day and one for after-school care. Eithne found public scrutiny of motherhood extends to childcare and she found crèche care is roundly condemned:

> And you know, we get a lot 'Oh, you have them in a crèche?'... A lot of people don't think crèches are very good for the child – in terms of the child's development; in that they don't get the one to one care that they would get in a home environment; and that your child is deprived somewhat by being in a crèche; or that you dumped them in the crèche from eight in the morning to six in the evening, day after day (Eithne, interview).

As caring is gendered, these choices are women's responsibility and choosing crèche care is a socially unpopular decision that women are obliged to defend. Women's desire to have their children cared for and loved by their carers led to many women claiming to have preferred family care to engaging a paid childminder or crèche to care for their children. However, only eight women managed to achieve this at any stage. Kate reported that when her children were younger, she engaged au-pairs, but when the children started going to school, she changed to her sister providing childcare. Au-pair is a particularly middle class childminding arrangement and three women in this study engaged au-pairs at some stage during their childminding histories. Six women combined family care with paid care and six women described their husbands as being actively involved in the care of their own children, which may suggest men are challenging and valuing care. This is consistent with the national data. In 2008, men spent on average 4 hours and 40 minutes per day on paid work and just under two hours per day on caring and housework.[46] Joy only works when her husband is home in the evenings and weekends to care for their children. Faye's husband is taking parental leave one day every week, while other husbands are available to older children after school.

In a minority of cases, women's care patterns changed with the birth of their second child. Four women had their own parents minding the first child, but moved to childminding or combination of crèche and childminding when the second child was born. Jasmine had her sister-in-law caring for her children when they were pre-school age but now combines after-school care with her husband, who has recently changed to working nights:

> I suppose I'm very lucky now at the moment, because Patrick is working in a different job now and he's working mostly at night, and he collects them mostly in the afternoon and that gives me the freedom not to be rushing home from work either, you know, that I can take an hour, whether it's to do a bit of extra work or ... just to meet a colleague ... so I'm kind of lucky enough (Jasmine, interview).

While Jasmine is privileged in relation to childcare because her husband is available to care for their children during the day, there is an inequality which arises from this position – Jasmine and her husband rarely spend time together. Both Eithne and Joy, whose husbands are involved in caring for their children, also reported spending very little time together as a family, as one parent was working while the other was caring for the children. Having family available for childcare is completely arbitrary and maintains caring as a private issue, which is not commoditised, and fits with traditional expectations of caring as outside the remit of the market. With the exception of six women who described their husband's involvement in childcare, all other care was provided by grandmothers, sisters, paid childminders and crèche workers, all women.

Joy believed only family care was good enough for her children, and claimed women who went outside family for childcare were neglecting their children, by 'dumping' them. 'So and so's dumping their children to be reared by other women' (Joy, focus group). In this research, family care is the most preferred form of childcare, followed by private childminders, and then crèche care, reflecting similar findings on research with middle class families in the UK.[47]

Women were concerned that the people they engaged as childminders would care for their children to the same extent as they themselves, did. However, sourcing and retaining suitable childminders who will care for children, physically and emotionally to the level women desire is difficult, because registered childcare is primarily available in the form of crèche care. Most participants expressed a preference for more personal forms of care and sought individual childminders who would develop long term relationships with their children. A private childminder is the most common form of care the women in this study utilised. Fifteen women engaged childminders either in the minders' home or in the woman's home, while four other women engaged childminders in shared arrangements:

Childminding has been a hidden part of the economy for a very long time, so we're not surprised at the numbers … it also suits society to have it this way, to have cheap, accessible childcare available.[48]

There is an implication by Childminding Ireland that because childminders are not registered, they are providing an inexpensive service. There is also an implication that childcare is accessible. It is not. Sabine had a distressing experience with a private childminder:

> Because, now we had a child minder here and the whiskey was going down and one day I came home and the child had a stain on the bib, that was cough bottle, adult cough bottle … with alcohol in it, given to the baby (Sabine, interview).

However, Amy had a situation which was dangerous, and which had a long term effect on her family:

> I suppose just the care here isn't good, you know … Safe childcare. Safe. I think, like you know, we don't know what our children are going into, and we don't know where it's going to take us if anything within that is going to change our lives forever, I think. And for me, that's what happened. My first childcare placement here, was with somebody who changed, utterly changed my whole life. It was a bad, bad experience … it was a price I paid, that I didn't expect that I had to pay, and I suppose I resent the fact that there was no (…) there was nothing in place to prevent that from happening (Amy, interview).

Choosing childcare is gendered, and if the choice, as in Amy's case, does not work, then Amy blames herself for making a bad decision. However, Amy also acknowledges the failure of the State to regulate private childminders and put structures 'in place to prevent that from happening' (Amy, interview). O'Connor and Murphy[49] argue this delay in developing a childcare policy, combined with the lack of State intervention to support parenting and care work has reinforced women's disadvantaged position in society. In all paid care arrangements, childminders are women, and all 'working mothers' have responsibility for sourcing, arranging and paying for childcare demonstrating the way caring work is gendered, even if it is commoditised somewhat by being undertaken by paid care workers.

'To have good public services, including caring services, a state must invest in them'.[50] Women who attempt to combine motherhood with paid employment experience difficulties sourcing safe childcare because of the lack of state provision, support or regulation of private childminders. These women's different views on childcare and the dilemmas they experience are not idiosyncratic. Discussions on mothers' websites[51] reveal that women's dilemmas in relation to finding and choosing the best care for their children are widespread. The state's lack of childcare provision and its lack of regulation creates inequalities for 'working mothers', because they are charged with full responsibility for choosing childcare in a situation where the state is less than helpful.

CONCLUSION

The availability of safe, affordable, childcare is essential if women are to combine motherhood with paid work. Women's preferred form of childcare was family care, the next most popular form of childcare was private childminders and crèche care was the least preferred form of care. Family care is arbitrary, private childminders are unregulated, and crèche care is a socially unpopular choice. However, there is some cause for optimism in that some fathers are involved in the care of their own children.

In this research, women are responsible for choosing, arranging and paying for childcare. When childcare arrangements are unsatisfactory, women blame themselves for poor decisions. The greatest inequality women experienced is that their children were unsafe in the care of private childminders. This inequity is the responsibility of the State, however, individual women and children bear this inequality. Women bear the responsibility of caring for children and arranging childcare if they engage in paid work, therefore the gender system has not changed because of women's participation in paid work. The persistent view that care work is predominantly a private concern and a female responsibility contributes to the complex inequality 'working mothers' experience in Irish society.

SOURCES

1   Government of Ireland, *Civil Service (Employment of Married Women) Act* (Dublin, Government Publications, 1973).

2   CSO, *Quarterly National Household Survey, Q1 2009: Married Women's Participation Rates*. 2009 [online] www.cso.ie.

3   A. Hochschild, *The Second Shift: Working Parents and the Revolution at Home* (London, Piatkus, 1990).

4   K. Lynch and M. Lyons, 'The Gendered Order of Caring', in U. Barry (ed.), *Where Are We Now? New Feminist Perspectives on Women in Contemporary Ireland* (Dublin, Tasc at New Island, 2008), pp 163–183.

5   C. Jones, L. Tepperman and S. Wilson, *The Futures of the Family* (New Jersey, Prentice Hall, 1995), p. 110.

6   Jacobs and Gerson, *The Time Divide: Work, Family, and Gender Inequality* (Harvard, Harvard University Press, 2004).

7   K. Gerson, *The Unfinished Revolution: Coming of Age in a New Era of Books: Gender, Work, and Family* (New York, Oxford University Press, 2011).

8   K. Davies, *Women, Time and the Weaving of the Strands of Everyday Life* (Aldershot, Gower, 1990).

9   L. Smyth, *The Demands of Motherhood* (Basingstoke, Palgrave Macmillan, 2012).

10   M. Blair-Loy, *Competing Devotions: Career and Family Among Women Executives* (Harvard, Harvard University Press, 2003).

11   F. Williams, 'Time to Care, Time not to Care', ESRC 4th National Social Science Conference. London, 28 November 2000.

12   O. O'Connor and M. Murphy, 'Women and Social Welfare', in U. Barry, *op cit*, pp 30–52.

13   C. O'Hagan, *Complex Inequality and 'Working Mothers'* (Cork, Cork University Press, 2015).

14   European Anti Poverty Network, *Access to Affordable Childcare for Low Income Families*, November 2007 [online] http://www.eapn.ie/eapn/wpcontent/uploads/2009/10/access-to-affordable-childcare-for-low-income-families.pdf.

15   Government of Ireland, *National Action Plan for Social Inclusion 2007–2016* (Dublin, Government Publications, 2007), p. 30.

16   Government of Ireland, *Early Childhood Care and Education Scheme* (Dublin, Department of Children and Youth Affairs, Government Publications, 2010).

17   Government of Ireland, *Budget, 2016* (Dublin, Department of Finance, Government Publications, 2015).

18   Government of Ireland, *Right from the Start: Report of the Expert Advisory Group on the Early Years Strategy* (Dublin, Department of Children and Youth Affairs, Government Publications, 2013).

19   Government of Ireland, *National Development Plan 2000–2006* (Dublin, Government Publications, 2000).

20   Government of Ireland, *Child Care Act 1991* (Dublin, Government Publications, 1991).

21   Government of Ireland, *Childcare Regulations* (Dublin, Department of Health and Children, Government Publications, 2006).

22   Government of Ireland, *National Childcare Strategy 2006–2010: Guidelines for Childminders*, Revised Edition, August 2008 (Dublin, Department of Health and Children, Government Publications, 2008).

23   Start Strong, *Policy Brief*, October 2012 [online] http://www.star tstrong.ie/files/Childminding-Regulation_and_Recognition.pdf

24   Goodbody Economic Consultants, *Children 2020: Cost-Benefit Analysis* (Dublin, Goodbody Consultants, 2011).

25   OECD, *Thematic Review of Early Childhood Education and Care: Background Report. Ireland.* 2002 [online] www.oecd.org/\els\social\family\database.

26   J. Hearne, 'Ratios and regulations: how crèches are controlled', *Irish Independent*, 8 August 2012.

27   European Commission, *Rationale of Motherhood Choices: Influence of Employment Conditions and Public Policies* (Brussels, European Commission, 2004).

28   OECD, *Thematic Review of Early Childhood Education and Care Policy in Ireland* (Paris, OECD, 2004).

29   OECD, *Babies and Bosses: Reconciling Work and Family Life: A Synthesis of Findings for OECD Countries* (Paris, OECD, 2007).

30   M. Fine Davis, *Childcare in Ireland Today*. Social Attitude and Policy Research Group (Dublin, Trinity College, 2007).

31   J. Murphy-Lawless, 'Changing Women's Lives: Child Care Policy in Ireland', *Feminist Economics*, 6, 1 (2000), pp 89–94.

32   OECD, *Employment Outlook Study* (Paris, OECD, 1990).

33   E. Coveney, J. Murphy-Lawless and S. Sheridan, *Women, Work and Family Responsibilities* (Dublin, Larkin Unemployed Centre, 1998).

34   S. O'Sullivan, 'Gender and the Workforce', in S. O'Sullivan (ed), *Contemporary Ireland: A Sociological Map* (Dublin, University College Dublin Press, 2007), pp 265–282.

35   CSO, *Socio Economic Groupings, Census of Population 1996* (Cork, Central Statistics Office, 1996).

36   SOC, *Standard Occupational Classification*, 2nd Edition (London, Her Majesty's Stationery Office, 1995).

37   K. Lynch, 'Solidary Labour: Its Nature and Marginalisation', *The Sociological Review*, 37, 1 (1989), pp 1–14.

38   K. Lynch, 'Love Labour as a Distinct and Non-Commodifiable Form of Care Labour', *Sociological Review*, 54, 3 (2007), pp 550–570.

39   D. E. Bubeck, *Care, Gender and Justice* (Oxford, Oxford University Press, 1995).

40   G. Collins and J. Wickham, *What Childcare Crisis? Irish Mothers entering the Labour Force*. ERC Labour Market Observatory (Dublin, Trinity College, 2001).

41   Women's Health Council, *Women's Mental Health: Promoting a Gendered Approach to Policy and Service Provision* (Dublin, The Women's Health Council, 2004).

42   Lynch, 'Solidary Labour', *op cit*.

43   C. Vincent and S. Ball, *Childcare, Choice and Class Practices: Middle Class Parents and their Children* (London, Routledge, 2006).

44   RTÉ, 'Breach of Trust', *Prime Time*, RTÉ, 28 May 2013.

45   C. O'Brien, 'Crèche Crisis: The Staff Speak', *Weekend Review, The Irish Times*, 1 June 2013.

46   F. McGinnity and H. Russell, *Gender Inequalities in Time Use: The Distribution of Caring, Housework and Employment Among Women and Men in Ireland* (Dublin, Equality Authority, 2008).

47   Vincent and Ball, *op cit.*

48   Childminding Ireland, Patricia Murray quoted by C. O'Brien in 'Most childminders not declaring income', *The Irish Times*, 4 July 2009.

49   O'Connor and Murphy, *op cit.*

50   Lynch and Lyons, *op cit.*

51   Rollercoaster (2013) [online] http://www.rollercoaster.ie/Disc ussions/tabid/119/ForumThread/141392186/Default.aspx, 2013; Magic Mum (2013) [online] http:///www.magicmum.com/php BB/vietopic/php?f=117&t=566863, 2013.

IRISH WOMEN, POVERTY AND THE GREAT RECESSION

Mary P. Murphy

INTRODUCTION

In anticipating a future of austerity Rubery is concerned that:

> shrinkage applies, particularly to the state's social roles as: a source of income support; a provider of free or subsidised public services; a direct employer; and a defence against the marketisation of society. All four areas have specific significance for women such that we cannot envisage progress towards gender equality in Europe, understood as a socially progressive objective, without a reversal of the austerity trends and an active social state.[1]

This paper primarily focuses on Irish women and poverty in the context of the Great Recession. It first sets the international context by referring to the position of women globally and the degree to which disparities in global wealth and income inequality are deeply gendered, by drawing attention to wealth and how macroeconomic policy and decisions about taxation and distribution of resources are gendered and by examining the relationship between poverty, inequality and care as the deeper structural cause of women's poverty and inequality. Having set this larger context the paper then focuses on the Irish economic and social crisis, focusing first on women who experience particular vulnerability in relation to poverty, including women with disabilities, women asylum seekers in direct provision centres, Roma women, and qualified adults, before focusing in more detail on lone parents who have been heavily impacted by austerity. We examine how a range of cuts over the crisis years have fundamentally shifted social protection for lone parent families, commodified those families and left them more dependent on a precarious labour market. The paper then unpacks the mantra 'a job is the best route out of poverty' and points to the degree to which low paid, part time and precarious work is a reality for many women. The paper ends by exploring women's agency in resisting austerity, celebrating victories achieved and arguing solidarity is necessary to end a future of austerity that will have major implications for women.

A GLOBAL PERSPECTIVE

Our starting point is the global position of women in poverty. Oxfam draw attention to the 80 people who own over 50% of the global wealth.[2] This pattern of high income and wealth inequalities is also gendered, for example the top global 50 stock broker hedge fund earners are all male, 90% of the *Forbes* rich list are male, and Ireland's annual rich list is a predominantly male affair. While significant data gaps remain in what we know about the wealthy we can be confident that any agenda that addresses gender equality will also make the world more equal.[3] The inverse is also true. Policies that address inequality will also address gender income, pay and pension gaps. As Fraser observes this offers women the possibilities of new 'triple movements', alliances and coalitions working with others to challenge macro-economic decisions that commodify social reproduction and increase inequalities.[4] Women are comfortable talking about and good at stretching household budgets – we excel in home economics. However one lesson from the crisis is that collectively we need to 'macro it up' and get better at talking about national political economy policy choices. Feminist women need to talk about poverty in parallel with talking about economic decisions that structurally create and perpetuate poverty and inequality. We need more fiscal feminism. The Centre for Women's Global Leadership focus on 'Maximal Available Resources' (MAR). Their 'MAR STAR' assists in bringing women's rights into macroeconomic policy.[5]

Fig 1: MARSTAR

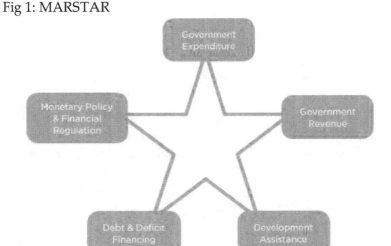

Source: Balakrishnan *et al*, 2011

This human rights approach means holding government to account about generating the maximum possible available resources and revenue and putting this to good effect to progressively realise human rights. Feminists need to pay greater attention to how government expenditure, regulation, taxation, deficit financing and development aid are used to perpetuate or increase inequality and poverty. This means building up our own skills and working in alliances with other actors. Ireland, like all national sovereigns, is increasingly subject to international governance processes such as the EU European semester and Sixpack regulations and the Transatlantic Trade and Investment Partnership (TTIP) and these need to be scrutinised by feminists.[6] At a national level feminists need to continue to demand gender sensitive budgeting and social impact assessments. The United Nations argues for a series of principles to be applied to macro-economic policy making. Collectively known as 'PANTHER' these include principles of Participation, Accountability, Non Discrimination, Transparency, Human Dignity, Empowerment, Rule of Law. In practice applying these principles would mean gendering all government policy and budgets and bringing greater transparency about social welfare, tax policy and labour market policy. This can only be done if data is effectively disaggregated to enable examination of the gendered impact of policy decisions. In particular more can be done; to ensure public procurement social clauses support gender equality; condition government funded foreign and indigenous enterprise and employer initiatives with gender equality targets and decent employment standards; develop the role of regulatory agencies to protect public interests in the context of privatisation of public services.

CARE

Simply ending austerity will not end women's poverty and inequality. When we examine the root causes of women's global poverty we find everywhere the reality that the unfair burden on unpaid care work means women have less access to economic resources and power. Sepúlveda Carmona and Donald argue we cannot make significant progress on women's poverty without redefining what we value as society; this means recognising and measuring unpaid care work and redistributing and reducing the inequalities and intensities of unpaid care through gender-sensitive public services and infrastructure.[7] Applying a care perspective in policymaking would, they argue, lead to greater understanding of the impact of heavy, intensive and unequal burdens of unpaid care work on the human rights of women living in poverty and the impact of care obligations on women's ability to access decent work. On average compared to men, women devote one to three hours more a day to housework and two to ten times more time a day to care of children, elderly and the sick, and one to four hours less a day to market activities.[8] Duflo finds women spend nearly twice as much time on household work as men, and five times as much time on childcare.[9] Not only is there less time for paid work but the constraints imposed by care across the life cycle also contribute to the concentration of women in lower-quality, informal and insecure jobs, due to the time women spend out of the workplace and their need for flexible work arrangements. These jobs are consequently less likely to enable women to lift themselves out of poverty,[10] a point we come back to when discussing the reality facing Irish lone parents later in this chapter. Rubery, assessing how austerity has damaged societies' capacity to care, anticipates a dystopian future without care:

> If austerity policies are not reversed the implied deficits in
> both public and private life will mean a squeeze on public

support for care leaving older people vulnerable and without care as women are often unable – due to geographical distance and work pressures – to provide substitute care. Children may be cared for informally or in overcrowded nurseries or even become a new generation of latch key kids – but the other alternative is for fertility rates to plummet further, exacerbating the demographic problems.[11]

However the longer term and deeper transformation we are experiencing cannot be captured by simple austerity, or a sole focus on 'care'. Fraser paints a stark picture of reality:

In a further turn of the screw, much of the formerly unwaged activity of social reproduction is now being commodified – witness the burgeoning global markets in adoptions, child-care, babies, sexual services, elder care and bodily organs. Now add to this the fact it is increasingly women who are being recruited today into waged work. Thus, neoliberalism is proletarianizing those who still do the lion's share of the unwaged work of social reproduction. And it is doing so at the very moment when it is also insisting on reduced public provision of social welfare and curtailed state provision of social infrastructure. The overall result is a deficit of care. To fill the gap, global capitalism imports migrant workers from poorer to richer countries ...[12]

Progress requires greater value on care both as paid and unpaid work. A 'careful' society will place greater value on care, children, family and community. However, this alone would not be sufficient. We also need to redistribute unpaid care work between men and women; this means maternity, paternity and parental leave and more creative work-life balance policy. In this context the Budget 2016 introduction of paid paternity leave is welcome. Finally, globally and in Ireland we need to resource childcare. Ireland is like an ostrich if it thinks it can be the best little country in the world to do business in while being the most expensive country out of 34 in the OECD to purchase childcare.[13] The European Commission has identified 'limited access to affordable and quality childcare' as 'a barrier to increased female labour market participation' and it has recommended that the State take action to address this issue.[14] The Irish Government has failed to make any progress, albeit a working group on childcare under the Department of Children and Youth produced some policy momentum in Budget 2016.

WOMEN AND POVERTY IN IRELAND

The international financial crisis in 2007/8 combined with indigenous Irish factors related to poor banking regulation and unbalanced fiscal policy hit Ireland hard. The Irish economy experienced one of the most severe financial crises of any high income country and subsequently came under a conditional international lending programme. Between 2008–2015 Ireland implemented seven years of austerity budgets. Even in this extreme context the Irish government, when faced with recession and fiscal deficits, still had choices. It could choose to raise more through taxation to address the fiscal deficit, or it could choose to focus on reducing public expenditure as the primary mechanism to reduce the fiscal deficit. After some debate in the 2011 general election the government settled on a 2:1 ratio with more focus on reducing expenditure than increasing taxation. Any strategy and policy that chooses to place the burden of fiscal adjustment on reducing public expenditure is inevitably gendered in its impact.[15] This gendered impact is felt in three ways; more women depend on social welfare, more women work in public services and more women rely on public services.[16] Government did not undertake a gender analysis of austerity budgets, however analysis by Barry and Conroy, the Equality Authority and Economic and Social Research Institute, Murphy and Loftus, and Murphy allows us fill in the gendered picture of Irish austerity.[17]

McGinnitty *et al* found gendered impacts with women in couples experiencing a 14% drop in income compared with 9% of men during the recession.[18] In Ireland the latest EU SILC data (fig 2 below) shows women comprise 52% of those in different forms of poverty and are slightly more likely than men to experience all forms of consistent, relative and deprivation-based poverty.[19] However these macro figures hide the reality that many women (and men) are vulnerable to extreme poverty. We also see a serious growth in child poverty – an issue that impacts on women as the family managers of poverty and in particular on lone parent families, over 90% of whom are headed by women and 63% of whom experience deprivation.

Fig 2: Risk of Poverty, Deprivation and Consistent Poverty by Gender 2006–2014

	2006	2008	2010	2012	2013	2014
Risk of Poverty All	17.1	14.4	14.7	16.5	15.2	16.3
Male	16.6	14	14.3	16.3	15.1	16
Female	17.4	14.9	15.1	16.7	15.4	16.5
Deprivation All	14	13.7	22.6	26.9	30.5	29
Male	13.6	13.1	21.7	26.4	29.6	27.9
Female	14.4	14.2	23.5	27.4	31.4	30.1
Consistent Poverty	6.6	4.2	6.3	7.7	8.2	8
Male	6.5	4	5.8	7.8	8	7.8
Female	6.7	4.4	6.8	7.6	8.5	8.3

IHREC found some groups of women have been hit harder and are more susceptible to unemployment, lower incomes, poorer living standards and extreme poverty over the crisis.[20] This section focuses on women who experience particular vulnerability in relation to poverty, including women denied access to social protection (asylum seekers in direct provision centres and Roma women excluded by habitual residence rules), the often hidden women with disabilities, largely invisible qualified adults, and, finally, lone parents who have been heavily impacted by austerity.

Male and female asylum seekers living in the Direct Provision system rely on €19.10 per week, the same level of income support since 1999. The system of Direct Provision has been criticised by several international human rights bodies and domestic experts for not respecting the rights of residents. These cite how lack of autonomy in food choices or preparation impacts directly on the right of Direct Provision residents to enjoy an adequate or culturally appropriate standard of living.[21] The 2015 Countess Markievicz School heard haunting personal testimonies from lone parents living in direct provision, managing child poverty, struggling to parent, and often experiencing depression and a loss of both physical and mental health. The impacts of the Habitual Residence Condition coupled with Right to Reside criteria is also generating new vulnerable groups with the Roma population consistently excluded from access to social protection. The United Nations Independent Expert noted her 'utmost concern' as she found these rules represent 'a considerable obstacle for members of vulnerable groups … to access services to which they are entitled'.[22] Meanwhile Traveller women in Ireland experience an 80% rate of unemployment.

The crisis has intensified the disproportionately higher rate of unemployment for people with disabilities and especially those with a mental health disability. The unemployment rate for persons with disabilities 'increased from 8% in 2004 to 22% in 2010'.[23] These shifts reflected the underlying patterns of the labour market rather than changes for people with disabilities, many of whom find themselves working in sheltered workshops without recognition or protection as an employee. They also struggle to cope with a higher cost of living (approximately a third higher for people with disabilities) which is not reflected in social security payments. Women with disabilities often have a double burden of care which leaves them frozen out of the labour market and in high levels of poverty and inequality as well as deprivation.[24] The vast majority of those who care for people with disabilities are women and unpaid. Women comprise 80% of recipients of the Carer's Allowance payment and Census 2011 showed 61% of 187,112 persons providing unpaid assistance to others were women. These women suffered cuts to respite care grant, a key support for full-time carers.

Prior to the crisis Barry argued:

> what remains critical for women under the Irish social welfare system is *individual entitlement* to payments and benefits rather than the traditional household system which continues to characterise so many women as dependents.[25]

Over the crisis the number of 'qualified adults' attached to welfare claims rose from 118,100 in 2006 to 202,559 in 2013. Of particular interest are qualified adults coupled with job seekers as they are; a) subject to limitation rule which lowers the family payment to 1.7 adult payments and b) are more likely to be of working age and potentially labour market active. In 2006 there were 18,996 such qualified adults but in 2013 this rose to 88,457. While recession occasioned a greater focus on activation and transition from welfare to work, there was no parallel modernisation of the social protection system that might enable individualisation and economic independence or equal access to quality education and training as essential steps to secure decent paid work.[26]

LONE PARENTS

The invisible qualified adult can be contrasted to the much more visible lone parent who endured multiple cumulative welfare cuts over the crisis. In Ireland almost half a million people live in families headed by a lone parent and such families are much more likely to experience poverty and social exclusion. In 2013, for example 63% of lone parent families experienced enforced deprivation. Instead of intervening to protect these most vulnerable families, changes to the One-Parent Family Payment (OFP) have further impacted to exacerbate poverty and cause stress and panic. In Budget 2012 Government announced plans to restrict eligibility for the OFP to those parenting alone whose youngest child is under age seven. The same budget initiated phased reductions of income disregards for lone parents to equal those of people on Job Seekers Allowances (JSA), reducing the income disregard from €150pw to €60pw.

Reactions and protests from lone parents groups forced the Government to reconsider the severity of these decisions. In 2013 the Government introduced a Job Seeker's Transition Allowance (JSTA) scheme for lone parents with children aged 7 to 14 years,[27] and in 2014 government halted the final €30 cut to the one parent family income disregard. Over the same period, despite Government recognition that any structural changes to lone parents' payments needed complementary investment in afterschool childcare, only €14m was invested in the provision of childcare. After-school and holiday time childcare remain inadequate, inaccessible and unaffordable with low income families including lone parents paying up to 40% of their total income compared to 24% of the income of a family with two incomes.[28]

In 2015 the Government effectively ended access to the One-Parent Family Payment (OFP) for lone parents whose youngest child is seven or over. Up to 40,000 lone parents were expected to transition from OFP that year with 30,200 transitioning on 2 July 2015. Those lone parents whose youngest child is between seven and thirteen will be on the Job Seekers Transition Allowance with the same means testing rules as the job seekers payment, an exemption from having to seek full-time work and accommodation of part-time work. Those whose youngest child is fourteen or older are placed on the Job Seekers Allowance. They are obliged to seek and accept full-time work under the same conditions and rules as apply to single people with no children.

The activation strategy for lone parents was developed 10 years ago in *Supporting Lone Parents*.[29] In 2006 60% of lone parents worked but lone parents still experienced significant poverty. Policy (then and now) is based on the assumption that paid employment will lift lone parents out of poverty. However recent research highlights a paradox; activation strategies and increased labour market participation among single mothers has failed to bring down poverty rates,[30] therefore governments cannot solely rely on labour market participation to reduce lone parent family poverty. Realistically lone parent families have only 24 hours or half the time and resources to do the same amount of domestic, parenting and care work as a two parent family with 48 hours. This means practical paid employment options are often limited to part-time and local options which are likely to be low paid. Without the addition of measures targeted directly at single parents' income, the risks of single parenting are likely to become even more significant.[31]

Instead of working with this reality, government policy is attempting to disincentivise part-time work as a viable choice for lone parent households, and, at the same time is reducing support with costs of childcare. The net result may be even less lone parents in employment. Pre-crisis employment levels of 60% dropped to 49% in 2011 and to 36% in 2013 but increased to 45% in 2015. While some fluctuations mirror economic crisis and/or recovery patterns, the 2012 significant decline is also attributable to a decline in the number of lone parents participating in community employment. We do not know how many may have left employment anticipating the practical impact of a policy to reduce income disregards. This is ironic given the evidence suggests lone parents in Ireland want to work. The new government needs to review the overall policy direction that has been taken over the crisis period. Retaining the One Parent Family Payment would enable government to target support in a way that promotes but does not exclusively rely on paid employment as the mechanism to address poverty. Without the addition of measures targeted directly at single parents' income, the latent risks of single parenting are likely to become even more significant. As encouraging and enabling employment amongst lone parents, policy should ensure a mechanism to target both income support and public services at lone parents. Logically this means retaining a one parent family payment for one parent families who have distinct needs that are distinguished from both two parent families and single people.

The contrast between the treatment of lone parents and qualified adults over the crisis is telling. In 2013 there were 88,457 qualified adults linked to job seekers' claims; this can be compared to 78,256 one parent family claims. Both types of families have low work intensity and are vulnerable to poverty and in particular child poverty. Why has government focused wholly on one family type while ignoring the other? Universal unconditional Child Benefit, family-based taxation transfers and unconditional Qualified Additions all support the option or choice of one parent to care full time in the home. Irish policy supports the choice of coupled households for one parent (usually the mother) to care full-time, but is clearly uncomfortable with supporting a woman in a one parent household to choose to parent full-time. Some of this policy is clearly driven by cost-cutting austerity and social policy focused on employment as a route out of poverty but this does not explain the focus and preoccupation with the lone parent family and the wilful indifference to the qualified adult. Why does Irish public policy explicitly support some mothers to care full-time in the home and deny other mothers this choice? Might 'Ireland' be happy to support 'wifely labour' in coupled households but feel threatened by prejudices about 'promiscuous women' who dare to rear children outside marriage and independent of men?[32]

Individual decisions about managing paid employment and parenting are governed not just by economic criteria but by gendered moral rationalities. There are complex trade-offs between the right to work, the right to care, the right to parent and to be parented. There are also issues of rights to work part-time and equality between mothers and different family formations. Recent policy decisions clearly separates the partnered woman and the lone parent and may be questioned on legal grounds from the perspective of family status, for example under the Irish

Constitution (Art 40 equality, or Art 41 economic necessity), or ECHR (Art 14, Family Status). A policy built on a gendered moral rationale would be more inclusive of the centrality of care and reflect the need for a careful activation strategy.[33] The present policy trajectory is also built on the assumption that equality is built on 'sameness' and does not factor in the differential impact of labour market activation for people who care. This approach over-problematises dependency when the reality is that we are all interdependent at economic, societal and family levels. Ireland was an outlier in terms of retaining a targeted lone parent payment but this may offer opportunity in enabling a more appropriate policy response in the light of this research and understanding. Rather than achieving rapid catch up with countries that seek to merge one parent families into job seeker payments it is preferable to maintain a targeted one parent payment and to use this to promote and enable employment. In practical terms it would be preferable not to move any lone parent families with children over 14 onto JSA but to maintain them on OFP (JSTA) and, if considered necessary, to build employment activation into those targeted payments.

RIGHT TO DECENT WORK
This lone parent policy and broader activation policy also fails to take into account how the crisis changed the Irish labour market with more low hour, precarious and low-paid work.[34] This is especially problematic for lone parents and other women with care obligations who are often restricted in the hours they can work and can be trapped in local labour markets. The international evidence is that activation of low income women into gendered often precarious labour market is not a sustaining route out of poverty; rather there may even be health implications for

both adults and children who experience negative spillover from poor quality employment.[35] Government recently recognised the reality of precarity in the Irish labour market when the newly-established Low Pay Commission contracted University of Limerick to research the extent of low-hour contracts in Ireland.

While government ministers often champion the right to work and claim the best route out of poverty is a job, a life churning between low pay and no pay is no guarantee of ending poverty. In 2013, 12% of Irish workers were at risk of poverty, and of the total number of people living in poverty, 5% were in work.[36] Women are particularly vulnerable in this regard. IHREC note 'austerity policies will undermine hard-won progress on gender equality and will aggravate gender differences in employment'[37] and note problems of lower female employment participation rates, less women in senior positions than men, continued lack of affordable childcare, and ongoing gender segregation in different sectors.[38] Working patterns are highly gendered with 34% of women continuing to work part-time compared to only 12.7% of men and with men more likely to be involuntary part time than women. The lack of gender equality in the labour market over a life time creates a pension gender gap of 38.2%, up almost 6% since 2008.[39]

Both migrants and lone parents alongside young people are statistically likely to churn between low pay and no pay. Over 60% of those on low pay are women and 50% of women in Ireland are earning €20,000 or less. Sectors where women predominate such as hospitality or retail have been at the frontline of aggressive casualisation and job and wage erosion, with low pay compounded by precarious work and non-fixed hour contracts.[40] We now have a worrying situation where Ireland's gender pay gap is actually widening from 12.6% in 2009 to 14.4% in 2014.

Historically one of the few measures to significantly narrow the gender pay gap was the introduction of a minimum wage. This amount continues to fall short of the 'low pay threshold' that Eurostat recommended should be set at an hourly rate of €12.20 in 2010.[41] Women face a 34% risk of earning below the 'low pay threshold'. Dunnes Research carried out by Mandate in 2015 shows 76% of workers on part time flexible contracts and 98% want more stable hours,[42] while previous Mandate research showed the gendered nature of this type of employment contract.[43] Minimum hours are as important as minimum pay and Irish home helps and their trade union SIPTU are to be congratulated at winning an important victory in this regard securing from the Health Services Executive a minimum hour employment obligation. The NWCI argue it is crucial that the Low Pay Commission be mandated to 'have regard to' gender and other equality factors as a named aspect of its deliberations and that the potential impact of any order on gender equality also be considered.[44]

CONCLUSION

The crisis has made more transparent the link between income inequality and power inequalities between national parliaments and international regulators and lenders. It has illustrated power inequalities between civil society including women's groups and economic actors representing business. The human rights principle of participation and voice requires sustainable government funding of women's groups and vulnerable marginalised communities. Even before austerity, government cuts, policy restrictions and privatisation strategies have hugely reduced and damaged such capacity. Harvey outlined how a number of independent statutory agencies with mandates of relevance to gender, human rights, equality, poverty, racism and interculturalism were closed, scaled down or absorbed into government departments.[45] Since the onset of the recession in 2008, the community and voluntary sector, including key community development programmes, has been subject to funding cuts resulting in structural changes and significant staff losses, in particular impacting on locally-based initiatives designed to respond to poverty and social exclusion.[46] The NWCI suffered significant cuts in this regard as did many local women's groups. Some national women's groups like Banulacht and One Parent Family Network are now gone. Such cuts need to be reversed and multi-annual funding guaranteed.

These cuts damaged but have not stopped women's voices. We need to celebrate women's agency. Trade unions, lone parents, women in direct provision and homeless women deserve our commendation and respect for their determined action to protect their rights. However most of all, those groups who have suffered most over the crisis and who continue to suffer into recovery need solidarity. These cuts need to be reversed and people's rights and entitlements restored. Otherwise as Rubery[47] anticipates:

> austerity without end and a decline in political will to fund income replacement to support citizens over the life course has strong implications for gender equality. It would certainly mark the end of a progressive gender equality agenda and a world where increasingly women will be required to ... 'work like a man' while still 'caring like a woman'.[48]

SOURCES
1   J. Rubery, 'Austerity, the Public Sector and the Threat to Gender Equality. Geary Lecture 2014', *The Economic and Social Review*, Vol. 46, No. 1 (Spring 2015), pp 1–27.
2   OXFAM, 'Wealth: Having it all and wanting more'. 2015. https://www.oxfam.org/sites/www.oxfam.org/files/file_attachments/ib-wealth-having-all-wanting-more-190115-en.pdf.
3   *Ibid.*

4   N. Fraser, 'Can Society be Commodities All the Way Down? Post-Polanyian Reflections on Capitalist Crisis', *Economy and Society*, 43, 4 (2014), pp 541–558.

5   Radhika Balakrishnan, Diane Elson, James Heintz and Nicholas Lusiani (2011), *Maximising Available Resources and Human Rights* (New Jersey, Centre for Women's Global Leadership, 2011).

6   P. Cullen, 'The European Parliament as a useful context for feminist activism in Ireland', paper, *European Conference on Politics and Gender*, Uppsala University, 11–13 June 2015; M. O'Dwyer, 'Gender and economic surveillance after the Sixpack: A feminist exploration of the EU's Economic Governance', paper, *European Conference on Politics and Gender*, Uppsala University, 11–13 June 2015.

7   M. Sepúlveda Carmona and Kate Donald, 'What Does Care Have to Do with Human Rights? Analysing the Impact on Women's Rights and Gender Equality', *Gender and Development*, 22, 3 (2014), pp 441–457.

8   World Bank, *World Development Report 2012* (Washington, DC, The World Bank, 2012).

9   E Duflo, *Women's Empowerment and Economic Development*, (MIT and CEPR Discussion Paper, No. 8734, January 2012).

10 World Bank, *World Development Report 2012* (Washington, DC, The World Bank, 2012), Chapter 5.

11 J. Rubery, *op cit.*

12 N. Fraser, *op cit.*

13 OECD, *Benefits and Wages: Statistics* (Paris, OECD, 2014).

14 European Commission, *Country Report Ireland Including an In-Depth Review on the Prevention and Correction of Macroeconomic Imbalances* (Brussels, European Commission, 2015), p. 1.

15 M. Karamessini and J. Rubery, 'Economic Crisis and Austerity: Challenges to Gender Equality' in M. Karamessini and J. Rubery (eds), *Women and Austerity* (Abingdon, Routledge IAFFE Advances in Feminist Economics, 2014), pp 314–351.

16 J. Rubery, *op cit.*

17 U. Barry and P. Conroy, 'Ireland in Crisis: Women, Austerity and Inequality' in M. Karamessini and J. Rubery (eds), *Women and Austerity* (Abingdon, Routledge, IAFFE Advances in Feminist Economics, 2014), pp 186–206; F. McGinnity, H. Russell and D. Watson, *Winners and Losers? The Equality Impact of the Great Recession in Ireland* (Equality Authority and ESRI, p.

5); IHREC, *Policy Statement on the System of Direct Provision in Ireland* (Dublin, IHREC, 2014); M.P. Murphy and C. Loftus, 'A Gendered Right to Social Security and Decent Work? The Debate in the Context of Irish Austerity' in B. Goldblatt and L. Lamarche (eds), *Women's Right to Social Security* (London, Hart, 2014), pp 239–262; M.P. Murphy, 'Ireland's Lone Parents, Social Welfare and Recession', *Irish Community Development Law Journal* 3, 2 (2014), pp 6–20.

18 McGinnity, Russell, Watson, *op cit*; IHREC, *op cit.*

19 CSO SILC (Dublin, CSO, 2014).

20 Irish Human Rights and Equality Commission, *Submission to the Committee on Economic Social and Cultural Rights under the International Covenant on Economic and Social Rights* (Dublin, IHREC, May 2015).

21 *Ibid.*

22 UN Office of the High Commissioner for Human Rights, *Report of the UN Independent Expert on Extreme Poverty and Human Rights, Magdalena Sepúlveda Carmona to the Human Rights Council* (Geneva, OHCHR, 2011), p. 12.

23 D. Watson, G. Kingston and F. McGinnity, *Disability in the Irish Labour Market: Evidence from the QHNS Equality Module 2010* (Dublin, Equality Authority and ESRI, 2013), p. 19.

24 Irish Human Rights and Equality Commission, *op cit.*

25 U. Barry, *Where Are We Now: New Feminist Perspectives on Women in Contemporary Ireland* (Dublin, New Island, 2008), p. 42.

26 M. MacDonald, 'Gender and Social Security Policy: Pitfalls and Possibilities', *Feminist Economics*, 4, 1 (1998), pp 1–25.

27 M.P. Murphy (2014), *op cit.*

28 OECD (2014), *op cit.*

29 *Supporting Lone Parents* (Dublin, DSP, 2006).

30 K. Jaehrling, T. Kalina and L. Mesaros, 'A Paradox of Activation Strategies: Why Increasing Labour Market Participation Among Single Mothers Failed to Bring Down Poverty Rates', *Social Politics*, 22, 1 (2015).

31 Jaehrling, Kalina and Mesaros, *op cit.*

32 C. Hunt, 'Gaybo was right. This is about women and sex', *Sunday Independent,* 14 June 2015, p. 14.

33 M.P. Murphy, *From careless to careful activation: making activation work for women* (Dublin, NWCI, 2012).

34 Nevin Economic Research Institute (NERI), *Quarterly Economic Observer: Spring 2015* (Dublin, NERI, 2015) p. 47.

35 M.P. Murphy, *From Careless to Careful Activation, op cit.*

36 CSO SILC (Dublin, CSO, 2014).

37 Irish Human Rights and Equality Commission (2015), *op cit.*

38 H. Russell, F. McGinnity and G. Kingston, *Gender and the Quality of Work: From Boom to Recession* (Dublin, Equality Authority and the Economic and Social Research Institute, 2014), p. 58.

39 Irish Human Rights and Equality Commission (2015), *op cit.*

40 NERI, *op cit*; M.P. Murphy and C. Loftus, 'A Precarious Future: An Irish Example of Flex-Insecurity', in S. Ó Riain *et al* (eds), *The Changing Worlds and Workplaces of Capitalism* (London Palgrave, 2015), pp 122–138.

41 NERI, *op cit.*

42 Mandate, 2015, http://dunnesworkers.com/.

43 C Loftus, *Decent Work: The Impact of the Recession on Low Paid Workers* (Dublin, Mandate Trade Union, 2012).

44 NWCI Submission to Low Pay Commission, 10 April 2015.

45 B. Harvey, *Government Funding and Social Justice Advocacy* (Dublin, The Advocacy Initiative, 2014).

46 Irish Human Rights and Equality Commission (2015), *op cit.*

47 J. Rubery, *op cit.*

48 *Ibid*, p. 8.

WOMEN'S LIVES IN POST-CONFLICT
NORTHERN IRELAND

Goretti Horgan

INTRODUCTION

There was a time when, objectively, women in Northern
Ireland could be said to have more rights than those south
of the border. The famous 1971 contraceptive train[1] was an
attempt to shame the establishment in the Republic into
ending the ban against even condoms being available in
the country. During the Anti-Amendment Campaign of
the early 1980s, a common argument against the Eighth
Amendment to the Constitution was that a Yes vote would
send the message to Unionists in the North that Home
Rule was still 'Rome Rule'.[2] The availability of divorce in
the North was also mentioned during the referenda on
divorce.[3]

However, while the North may have had more formal
rights for women, the reality of how women were treated
in the course of a conflict, which saw what has been
described as an 'armed patriarchy'[4] has only recently

started to emerge – with the stories of women like Mairia Cahill.[5] A small insight into this reality had been glimpsed in the treatment of Women's Coalition elected members of both the Northern Ireland Forum (NI Forum) and later the Northern Ireland Assembly (NIA).[6] Women were heckled every time they rose to speak and were told on more than one occasion to 'get back to the kitchen'.[7] Further, the language in relation to abortion rights which was seen, as recently as 2013[8] as acceptable in the Assembly, gives the lie to the idea that rights for women in Northern Ireland are in any way in advance of those in the south. Indeed, when it comes to reproductive rights, some advances can be recorded in the Republic, while abortion rights have gone backwards in the North.

Position of Women in Northern Ireland

Women make up 51% of the population of Northern Ireland. Despite the lack of abortion rights in the region, the fertility rate has not reached replacement level since 1991 – 2.1 children per woman. The average age of first time mothers in 2014 was 28.2 years, compared with 24.1 in 1984. The number of births to teenage mothers has more than halved over the last 15 years, from 1,791 births in 1999 to a record low of 839 in 2014. Much of this reduction has been due to the easier availability of the morning-after pill which became available over the counter in 2001. In 2014, some 40% of all births in the North were outside of marriage; in Belfast and Derry cities, 60% of births were outside marriage.

Women are considerably more likely to be in paid employment now than ten years ago. In 2014, the economic activity rate for men aged 16–64 was 79.4%, while for women it was 67.2%.[9] This gender gap is considerably lower than in 2004, when it was 20.6 percentage points. One of the most striking developments has been the increase in male part-time employment.[10] However, women still disproportionately occupy part-time jobs. Just under half of female jobs were part-time (49.7%) in 2014, compared to 21% of males.[11] While most men working part-time say they would prefer to work more hours, most women working part-time do not. Women's employment patterns are influenced by the number of children they have and the age of the children. In 2008, 73% of women with no children were in paid work compared to 64% for women with two children. Women with children under 10 years old were less likely to be in paid work than those with children in the 11–15 age group, while women who were lone parents were much less likely than women in two parent families to work outside the home.[12] Women are much less likely than men to be self-employed. Only 6% of females in employment in 2014 (26,000) were self-employed compared to 22% of males. This reflects little change from ten years ago. Occupational gender segregation remains stark in Northern Ireland. For example, there are over twice as many women as men working in public administration, education and health industries – 52% of women workers are employed in this sector, compared with 20% of males.[13]

Income inequality is even sharper in Northern Ireland than in the Republic. For example, in 2011/12, households in the top 20% of the income distribution had a weekly income 3.8 times higher than those households in the bottom fifth of the income distribution; while the bottom 53.4% of incomes were under £20,000 a year, the top 1.1% of incomes were over £100,000 a year and the top 0.3% over £200,000 a year.[14] Barclays Bank Wealth Report says that the number of millionaires in Northern Ireland increased by 40% from 2010–2015.

As in the Republic, the only families in Northern Ireland with a low risk of living in poverty are those where there are two adults in paid work. Those where at least one adult works have a very similar risk of poverty before and after housing costs, but for workless households with children housing costs increase poverty considerably. Most of these households are lone parents, over 90% of whom are women. Some 56% of lone parents are living in the private rented sector where rents far exceed levels of Housing Benefit.[15] Figures published in 2011 show just one in seven lone parents in Northern Ireland not in employment wants paid work, a smaller proportion than in any of the regions of Great Britain. Lack of infrastructure, such as childcare and public transport, as well as the quality of work available may be factors contributing to this.[16] Even when lone parents are in full-time work they have twice the rate of poverty of couple families – thus family poverty is overwhelmingly female poverty.[17]

Perhaps the most obvious example of how far women's position in the North is now behind that of women in the south is the fact that the first women High Court judges were appointed only in October 2015. The appointment of Denise McBride QC and Siobhan Keegan QC to the High Court came about after the Equality Commission complained that women are 'underrepresented in the highest offices of the judiciary'.[18] Eleven High Court judges had been appointed between 2001–2015, and five Appeal Court judges since 2007; all were men.

Like the south, Northern Ireland has suffered swingeing cuts to public services and to the community and voluntary sector since 2007. Women and children have suffered disproportionately from the cuts; the community women's sector has all but disappeared as funding has been withdrawn. The range of services provided by women's groups and organisations is extensive and include trauma counselling, support for those affected by domestic and sexual abuse, mental and physical health, education, training and employability, childcare, early years, after school and family support, diversity, community planning services and health promotion programmes. Services on which women rely to allow them to work, such as the childcare provided by Gingerbread for lone parents, have closed. Even the larger, regional agencies have seen their budgets cut again and again. For example, the education and training which the women's sector has provided for decades to women in disadvantaged communities has all but disappeared as a result of the Department for Education and Learning changing the criteria by which the women's sector could access the European Social Fund (ESF). Instead, ESF funding is being used to fund courses in Further Education colleges.[19] Because many groups that deliver services to women had smaller pots of funding provided by several different government departments, the cumulative effects of cuts by every department has seen many women's groups forced to close.[20]

It is hard to predict what the precise impact of all these cuts will be on society in general in the North. We can say for sure that it will be more difficult for women who left school without qualifications to resume their education, with all that this means for their children's prospects – since there is clear evidence that improved maternal educational attainment improves children's chances of academic success.[21] There is also evidence that community women's groups contribute to the mental well-being of disadvantaged women, a vital role in a society which has very high levels of post-traumatic stress disorder (PTSD) and extraordinarily high rates of anti-depressant and anti-anxiety medication.[22]

LEGACY OF THE CONFLICT

The 1998 Belfast ('Good Friday') Agreement included a specific affirmation of 'the right of women to full and equal political participation'. Side argues that these measures in the Agreement gave cause for a 'climate of guarded optimism' about the potential to advance women's social citizenship rights in Northern Ireland.[23] This optimism turned out to have been misguided.[24]

UN Security Council Resolution 1325 formally acknowledges women's right to participate in all aspects of conflict prevention and resolution, post conflict reconstruction and peace-building. When asked in 2013 by the monitoring committee[25] of the Convention to Eliminate Discrimination Against Women (CEDAW) why the resolution had not been implemented in Northern Ireland, the UK Head of Delegation replied that:

> the position of her Government, which had been endorsed by the First Minister of Northern Ireland and the Democratic Unionist Party but not by the Deputy First Minister of Northern Ireland or Sinn Féin, was that the situation in Northern Ireland did not constitute an armed conflict as defined under international law.[26]

After a Westminster inquiry into the (non) implementation of the Resolution was dropped due to lack of funds in 2011, the Northern Ireland Women's European Platform (NIWEP) continued the work. A panel of experts on women and conflict, women and decision-making and gender equality was established to undertake an 'Inquiry into the Actions and Level of Implementation of UNSCR 1325 Women, Peace and Security for Women in Northern Ireland since the Peace Process' at Stormont in December 2013.

The Inquiry heard directly from women from local communities and from women's NGOs across Northern Ireland in open and closed sessions. The inquiry called witnesses from a range of public and civic organisations including equality and human rights bodies, trade unions, statutory agencies and NGOs. The Office of the First

Minister and Deputy First Minister (OFMDFM), with responsibility for the Gender Equality Strategy, was invited to give evidence, however, it did not do so. The inquiry took into account a broad range of issues, including the impact of the conflict on women's continuing economic inequality in Northern Ireland; the fate of women's groups; the level of implementation of the Good Friday Agreement's commitment to the 'full and equal political participation of women', and the rights of women victims of the conflict. However, in spite of the evidence gathered by the Inquiry and by the United Nations commissioned Global Study on the Implementation of Resolution 1325, no progress has been made in relation to Northern Ireland. Thus, women in Northern Ireland suffer the consequences of living in a region which 'is not yet a society at peace as the legacy of the past continues to overshadow our present',[27] but without any of the protections enjoyed by women in other areas emerging from conflict.

REPRODUCTIVE RIGHTS

Until the 1998 Belfast Agreement, and particularly until the devolution of powers to the Stormont Assembly in that year, women's reproductive rights in the North were ahead of the South. So, in 2002, when Deirdre Conroy received the tragic news that one of the twins she was carrying had died and the other had Edwards Syndrome, a condition which usually ends in miscarriage or death shortly after birth, she was able to travel to Belfast and get the termination she sought there. That is because abortions were carried out routinely in hospitals in the North for reasons of foetal impairment generally, not only for fatal conditions. However, she would not be able to get the abortion she needed in Belfast today because women's rights have regressed since the Agreement.

This regression should be blamed on the 'chill factor' in relation to abortion which has been encouraged by Northern Ireland's fundamentalist politicians such that the number of legal abortions carried out in the North has dropped from 80–100 each year until 2002 to 30–40 in 2012. The law governing abortion in the North comes from the time before the light bulb was invented. The 1861 Offences Against the Person Act criminalises abortion and endorses life imprisonment as the punishment; however the law has been updated somewhat by the 1937 'Bourne judgement' and by a series of court cases in the 1990s. The 'Bourne judgement' refers to the acquittal in England of a doctor who had performed an abortion on a fourteen-year-old girl pregnant as a result of multiple rape. The judgement accepted that abortion is legal if continuing the pregnancy would leave the woman 'a mental or physical wreck'. The Bourne judgement, like the judgement in the X Case in the south, is notoriously unclear, which is why the 1967 Abortion Act had to be introduced in Britain.

Four judgements in the NI High Court between 1993 and 1995 suggest that abortion is legal in Northern Ireland in many more circumstances than is generally realised.[28] In an effort to gain some legal clarity, the Family Planning Association (fpaNI) used the Agreement's obligations on gender equality in 2001 to secure a Judicial Review of the failure of the Department of Health, Social Services and Public Safety (DHSSPS) to issue guidance clarifying when abortion is legal in Northern Ireland. In 2004, the Court of Appeal instructed the Department to issue such guidance and investigate barriers to obtaining legal terminations. In January 2007, Ulster Unionist Michael McGimpsey, then Health Minister in the Assembly's power-sharing Executive, issued guidelines for consultation. These stated that abortion was legal when a woman's mental or physical health is in 'grave' danger of 'serious and permanent damage' due to a pregnancy.[29]

At the time, Iris Robinson of the Democratic Unionist Party was chair of the Assembly's multi-party Health Committee. In October 2007, Robinson challenged Minister McGimpsey's guidelines by moving:

> That this Assembly opposes the introduction of the proposed guidelines on the termination of pregnancy in Northern Ireland; believes that the guidelines are flawed; and calls on the Minister of Health, Social Services and Public Safety to abandon any attempt to make abortion more widely available in Northern Ireland.[30]

The DUP, Sinn Fein and the Social Democratic and Labour Party (SDLP) supported the motion. Unsurprisingly, since McGimpsey was its appointee as Health Minister, the Ulster Unionist Party (UUP) opposed it, but emphasized that this position did not signal support for liberalised abortion access. Alliance had a free vote. Robinson's motion was passed without difficulty. She subsequently wrote to Minister McGimpsey that the Assembly's Health Committee 'fully endorsed' advice from the Association of Catholic Lawyers of Ireland that:

> The starting point of the Guidance should have been a clear statement of the illegality of abortion in Northern Ireland: that it is a crime punishable by a maximum of life imprisonment ... The Guidance should then have recalled the central if not sole purpose of this prohibition: the protection of the unborn child, a purpose which has informed the law against abortion for over 700 years. Only when the rule had been clearly stated should the scope of the exception have been considered.[31]

In March 2009, guidelines for medical staff were finally issued. These were minimalist statements of when abortion is lawful in Northern Ireland, for example only where 'it is necessary to preserve the life of the woman' or where 'there is a risk of real and serious adverse effect on her physical or mental health, which is either long term or permanent'.[32] The Guidelines reminded medical practitioners that performing an abortion illegally or assisting in such a procedure carries a maximum penalty of life imprisonment.[33] But McGimpsey's guidelines did reflect the law as laid out in the court cases and, as the courts had ruled, provided information on care pathways. For example, it explained what doctors should do if they thought a woman qualified for an NHS abortion because of her physical or mental health. They indicated that if you are a doctor who doesn't want to be involved in abortion, you need to pass the woman onto another doctor. It really seemed that women would have access to abortion in the North under limited circumstances, and that the most difficult cases at least would be looked after in their local hospitals.

Those Guidelines were challenged in court by the Society for the Protection of the Unborn Child (SPUC), leading to the guidelines being withdrawn. The courts backed the interpretation of the substantive law and the Guidelines' description of when abortion is legal, but they fell on the adjacent issues of conscientious objection and counselling requirements. Revised guidance with provisions on conscientious objection and abortion-related counselling was issued for consultation in July 2010, with a final date for responses to the consultation set for 22 October 2010.[34]

After Assembly elections in May 2011, the Reverend Ian Paisley's Democratic Unionist Party made sure that it took the Health Ministry. To the delight of anti-abortionists, every Health Minister appointed since then has been a fundamentalist, evangelical Christian. The three DUP Health Ministers from 2011, Edwin Poots, Jim Wells and Simon Hamilton are all associated with the Caleb Foundation, an organisation set up in 2009 to promote law and government in line with biblical thinking – whose associates refer to themselves 'jokingly' as 'The Caleban'. Liam Clarke of the *Belfast Telegraph* described the position of Caleb's supporters thus:

> [W]here the Taliban is pushing for an ultra hardline version of Sharia law based on its own reading of the Koran, Caleb wants to see a Bible-based society with every law measured against scripture.[35]

In April 2013, only after the intervention of the courts, Edwin Poots issued completely new guidelines. These bore little resemblance to those on which his predecessor had consulted. The very title – 'The Limited Circumstances for a Lawful Termination of Pregnancy in Northern Ireland' was designed to maintain the 'chill factor'. The advice to clinicians in the Guidance echoes the language the Association of Catholic Lawyers of Ireland used in their response ('Dedicated to God and his Holy Mother') to the 2010 consultation. The opening clause reads:

> The aim of the health and social care system must be *protection of both the life of the mother and her unborn child*. The objective of interventions administered to a pregnant woman must be to save the mother's life or protect against real and serious long-term or permanent injury to her health. *Intervention cannot have as its direct purpose the ending of the life of the unborn child*.[36]

Anyone who has followed the tortuous debate on abortion in the Republic will know that the final sentence of that clause upholds Roman Catholic teaching that only 'indirect' abortion is permissible; if doctors remove an embryo or foetus in the process of removing a fallopian tube or a uterus then that is not an abortion under Catholic teaching. But removing the embryo or foetus to save a fallopian tube or uterus is a 'direct' abortion and not allowed under Catholic teaching. Thus we have the bizarrely ironic scenario of the Rev Ian Paisley's party ensuring that the very 'Rome Rule' which he campaigned against for a lifetime applies in Northern Ireland.[37]

It is difficult to conclude other than that the point of the Poots' Guidance was to scare doctors from providing abortions to women who need them. Some abortions for reason of foetal abnormality continue but are hidden, while some couples from the North seeking abortions on the ground of foetal abnormality are forced to travel to England, like their southern counterparts.

Meanwhile, women in the North have easier access to the abortion pill than do those in the south and the number of women choosing not to travel to England but to self-administer a safe but illegal abortion with the online support of Women on Web or WomenHelp.org is growing year on year. Some women have gone to hospitals, admitted to doctors that they had taken abortion pills and been reported to the police; some have been told they would be charged but no woman has yet been charged with inducing an abortion herself. However, a mother in Belfast was charged in June 2015 with obtaining abortion pills for her underage daughter and faces a potential five year prison sentence for helping her daughter. The news of her court appearance came just a week before the Appeal Court in London turned down the case of another Northern Irish mother and daughter[38] – the A and B case. A, a teenager, had sought through B, her mother, a ruling that she should have been entitled to an NHS abortion in England since she could not get one at home in Belfast. Her mother could not get the money together to bring her to England and, by the time they had found the Abortion Support Network and got financial help from that source, A was 15 weeks pregnant. Both mother and daughter were distraught by this time as they feared she would be forced to continue the pregnancy.

It was not surprising then that the response of many in the North was to ask 'what is the mother of a pregnant teenager supposed to do?' If she can't afford to travel and pay for a private abortion in England, her daughter will become a mother while still a child herself; if she gets pills to cause an early miscarriage at home, she could face a prison sentence.

Over the last twenty years, Professor Colin Francome of Middlesex University has carried out several studies of attitudes to abortion among the medical profession in Northern Ireland. His 1994 survey of gynaecologists reported that 59% of respondents believed abortion should be legal in Northern Ireland if a woman had been raped, while 70% believed it should be legal where there was evidence of foetal abnormality.[39] A follow-up survey in 2009, to which thirty-seven of forty-two gynaecologists working in Northern Ireland responded, found that a majority of respondents would support liberalising the current abortion law, with only 32% saying the law should stay as it is.

Francome's 1994 survey of GPs in Northern Ireland found that 70% said the decision whether or not to continue a pregnancy should be left to the woman in consultation with her doctor. One worrying statistic from the survey of GPs is that 11% of them had seen evidence of attempts at amateur abortion.[40] Hopefully such dangerous practices are no longer happening since the abortion pill became available over the internet.

Opinion polls suggest that the politicians in the North are even more out of step with public opinion than their southern counterparts. An October 2012 poll for the *Belfast Telegraph* found that 45% of those polled wanted to see abortion law liberalised, with just over one in four thinking it should be a woman's right to choose. While a substantial group (26.5%) believed that abortion should only be allowed 'if the mother is likely to die if the pregnancy continues' which would mean a tightening of current law, only 2% of the sample – all of them men – agreed that: 'Abortion is no better than shooting a child in the head and should be treated as murder'.[41]

A November 2015 poll carried out for RTÉ and the BBC found that 20% of people in the North and 14% in the south thought that abortion should never be available, with 56% in the North and 64% in the south thinking that it should be available 'sometimes'. A further breakdown of these figures shows that there was most support for abortion for reasons of fatal foetal impairment (more than 4 out of 5 people in both jurisdictions), rape and when a woman's health is at risk.

On 30 November 2015, the High Court in Belfast ruled that current NI legislation criminalising abortion breaches Article 8 (the right to private and family life) of the European Convention on Human Rights because it does not provide for rape or fatal foetal abnormality (FFA) exceptions. However, the judge's declaration, which can be appealed, puts the onus back on the Assembly to legislate to make the law Convention compliant. Although the core of the judgement would return the North to the *status quo ante* – before the 'chill factor' described above, rather than being a real step forward for women in the region, there were a number of useful points made in Mr Justice Horner's judgement. In cases of FFA, he concluded that the woman's inability to access an abortion was a 'gross interference with her personal autonomy'. Further, he suggested that the current situation 'smacks of one law for the rich and one law for the poor'.

LIFE AFTER BIRTH IN NORTHERN IRELAND

As with the south, having anti-abortion policies does not mean that Northern Ireland is 'pro-life' or 'pro-child' in its policy approach. Rather, it is 'pro-birth'. For example, the North is the only part of the UK not to have a fully-funded childcare strategy. Again as with the south, childcare in the North is horrendously expensive; it is also scarce. In 2013, there were only 56,000 registered childcare places and some 355,000 children in the 0–14 age range: only one registered childcare place for every six children. In 2014, the cost of a full-time average childcare place in NI was £162 per week – this is 44% of the median net weekly earning, and almost FOUR times the average cost for childcare in OECD countries. For over half of families, the monthly childcare bill exceeded the mortgage/rent payment.[42]

Save the Children research into spending on services for children across the UK found that expenditure per child on early years' services was significantly higher in Britain at c£2,000 per child, compared to £630 per child in Northern Ireland. In relation to SureStart services, the Six Counties did very poorly compared to England at nearly £600 per child, Scotland (£380 per child) or Wales (between £270–£350 per child). The figures for Northern Ireland are very low by comparison, at £80 per child.[43]

As we have seen above, the position of women in the North is such that mothers and especially lone mothers are more likely to be living in poverty. Now, it is women and their children who are being hardest hit by the cuts to public services and to welfare benefits.[44] The 'Fresh Start' agreement between Sinn Féin and the DUP to extend welfare reform, even with the temporary supplementary payments to ease the impact of cuts, will make many women's lives more difficult and will act to prevent the 'full and equal political participation' promised in the 1998 Agreement. The cuts to benefits being introduced as part of welfare reform will have the most devastating effects on women – because women manage family poverty, they do most of the worrying when ends simply won't meet. Women with large families are most at risk of being in severe and persistent poverty. Yet the 'Fresh Start' accepts the imposition of a £20,000 benefit cap on households, regardless of how many children there are in them. While in London the cap has affected those claiming Housing Benefit, in Northern Ireland where housing costs are lower, families with three or more children will be hit by the cap. So, in a region where abortion is not available and childcare is scarce and expensive, a woman faced with a third or subsequent pregnancy will know that she will not receive a brass farthing towards the upkeep of that child, should she and her partner lose their jobs or be unable to work due to illness or disability.

Welfare reform will bring Universal Credit, a new benefit which will replace six benefits with one single household payment. One of the worrying elements of Universal Credit is that this payment is to go to one member of the household and, traditionally, this has been the man in a couple household. While it is possible for those in abusive relationships to ask for the payment to be split, many women in abusive relationships would not be able to do this safely. Even in the most equal household, paying all benefits to one person will represent a loss of independent income for women, as it includes Child Benefit which has traditionally gone to the purse rather than the wallet. Universal Credit (UC) changes could mark the start of a return to a 'male breadwinner' model in couple households. Universal Credit aims to 'make work pay' through a system of earnings disregards and a tapering of withdrawal of benefits as earnings rise. However, this help towards making work pay is available to only one person in a couple household and the income of a second low paid worker will be taxed at a very high marginal rate. While this improves the incentive for one person in a couple household to move into employment, it may be a disincentive to second earners – mainly women entering or continuing to work.[45]

Part of the austerity being imposed on the population in the North is a programme of redundancies in the public sector. These cuts are a big blow to young women studying today in the hope of getting a decent job in the future. While the redundancies are 'voluntary', up to 20,000 jobs will be gone forever. Women make up 65% of the public sector workforce, which provides the best quality work for women; the gender pay gap for full time employees is half that in the private sector. Family-friendly policies are more available in the public sector. Even if jobs become available in the private sector for women, it is unlikely they will match the pay and conditions of the jobs lost. This would result in a widening of the overall gender pay gap and worsening levels of female poverty.

CONCLUSION

Women's lives in the North were extremely difficult during the Troubles and what has happened since the 1998 Agreement has done nothing to recompense them for that time. Instead, women have seen their reproductive rights worsen, their jobs cut and their living standards driven down. The nature of politics in the region, particularly since the 1998 Agreement, has meant that politics has focused almost entirely on Orange-Green issues, even if the controversies often seem contrived. The consociational form of government has led to a 'policy impasse', even on issues which are relatively uncontroversial.[46] When policy decisions are taken, they have been largely based on a 'lowest common denominator' approach[47] and all too often take a neo-liberal approach which serves only to make the lives of women more difficult.[48] In this scenario, it is hard to envisage any early improvement in the rights of the majority of women in Northern Ireland.

SOURCES
1   In 1971, members of the Irish Women's Liberation Movement travelled to Belfast to buy contraceptives which were illegal in the Republic of Ireland. They declared the condoms,

spermicides and pills which they brought on the return journey to Customs officers at Connolly Station Dublin, while refusing to hand them over. Their action helped to break the silence about the lack of contraception in the south.

2   T. Hesketh, *The Second Partitioning of Ireland: The Abortion Referendum of 1983* (Dublin, Brandsma Books, 1990).

3   D. Keogh and M.H. Haltzel, *Northern Ireland and the Politics of Reconciliation* (Cambridge, Cambridge University Press, 1993).

4   Y. Galligan, 'Women in Northern Ireland's politics: feminising an "armed patriarchy"', in M. Sawer, M. Tremblay and L. Trimble (eds), *Representing Women in Parliament* (London, Routledge, 2006).

5   BBC, 'Mairia Cahill "told Gerry Adams" of IRA rape claim', 2014. http://www.bbc.co.uk/news/uk-northern-ireland-29631344.

6   The NIA is a legislative assembly to which power over most social policy issues was devolved in 1998 following the Belfast Agreement of April 1998.

7   A. Kilmurray and M. McWilliams, 'Struggling for Peace: How Women in Northern Ireland Challenged the Status Quo', *Solutions Journal*, Volume 2, Issue 2 (February 2011).

8   *Northern Ireland Assembly Debate* (Official Report). 12 March 2013.

9   Department for Enterprise, Trade and Investment NI. *Labour Force Survey*, April 2015. http://www.detini.gov.uk/index/what-we-do/deti-stats-index/labour_market_statistics/labour_force_sur vey.htm.

10   DETI. *Northern Ireland Labour Force Survey Quarterly Supplement Oct-Dec 2013*. 2014. http://www.detini.gov.uk/lfs_quarterly su pplement_october-december_2013.pdf.

11   Department for Enterprise, Trade and Investment NI. *Quarterly Employment Survey*, March 2015. http://www.detini.gov.uk/ind ex/what-we-do/deti-stats-index/labour_market_statistics/stats-qes.htm.

12   A.M. Gray and G. Horgan, *Figuring it Out: Looking Behind the Social Statistics in Northern Ireland* (Belfast, ARK, 2009).

13   A.M. Gray, G. Horgan and A. Leighton, *Figuring It Out, Social Statistics in Northern Ireland, Volume 2* (Belfast, ARK, 2015).

14   NERI (2012), *Quarterly Economic Facts*, Autumn 2013.

15   P. Gray, U. McAnulty and M. Keenan, *The Private Rented Sector in Northern Ireland, Report 1* (Belfast, NIHE, 2009).

16   B. Hinds, *Northern Ireland Economy: Women on the Edge? A Comprehensive Analysis of the Impacts of the Financial Crisis* (Belfast, WRDA, 2011).

17   L. Davies, 'Lone Parents: Unemployed or Otherwise Engaged?' *People, Place and Policy Online*, 6, 1 (2012), pp 16–28.

18   ECNI, *Summary: DRAFT Policy Positions on Gender Equality October 2015* (Belfast, Equality Commission NI, 2015).

19   Women's Views, *In Northern Ireland, Women Don't Matter*. 2015. http://www.womensviewsonnews.org/2015/05/in-northern-ire land-women-dont-matter/.

20   WRDA, *WRDA Director Represents Women at Joint Forum Meeting*. 2015. http://www.wrda.net/WRDA-Director-Represen ts-Women-at-Joint-Forum.aspx.

21   Jere R. Behrman and Mark R. Rosenzweig, 'Does Increasing Women's Schooling Raise the Schooling of the Next Generation?' *American Economic Review* 92, 1 (2002), pp 323–334; A. Chevalier, C. Harmon, V. O'Sullivan, I. Walker, *The Impact of Parental Income and Education on the Schooling of their Children*, IFS WP 05/05; J. Ermisch and C. Pronzato, *Causal Effects of Parents' Education on Children's Education*, ISER Working Paper 2010–16. 2010. https://www.iser.essex.ac.uk/ files/iser_workingpapers/2010-16.pdf.

22   F. Ferry, D. Bolton, B. Bunting, B. Devine, S. McCann and S. Murphy, *Trauma, Health and Conflict in Northern Ireland: A Study of the Epidemiology of Trauma Related Disorders and Qualitative Investigation of the Impact of Trauma on the Individual* (Omagh, University of Ulster and NICTT, 2008); NI Audit Office, *Primary Care Prescribing* (Belfast, NIAO, 2014).

23   K. Side, 'Contract, Charity, and Honorable Entitlement: Social Citizenship and the 1967 Abortion Act in Northern Ireland after the Good Friday Agreement', *Social Politics*, 13, 1 (2006), 89–116.

24   G. Horgan and J.S. O'Connor, 'Abortion and Citizenship Rights in a Devolved Region of the UK', *Social Policy and Society*, 13, 1 (2013).

25   The United Nations Committee on the Elimination of Discrimination against Women (CEDAW), an expert body established in 1982, is composed of 23 experts on women's issues from around the world, with a mandate to watch over the progress for women made in those countries that are the

States parties to the 1979 Convention on the Elimination of All Forms of Discrimination against Women.

26 E. Law and A.M. Gray, *The Politics of Defining Armed Conflict in Northern Ireland*. 2014. https://www.opendemocracy.net/5050/ elizabeth-law-ann-marie-gray/politics-of-defining-armed-confl ict-in-northern-ireland.

27 M. Ward, 'Excluded and silenced: Women in Northern Ireland after the peace process'. 2013. https://www.opendemocracy.ne t/5050/margaret-ward/excluded-and-silenced-women-in-north ern-ireland-after-peace-process.

28 Horgan and O'Connor, 2013, *ibid*.

29 http://archive.niassembly.gov.uk/record/reports2007/071022 .htm#11.

30 NIA Debate, 22 October 2007, 26.

31 I. Robinson, Letter to Michael McGimpsey MLA, on behalf of the Committee for Health, Social Services and Public Safety. 2008.

32 DHSSPSNI, *Guidance on the Termination of Pregnancy: The Law and Clinical Practice in Northern Ireland* (Belfast, DHSSPS, 2009), 1.4.

33 *Ibid*, 1.8.

34 Horgan and O'Connor, 2013, *ibid*; Fiona Bloomer and Eileen Fegan, 'Critiquing Recent Abortion Law and Policy in Northern Ireland', *Critical Social Policy*, 34, 1 (2014), pp 109–120; DHSSPSNI, *Guidance on the Termination of Pregnancy: The Law and Clinical Practice in Northern Ireland* (Belfast, DHSSPS, 2010).

35 L. Clarke, 'The rock the DUP was built on, but now "the Caliban" may cost votes'. 2012. http://www.belfasttelegraph.c o.uk/news/politics/creationist-bible-group-and-its-web-of-infl uence-at-storm ont-28787760.html.

36 DHSSPSNI, *The Limited Circumstances for a Lawful Termination of Pregnancy in Northern Ireland: A Guidance Document for Health and Social Care Professionals on Law and Clinical Prctice* (Belfast, DHSSPS, 2013), 1.1, author's emphasis.

37 G. Horgan, 'A Holy Alliance? Obstacles to Abortion Rights in Ireland North and South', in Quilty, Kennedy and Conlon (eds), *The Abortion Papers Ireland Vol II* (Cork, Cork University Press, 2015).

38 On 23 December 2015, the Supreme Court in London agreed to hear A and B's appeal against the Appeal Court's findings. The hearing is likely to take place mid-2016.

39   C. Francome, *Abortion in the USA and the UK* (Aldershot, Ashgate, 2004).

40   *Ibid.*

41   Belfast Telegraph, 'Abortion: 45% want a liberalisation of the law in Northern Ireland'. 2012. *http://www.belfasttelegraph.co.uk/news/northern-ireland/abortion-45-want-a-liberalisation-of-the-law-in-northern-ireland-28999931.html.*

42   Employers for Childcare, *Childcare Costs Survey*, 2014 (Belfast, 2014).

43   Save the Children, *A Child's Portion, UK Briefing*, SC (London, 2010).

44   G. Horgan and M. Monteith, *A Child Rights Impact Assessment of the Impact of Welfare Reform on Children in Northern Ireland* (Belfast, Northern Ireland Commissioner for Children and Young People, 2012).

45   Engender, *Gender and 'Welfare Reform' In Scotland: A Joint Position Paper* (Edinburgh, Engender, 2014).

46   A.M. Gray and G. Horgan, 'Devolution in Northern Ireland – a Missed Opportunity?' *Critical Social Policy* 32, 3 (2012), pp 467–478.

47   A.M. Gray and D. Birrell, 'Coalition Government in Northern Ireland: Social Policy and the Lowest Common Denominator Thesis', *Social Policy and Society*, 11, 1 (2012).

48   G. Horgan, 'Devolution, Direct Rule and Neo-Liberal Reconstruction in Northern Ireland', *Critical Social Policy*, 26, 3 (2006), pp 656–668; J. Nagle, 'Potemkin Village: Neo-Liberalism and Peace-Building in Northern Ireland?' *Ethnopolitics*, 8, 2 (2009), pp 173–190.

VIOLENCE AGAINST WOMEN

Margaret Martin

Countess Markievicz, a woman of activism and authority, was the first Irish woman Cabinet Minister in 1919, and almost a century later, four of our Cabinet Ministers were women. In fact as of early 2016, we had a constellation of women in key positions of power and authority, particularly in the justice arena: Tánaiste Joan Burton; Minister for Justice and Equality Frances Fitzgerald; Garda Commissioner Nóirín O'Sullivan; Chief Justice of the Supreme Court of Ireland Susan Denham; Attorney General Máire Whelan and Director of Public Prosecutions Claire Loftus. These are major strides forward for gender equality, but to paraphrase Yeats, change comes dropping slow.

Women's Aid was first established by another activist, Nuala Fennell, who later became Minister of State with special responsibility for Women's Affairs and Family Law. Nuala was struck by hearing the voice of women's experiences who fled domestic violence and were left with nowhere to go. She took it upon herself to enlist the help of other women who saw this situation for what it was: terrifying, unacceptable, disempowering. Together, this newly-formed collective began to listen to the voices of women experiencing domestic violence, and to make changes for the better.

A woman recently contacted Women's Aid who had been involved in those early days and was keen to hear about what has changed since the 1970s. Back then she sincerely believed that once people knew how tough it was for battered women things would change dramatically. Now she wondered what, if anything, had changed? I was able to reassure her that some significant improvements have been achieved and that protection and support for women and children is provided daily, but unfortunately the situation is far from satisfactory especially given the current homeless crisis. For example, Ireland now has one third of the EU recommended amount of refuge accommodation. However, this begs the question that if it has taken us 40 years to provide one-third of the protection needed, will it take another 80 years to achieve the other two-thirds? And this is just one of the many things that needs to improve. I hope a constellation of powerful women in key justice posts will hurry Ireland along the way so that change will blow in like a gale and women and children will be significantly safer.

Women's Aid has worked to provide hope and support to women experiencing abuse at the hands of a partner, and to lobby for justice and social change, since 1974. While opportunities have opened up to women across many areas of society since then, unfortunately the abuse they experience remains much the same. Take for example a young woman called Cara who was 21 when she met her college boyfriend Colm. At first, he was charismatic and charming, easy company and fun to be around. But gradually, his behaviour became more and more controlling. Cara said, 'At first I thought his concern was sweet but it quickly became suffocating'. Colm began to exert influence and control over every aspect of her life. 'He wanted to know my every move. I felt under constant surveillance'. Things escalated when Cara finally decided to end the relationship. He began stalking her and following her.

Cara lived in fear of her ex, and worried for her safety. 'I became a shell of myself. I was alone, isolated from my friends and felt like I was going crazy. My life was dominated by my ex'. It was then that she decided to reach out for help. She confided in her family and phoned the Women's Aid Helpline. Women's Aid listened and explained her options to Cara. We told her we would support her in whatever course of action she decided was right for her. 'They told me it was not my fault. Life is getting better step by step. I feel safe'.

At Women's Aid we have been providing continued support to thousands of women like Cara, who feel frightened and alone, for more than 40 years. We now run the National Freephone Helpline 24 hours a day, 7 days a week, with translation available in 170 languages and a text service for deaf or hard of hearing women. All of our work is informed and shaped by the voices of the women who find the strength to pick up the phone and give voice to their suffering.

There is, unfortunately, still a great deal of work for Women's Aid to do. The magnitude of the problem of domestic violence has been illustrated again and again. Particularly important in this respect was the major study carried out by the European Union's Fundamental Rights Agency (FRA) in 2012. This was a transnational project that investigated women's experiences of domestic abuse throughout the EU, by carrying out a staggering 42,000 face-to-face interviews in all.

The FRA study used unambiguous numbers to illuminate the story that Women's Aid tells. Intimate partner violence is a daily reality for vast numbers of women in Ireland. It is happening to every type of woman, from every background, and every upbringing. Each of us probably knows at least one woman who has had to endure this form of suffering.

How did the Irish data compare with the rest of Europe? 69% of women in Ireland avoid certain places or situations for fear of being physically or sexually assaulted. This is higher than the EU average of 53%. 52% said that they avoid certain streets or areas for fear of assault, compared with 37% on average across the EU. The study also highlighted that Ireland has the worst record of all the countries surveyed for meeting the needs of women who have managed to get themselves to a place where they can reach out for help.

The Irish data showed that almost one in every three Irish women had experienced at least one incidence of psychological abuse by a partner since the age of 15. In real numbers, this makes up just short of half a million women (470,157). The psychological abuse of women in Ireland, reported by the study, included being locked inside their homes, restricted in their access to their cars, isolated from friends and family, threatened, belittled and insulted. Women often tell us at Women's Aid that it is this form of abuse that can be the most difficult to talk about, and that takes the longest to heal.

One in every 16 women (90,000; 6% of those surveyed) reported an incidence of sexual violence by a partner. Women's descriptions of sexual abuse included the partner forcing her or attempting to force her into sexual intercourse by holding her down or hurting her in some way, or forcing her to take part in other forms of sexual activity when she did not want to, or was unable to refuse.

One in every seven women experienced physical violence at the hands of a partner. This abuse involved pushing, shoving, slapping, being beaten with fists or hard objects, being burned, stabbed, choked and shot at. Over 50% of women surveyed who reported experiencing physical violence were left with bruises or scratches. 15% had wounds, sprains and burns. 14% had fractures, broken bones and broken teeth. 4% were inflicted with internal injuries. 3% suffered from concussion or brain injury. Four women in the study reported a miscarriage as a result of the most serious incident of physical violence.

The impacts on women of being subjected to these types of abuse are devastating and unquantifiable. Women's health and lives are being put at risk every day as long as they are subjected to this terror in their own homes.

In particular, Women's Aid remains gravely concerned about strangulation as a form of violence. Too often, we hear it being brushed off as 'no worse' than being punched or slapped. We hear of men who say 'I've never even beaten you. I haven't put a bruise on you'. This might be true, because when he puts his arm around her neck, or his hand on her throat, he probably won't leave any marks. One US study showed that most survivors of strangulation had no marks. 22% had injuries too faint to photograph. 20% reported pain only, while only 16% displayed visible injuries.

It takes only 11lbs of pressure to stop a person's blood supply, while almost double at 20lbs is needed to open a can of Coke. This is not difficult, it does not require a great degree of strength. After 20 seconds of pressure to the throat there is loss of consciousness. After 50 seconds the victim rarely fully recovers. The supply of blood to the brain controls our swallowing, speaking and our breathing. It controls our blood pressure and our bowel function. How does a woman recover from the trauma of being choked? How does she recover her confidence and sense of self-esteem when his hands are around her throat, she can't breathe, she loses consciousness and control of her bowel or bladder? She wakes up to find that she has soiled herself, and he is standing over her calling her a worthless piece of shit. How can you begin to speak about this abuse? In the past, the Dublin Rape Crisis Centre has appealed to survivors to 'speak the unspeakable', and this is what women who endure this kind of intimate partner terrorism try to find it within themselves to do.

Over four decades thousands of women have done just this: they have told us their stories. While every woman's experience is unique, they usually have one thing in common. Their partner will minimise the abuse and blame them: 'you made me do it', 'don't be a baby, it's nothing', 'if you weren't such a bad mother/a bitch/a slut I wouldn't have needed to hit you'. When you are told this over and over again you start to believe it. It becomes your reality. You lose your confidence. You lose your voice.

This abuse is supported and compounded by our victim-blaming culture. Classic comments include 'she must have deserved it' and 'if it's so bad, why doesn't she just leave?' These remarks minimise and even tacitly condone the abuse of women. They contribute to a culture of silence and shame, and prevent women from being able to come forward unashamedly and seek help. We know that about one-third of women experiencing abuse never tell anyone what they are going through. Our victim-blaming culture creates a wall of stigma. This often means that it is the woman who feels ashamed, not the perpetrator.

As well as feeling a sense of guilt or blame for their abuse, many women are made to feel that this abuse is only happening to them, that it is not happening to other women. That's why it is important to look at prevalence and to give platforms to women's voices when they want to share their testimonies in their own way, on their own terms. The FRA study showed us that psychological abuse is an experience shared by one in every three women in Ireland – close to half a million women. One in seven are physically abused – almost a quarter of a million. These are women you know, from all walks of life. None of them deserves what has happened to them. All of them need support.

We all have a responsibility to recognise this, and if a woman asks for help or support we have a responsibility to listen, to respect and to believe. If someone you care about tells you they are in an abusive relationship, give her the space to express herself – listen to her, try to understand and take care not to blame her. Don't push her for details – allow her to make sense of her experience in the way that feels right for her at that time. Allow her to make her own decisions. Don't tell her to leave the relationship if she is not ready to do so. Encourage her to call the free confidential Women's Aid Helpline to speak to an experienced listener where she can talk about her experience without being judged or pressurised.

While we all have a responsibility to recognise and respond to victims of domestic violence, those among us who are in positions of power are able to do more. Minister Fitzgerald recently published the heads of a new Domestic Violence Bill and there is much in it to be welcomed, including the removal of the property requirement for victims in crisis situations. This means it is no longer required that the woman has an equal or greater property interest in the home; making it easier to obtain an Interim Barring Order which provides protection for 8 days. Minister Fitzgerald made a strong commitment to protecting and supporting victims and the Bill includes a range of measures to make the courts process easier for them, such as mandating the court to provide applicants for domestic violence orders with information about and contact details of specialist domestic violence services.

It is particularly good to see that the new Bill will address the issue of intimidation and abuse by phone and electronic means for the first time. This is a concern that Women's Aid has been highlighting for a number of years. Our old laws are simply unfit to meet twenty-first century challenges such as cyber stalking and revenge porn. However, we would like to see this Bill going even further. In addition to the court being enabled to prohibit communication between both parties, communication through electronic means to third parties about women should also be addressed. We also feel that there is a missed opportunity to address a key gap in legal protection for younger victims of domestic violence with this Bill. Many young women experiencing abuse in dating relationships cannot avail of any legal protection under the Domestic Violence Act, current or proposed, because they have not lived together. Women's Aid frontline services hear about these experiences every day. They are women like Cara who are forced to live with constant fear and intimidation. Research has shown that while young women can be at even higher risk of abuse in a relationship than their older counterparts, there is low recognition of controlling and coercive relationship behaviour among young women. We know that in a national survey on domestic abuse in Ireland, almost 60% of those who had experienced severe abuse in intimate relationships first experienced it when they were under the age of 25.

We must protect safe spaces where women can share their stories. We must see perpetrators' attempts to control and manipulate for what they really are and ensure they are held accountable. As feminists, we must give each other the opportunity and space, the voice and the courage, to stand together and to 'speak the unspeakable'.

GENDER ISSUES IN THE TRAVELLER COMMUNITY

National Traveller Women's Forum

The National Traveller Women's Forum (NTWF) is the national network of Traveller women and Traveller women's organisations from throughout Ireland. The NTWF recognises the particular oppression of Traveller women in Irish society and is working to address this issue through the provision of opportunities to enable Traveller women develop collective strategies and skills to work towards the enhancement of their position in society.

This position paper sets out the principles which underpin the NTWF's approach to working with Traveller women and outlines some of the primary gender issues which affect Traveller women. In so doing, the NTWF recognises that Traveller women as members of Irish society are subject to the same systematic and structural barriers to equality as women in the settled population. The issues outlined in this paper document the additional dimensions of inequality which are specific to Traveller women.

PRINCIPLES

The following principles underpin our work:

We believe all women have a right to equality, dignity and respect. This value base lies at the heart of our work.

Our ethnic status as members of the Traveller Community is the foundation on which all our work is built. We are proud of our identity as Travellers. We recognise that in highlighting issues which we face as Traveller women we risk inviting criticism or re-enforcing stereotypes from the settled population. This will not inhibit our work. We embrace this challenge as we do not compromise on our rights to equal status either as Travellers or as women.

We recognise the diversity of women's experience within the Traveller Community which varies according to age, socio-economic status, educational levels, economic activity and other factors. We value the diversity of those experiences equally and welcome debate which helps to reach a deeper understanding of these differing perspectives.

Our work is informed by the reality of women's experience, recognising that the inequalities we experience are derived from complex structures and systems, both internal and external to the Traveller community, which limit and influence personal choice and freedom.

We work from a rights-based approach. We see equality and freedom from discrimination and oppression as part of our core human rights, both as women and as members of an ethnic minority.

We are committed to the creation of women only spaces for dialogue and debate as a means of refining and defining our own analysis as Traveller women. These will be safe, confidential spaces in which all voices are valued.

We recognise the importance of building strategic alliances with other organisations and with women in the settled community as part of our commitment to drive social and societal change. We recognise the fact that gender inequality is an issue that must be addressed in all sectors and at all levels of Irish society.

We are committed to representing the needs, interests, experiences and priorities of Traveller women. Our policy and practice will be based on an informed analysis of those. We will provide leadership to and for Traveller women, both amongst Travellers and within wider society.

GENERAL PROFILE – TRAVELLER WOMEN

The National Traveller Health Study conducted in 2008 states the Irish Traveller population as 40,129; 36,224 in the Republic of Ireland and 3,905 in Northern Ireland.[1] The population profile of Travellers is similar to that of developing countries with a high birth rate and a young population coupled with high mortality rates and a life expectancy much lower than that of the general population.[2] For example, 62% of the Traveller population is aged less than 25 years compared with the national figure of 35.3%, while 2.6% of the Traveller population is over 65 years of age compared to 11% of the national population. Only 25 Travellers were over 85 years of age when the field work was conducted in 2008.

Traveller women have a life expectancy of approximately 71 years, which is 11.5 years less than women in the general population, and is equivalent to the life expectancy of the general population in the early 1960s. This is despite an improvement from 1987 when life expectancy for Traveller women was 65 years.

Travellers, in particular males, continue to have higher rates of mortality for all causes of death. Traveller women, despite there being a 35% reduction in mortality rates since 1987, have a mortality rate 3.1 times that of women in the general population.

Traveller infant mortality is estimated at 14.1 per 1,000 live births. This is a small decrease from an estimated rate of 18.1 per 1,000 live births in 1987. Over the same time period, the general population infant mortality rate has reduced from 7.4 to 3.9 per 1,000 live births.

These headline statistics provide an overarching indicative demographic profile of Traveller women, one which is characterised by a significant disparity in health status compared with women in the overall population in Irish society.

GENDER ISSUES

While this position paper will discuss some areas where discrimination exists for women within the Traveller population, gender issues or differences do not always involve discrimination. Identification of a gender dimension to an issue will sometimes simply draw attention to the fact that women and men have different experiences of that issue. This means it needs to be addressed differently (requiring a different practice or policy response) for women and men. It may also mean that Traveller women who experience an issue experienced by women in wider society such as domestic violence will experience it differently as Traveller women.

In other words, the experience of a Traveller woman will sometimes be distinctive because she is a woman, sometimes because she is a Traveller, and sometimes because she is both.

ROLE OF TRAVELLER WOMEN

Traveller women play a central role in Traveller society. In the domestic sphere, they assume responsibility for child rearing, care of the home and the welfare of both their immediate and extended families. In 2011 one in three Irish Traveller women (32.7%) were looking after the home and family, nearly twice the rate of the general population (17.5%).[3] Similar to women in the settled community, they are often the key point of contact with frontline service providers such as GPs, PHNs, local authority personnel with responsibility for accommodation, schools, etc. In this context, the well documented existence of institutional discrimination and prejudice directed at members of the Traveller Community is more likely to affect Traveller women than Traveller men.

Within the Traveller movement in Ireland, Traveller women have played a significant role in the development of Traveller organisations and in this arena have made a valuable contribution to the improvement of the lives of Travellers in Ireland. Over the last ten years, a significant number of Traveller women working in Traveller organisations have progressed from a voluntary to a paid capacity, representing a significant and positive development for both Traveller women and Traveller organisations alike.

Broadly speaking, gender roles are clearly divided in the Traveller Community with distinct divisions between experiences, expectations, decision-making authority and the sense of value associated with each sex. In the main, and undoubtedly with exceptions, men are the dominant grouping, with more access to power, control and decision-making authority. However this is a changing dynamic and the increased number of Traveller women in voluntary work, paid employment and education is having a positive effect on the choices and experiences of Traveller women.

TRAVELLER IDENTITY

For ethnic minority groups, expression of identity and pride in identity is an important feature of creating a sense of belonging to society. That identity being positively received and welcomed by the majority population is also a critical factor in the extent to which people experience a sense of place in society. The extent to which that experience is positive or otherwise will affect confidence and self esteem both on an individual level and on a collective level as a community. The extent of discrimination against the Traveller community in Irish society is such that it is not uncommon for Travellers to make deliberate attempts to hide their identity (in a physical sense), to deny their identity, or to choose not to disclose it. In the main, this affects Traveller women more than Traveller men because of physical characteristics or traditional style features. In other words, because women may be more readily identifiable as Travellers because of their physical appearance, they are more susceptible to discrimination and may be more likely to conceal their identity to prevent that discrimination from taking place.

SOCIAL AND SEXUAL FREEDOM

Strongly-held beliefs, traditions and expectations around accepted social and sexual practice remain prevalent within the Traveller population. This, combined with Roman Catholic beliefs[4] around sexual practice and a strong sense of family honour, can create a limiting social environment for Traveller women. The extent to which this is the case varies greatly and can be dependent on factors such as age, the value attached to Catholic teachings within the family, etc. Issues of social and sexual freedom are matters on which there are diverse opinions, attitudes and perceptions amongst Traveller women and which benefit from ongoing debate to ensure that those differences are respected. As in most communities, issues around sexual practice and social freedom are highly sensitive. Change in this area, as well as failure to change, can create difficulties for women who attempt to negotiate their way around differing expectations and possibilities.

CHANGING ROLES/YOUNGER WOMEN

Young Traveller women are faced with the challenge of re-defining their role as young women in the Traveller community. There are more young Traveller women in formal education than in previous generations. They are remaining in school for longer and are achieving a greater degree of educational success. There are a number of consequences to this increased level of engagement with the education system. In the first instance, there is a higher degree of interaction with members of the settled community which creates exposure to different value sets and moral codes, both of which can be at considerable variance from those in the Traveller community. This can create some of the challenges alluded to in the section above on 'social and sexual freedom'.

Secondly, involvement in the formal education system creates a set of expectations and opportunities around individual potential which did not exist for most in the previous generations of Traveller women. Therefore, young Traveller women today have, relatively speaking, unprecedented scope and opportunity to realise their individual potential. They are, however, faced with the challenge of achieving this against a backdrop of a very different set of expectations of the roles they should assume amongst some in the older generation in the Traveller population. In some cases the realities of early marriage and the birth of children are still significant factors which inhibit access to and outcomes from education.

Furthermore, access to further education and employment opportunities necessitates increased engagement within mainstream society, a society which in the main does not affirm, celebrate or validate Traveller identity. Young Traveller women therefore essentially straddle two cultures, one which is affirming, welcoming and to which they belong by birth, and another which is often discriminatory, judgmental but within which educational and employment opportunities lie. These combined issues create a challenging situation for young Traveller women as they work through a number of complex, changing situations and in so doing, carry an enormous burden of responsibility in re-defining what it means to be a Traveller woman in contemporary Irish society.

ACCOMMODATION

Recent statistics from both the All Ireland Traveller Health Study 2010 and the 2011 Census show that the majority of Traveller families are accommodated in housing accommodation (both public and private) which is designed with the needs of the settled community in mind and as such is not the preferred accommodation choice of many Travellers. Furthermore, many Traveller women continue to live on sites which lack the most basic provisions required for a healthy and safe environment. The All Ireland Traveller Health Study 2010 shows that there are still significant numbers of Travellers living without access to running water.

One of the more striking developments has been the increase in the number of Traveller families living in private rented accommodation, a particular feature amongst young Traveller families. This creates a particular form of isolation for younger Traveller women as it involves removal from supports traditionally provided by the extended family. Year on year, these increases have accounted for approximately 25.1% of all families recorded.[5] In the 2010 Annual Count the number of families in private rented accommodation rose by 377 to 2,380.[6] This figure rose again in subsequent years to its peak in 2012 of 2,818. It has started to decrease in recent years – due to high demand generally for private rented accommodation and we are now seeing a subsequent rise in the numbers of families sharing.

Despite Government policies to the contrary, the Traveller Community as a whole cope with the challenge of living in a society which does not accommodate either a nomadic lifestyle or the preferred Traveller specific accommodation choices of members of the Traveller Community. To date, little progress has been made on the provision of Traveller accommodation following on from the publication of the Task Force Report on the Traveller Community in 1995. This report recommended 3,100 units of additional Traveller accommodation. The 2014 Annual Count of Traveller families conducted by the Department of Environment, Community and Local Government showed that 445 families were living in unauthorised sites and another 2,672 families were living in private rented accommodation, that is, a total of 3117 families were without permanent accommodation at the end of 2014. Also at this time, 727 families shared accommodation; many in overcrowded conditions.

The tragic deaths in Carrickmines in October 2015 are evidence of just how dangerous the living conditions of many Traveller families are. Three extended families were staying on the 'temporary' halting site when fire broke out. The site itself (which was never intended for use as Traveller accommodation) had three bays, but up to six families had been living there for seven years, in three portacabins and two caravans. In the aftermath of the fire the wider anti-Traveller bias and discrimination was evident – particularly within some of the print and online media.

The quality and quantity of Traveller accommodation and lack thereof is set against a backdrop of reduced resources, yet budgets are returned to central government. The funding for Traveller accommodation was reduced from €40 million in 2008 to €4 million in 2015 which is a cut of 85%.[7] Despite the significant demands for Traveller accommodation, there have been substantial underspends – in 2010 this figure was 54%, and in 2012 it was 34%.

The significantly high number of families living without permanent accommodation or in accommodation which is inadequate has significant consequences for Traveller women. Women spend more time in the home and are the primary carers, so they bear the brunt of having to cope with basic conditions such as lack of clean running water, lack of adequate refuse collection, poor sanitation and unsafe areas for children to play. Furthermore, problems with accommodation and poor living conditions can lead to ill health. In particular, it can have an effect on women's mental health as they cope with a challenging combination of tasks; looking after the family, dealing with the local authority, making sure the children have an education, etc, in difficult, challenging circumstances.

DOMESTIC VIOLENCE

Violence of one form or another is part of the real life experience of many Traveller women. The nature of this violence is broad and varied and is experienced within a domestic situation as a member of a community isolated from mainstream society or in the form of institutional violence where services and supports are not accessible or appropriate to the needs of Traveller women.

The report on the *National Study of Domestic Abuse* identifies that a disproportionate number of Traveller women use refuge accommodation and within this, there is also a need for greater awareness amongst Traveller women of the various support services that are available outside of the refuge model. The Safe Ireland study shows that 37.7% of all refuge users in 2009 were Traveller women.[8] Meetings with service providers undertaken by the NTWF during 2010 highlighted that the problem of finding accommodation for Traveller women post-refuge is a significant explanatory factor in why Traveller women access refuges so frequently and why their stay is prolonged. This also appears to be a factor in why Traveller women use the refuge model and do not access support services to the same degree. The National Women's Strategy identifies 'awareness raising' as a key priority and recommends that local, regional and national organisations be resourced to provide this awareness training/support to women.[9] It is commonly agreed that the issue of violence against women is no more prevalent within the Traveller Community than within the settled community, but factors such as educational attainment, employment, accommodation and different health status make it more difficult for Traveller women to move out of violent relationships and seek help through mainstream services. In some situations, poor relationships with service providers including the Gardaí, Social Welfare and Social Work Departments of the HSE have also been identified as factors which contributed to Traveller women returning home. Traveller women have cited a history of mistrust and a lack of understanding on the part of frontline services of the experiences and cultural practices of the Traveller community as being barriers to their safety in situations of domestic violence.

Whilst Traveller women are speaking more of their experiences of domestic violence there remains a significant taboo in relation to sexual assault, rape and childhood sexual abuse. Traveller women rarely access rape crisis centres for support or information. The national statistics provided by the SAVI report cite 20% of women have experienced sexual assault as adults.[10] In this context, the NTWF is concerned that Traveller women who have similar experiences are not accessing emotional, physical or legal support.

PUBLIC REPRESENTATION

The majority of development, advocacy workers and volunteer representatives within the Traveller community are women. As such, women occupy that interface between the Traveller population and service providers. The struggle to assert the needs and rights of the Traveller Community often lies with women. As a consequence, women are subjected to racism and discrimination more so than men because they are more involved in community and voluntary activities, participate on more committees and have a higher degree of engagement with mainstream services. Furthermore, frustration from within the Traveller Community at the lack of progress as a result of the work of various committees and initiatives is more likely to be directed at Traveller women as a result of the disproportionate nature of their representation.

Anecdotal information suggests that Traveller women are frequently treated differently to Traveller men on committees. Other committee members have pre-conceived ideas of Traveller women and this, combined with the societal tendency to attach different values to women and men's perspectives, often means that it is the voice of the Traveller man who is listened to and acted upon.

EDUCATION AND EMPLOYMENT

There continues to be a significant gap between the participation and attainment of Traveller children when compared with children from the wider settled society. The attainment and retention levels of Traveller students in second level education remains a serious concern. There are lower numbers of Traveller women engaging in higher and further education. In 2006 only 19 Traveller women had obtained a third level qualification at degree or higher level and only 3.1% of Travellers continued their education.[11] The 2011 Census revealed that only 3.1% of Travellers continued their education past the age of 18 compared with 41.2% of the general population and that the number of Irish Travellers who completed third level in 2011 was 115 or 1%. This compares with 30.7% of the general population, excluding Irish Travellers. Significant budget cuts have been a feature in the education sector also. From 2008 to the end of 2013 we saw an 86.6% cut to Traveller specific supports in education.

The 2006 Census records a low level of labour force participation for Travellers with 74.8% of Travellers in the labour force unemployed, compared with 8.5% unemployed amongst the national population. Census 2011 reveals that out of a total labour force of 4,144 Traveller women, 81.2% were without work. Access to and participation in mainstream employment opportunities for the most part continues to be outside the reach of Traveller women. This is due in part to low education attainment, traditional gender roles and discrimination by employers. For example, over 55.1% of Travellers who were interviewed as part of the National Traveller Health Study felt they had been discriminated against in attempts to secure work on one or more occasion.

Traveller women who do secure employment continue to face challenges for a number of reasons. Work environments are not necessarily multi-cultural environments and tend to be organised around the needs and expectations of the majority culture. In this context, Traveller women are frequently faced with decisions between honouring the norms of their culture or meeting the demands of their workplace. When these come into conflict, Traveller women are faced with the choice of letting themselves and their community down or letting down their employers.

Some of the challenges referred to above for young Traveller women are also faced by women in employment. In being engaged in fulltime employment, Traveller women have started to re-define what it means to be a Traveller woman. However, in many cases, they have done so with the expectation remaining in the Community that they will continue to fulfill primary roles in rearing children, managing the home and having overall responsibility for the welfare of their families. Therefore, working after normal working hours, at weekends or being involved in work which involves overnight stays away from home can be viewed as reneging on family responsibilities and can create tensions within the family. The fact that the number of Traveller women in fulltime employment is a small minority of the overall population makes the challenge of fulfilling both paid work and family roles all the more difficult. Traveller women in employment lack the critical mass necessary within the Community to create a sense that these changed roles may require a change in domestic arrangements involving both women and men. Traveller women have highlighted the impact of discrimination and racism in the labour market and the survival strategy of hiding one's identity to gain access to it. This strategy is a double-edged sword. It not only has negative consequences for the individuals concerned but also has wider social implications. Without the visible inclusion of Traveller women in the labour market there is little opportunity to challenge the prevailing negative stereotypes. Likewise without appreciable outcomes many Traveller parents regard engagement in formal education as a dead-end.

THE CHALLENGE FOR TRAVELLER WOMEN

Traveller women, like every other specific grouping in Irish society, are disadvantaged in multiple ways. However, challenging gender norms, expectations, stereotypes and discrimination is a complex issue for Traveller women.

The Traveller Community as a whole is subject to widespread negative stereotypes and perceptions within Irish society. This has far-reaching consequences in terms of access to education, healthcare, accommodation and other services which affect Traveller ability to realise their full potential and play a full and equal role in Irish society.

Despite much discussion on this in recent years, many government, public service and NGO agencies fail to collect and analyse data on an ethnic minority basis thus making monitoring the situation of Travellers virtually impossible. This significantly affects the ability of Government departments to equality proof their policies or programmes in a way which would respond to the needs of Traveller women. Where data is available, it is not gender disaggregated, making a clear analysis of the position of Traveller women in Ireland, the development of specific provisions for them and monitoring progress extremely difficult.

Over the decades, changes forced on the Traveller population by mainstream society, living within a system which is intolerant of a nomadic lifestyle, and persistent attempts at assimilation by successive governments has affected the integrity of Traveller culture. Despite this, Travellers have succeeded in retaining their status as a strong vibrant grouping with a distinct, proud identity. However, one of the outcomes of the pressure from mainstream society has been that members of the Community, both individually and collectively, are sensitive to, and affected by, perceptions of the Traveller population and of any developments which may result in a further erosion of Traveller culture.

Traveller women, in challenging gender discrimination within their own Community may find themselves in a position of divided loyalty. To highlight certain issues and opinions may contribute to re-enforcement of negative stereotypes of their own Community in mainstream society, possibly resulting in further experience of discrimination. Failure to highlight and address those practices may help ensure that discriminatory practices against women within the Traveller Community continue.

In addition, Traveller women are also conscious of the fine line between culturally-accepted norms and cultural practices which actively oppress women. Traveller women see the need to maintain their culture and to ensure it is passed down the generations, but are faced with an enormous challenge and burden of responsibility when that culture is used as justification or camouflage for the oppression of women within their Community. There have been significant changes over the past number of years to the human rights and equality infrastructure in Ireland as a result of major cuts imposed on the Equality Authority and the Irish Human Rights Commission – the two bodies have now merged. There have also been severe cuts in the resourcing of community development organisations and the Community Development Programme has been integrated into the Local Development Programme (Partnership), which had been further integrated into the Social Inclusion and Community Activation Programme. All of these changes have combined to diminish the dedicated time, resources and space available for development work within the Traveller Community. In this context, it is more important than ever to ensure that Traveller women-only spaces are retained and that the

Traveller women's agenda continues to develop and retain priority in the years ahead.

There remains a pressing need within the Traveller Community to further develop a sense of solidarity between Traveller women and to make positive links with the wider women's movement. The latter will be essential to ensure that the specific needs and issues of Traveller women are included in the gender thinking and analysis which informs the development of policy and practice.

SOURCES

1   All-Ireland Traveller Health Study, 'Our Geels' (2010), Dept. of Health.

2   http://pavee.ie/ourgeels/traveller-population.

3   http://www.cso.ie/en/census/census2011reports/census2011pro file7religionethnicityandirishtravellers-ethnicandculturalbackg roundinireland/.

4   Religion may be more important to Travellers than to the general comparable population. Religion is 'important' or 'very important' to 89.4% of ROI Travellers and 85.3% of NI Travellers. Source: All-Ireland Traveller Health Study, 'Our Geels' (2010), Dept. of Health.

5   National Traveller Accommodation Consultative Committee: Annual Report 2010. Table 1, p. 13.

6   Department of Environment, Community and Local Government Annual Count, p. 2.

7   B. Harvey, *Travelling with Austerity: Impacts of Cuts on Travellers*, Traveller Projects and Services, 2013.

8   Safety and Change: A national study of support needs and outcomes for women accessing refuge provision in Ireland, 2009, p. 17.

9   National Women's Strategy 2007–2016, Department of Justice, Equality and Law Reform, p. 86.

10   Sexual Abuse and Violence in Ireland Study (SAVI).

11   http://www.cso.ie/en/census/census2006reports/census2006 Volume5-ethnicorculturalbackgroundincludingtheirishtravelle rcommunity/.

WOMEN IN POLITICS

Justine McCarthy

The dearth of women in Dáil Éireann is most often discussed from the perspective of its optics, which are indisputably awful. The Dáil is the parliamentary version of socks with sandals and avocado bathroom suites. It is an out-dated look that will never be easy on the eye. Nothing captures the paternalism of Irish parliamentary politics as succinctly as the great, stonking, fossilised maleness of Leinster House. Where, a visitor to its hallowed chamber might wonder, has the other half of the population gone? No parliament can candidly call itself modern or progressive when few of its members have felt the common life experiences of 50% of the electorate. Contrary to Ireland's legendary, if mostly mythical, strong women – Mother Ireland, Grainne Mhaol, Queen Medb, Cathleen Ní Houlihan and the Mammy – what the Dáil says is that a woman's place is in the home, not in the House. To political strategists and commentators, the scarcity of women is an image problem in a politically-correct age. Party handlers try to dilute the excess Y chromosomes in Leinster House by positioning their paltry few women prominently in controlled media events. Some challenges, though, prove too great to overcome, as when Enda Kenny, as Taoiseach, failed to appoint any Fine Gael women to the junior ministerial ranks in 2014. In a routine week of a Dáil term, you can stroll into the chamber to find no woman at all among the serried male ranks.

Just 95 women had been elected to the Dáil in its history, until the 2016 election broke the century. Even then the Irish parliament still only ranked 17th out of 27 EU states.. It had got off to a promising start with the election of Constance Markievicz to the inaugural Dáil in 1918, making her the first woman elected to a European parliament. In the second Dáil, the number of female TDs climbed to six (Markievicz, Margaret Pearse, Ada English, Mary MacSwiney, Kathleen O'Callaghan and Kathleen Clarke) but dropped back to two of 128 in the third Dáil (MacSwiney and O'Callaghan). The next time it reached double figures, when 11 women were elected, was 1981. It took another decade to struggle past the 20 mark, to a grand total of 23, in the 1992 election. Recently, Ireland ties with Eritrea in 75th place in the world for the level of female representation in national parliaments, behind Turkmenistan, Suriname and Equitorial Guinea. Rwanda has more than any other country because of a quota system introduced there after the 1994 genocide.

Until the 2016 elections north and south of the border, Northern Ireland, despite having been frozen in time by the Troubles for three decades, surpassed the Republic of Ireland. Of 108 Assembly members in Belfast, 21 were women. That equated to 19.4% as compared to 16% (27 of 166 TDs) in the 2011–2016 Dáil. It is arguable that many women were radicalised within their communities during the Troubles, recognising that political activism was necessary if they wanted to bring about change. One of the North's most famous politicians of the Troubles was Bernadette Devlin. The Peace Women, Betty Williams and Mairead Maguire, won the Nobel Peace Prize in 1976 for their activism. The cross-community Women's Coalition, founded by Monica McWilliams and Pearl Sagar, sat at the negotiating table in the peace talks.

In the republic, the shallowness of the debate about the lack of women in political life seldom allows for deeper examination of its cause and effect. When western economies plunged in 2008, some people wondered what might have happened had Lehman Brothers, the bankrupt company that triggered a domino effect, been Lehman Sisters? While nobody can say it would have been better, undoubtedly it would have been different. The same can be said about the treatment of women by the Irish State since its foundation. There is no shortage of examples of how the absence of women's voices in the Dáil has had direct and damaging consequences for female citizens and for their families.

In the early 1950s, Noël Browne, a modernising minister for health, published the Mother and Child Scheme. It proposed free ante- and post-natal care for all expectant mothers and free healthcare for their children up to the age of 16. Browne's scheme was vehemently opposed by the avowedly celibate, men-only Catholic hierarchy. The bishops objected, in particular, to a provision allowing mothers to obtain family planning advice. They denounced the bill as 'anti-family'.

'Education in regard to motherhood includes instructions in regard to sex relations, chastity and marriage', the Bishop of Ferns, James Staunton, wrote to the Taoiseach, John A. Costello, in October 1950:

Gynaecological care may be, and in some countries is, interpreted to include provision for birth limitation and abortion. Doctors trained in institutions in which we have no confidence may be appointed as medical officers under the proposed services, and may give gynaecological care not in accordance with Catholic principle.

John Charles McQuaid, the powerful Archbishop of Dublin, had banned Catholics from attending Trinity College without his special permission and Browne's bill did not allow for a veto on Trinity-trained doctors participating in the scheme. McQuaid held more sway over Irish political life than most of the Dáil's members.

In the inter-party government that featured Browne, formed after the 1948 general election, just 5 of the 145 TDs were women: 3 Fianna Fáil, 2 Fine Gael and all representing rural constituencies. Thirty four constituencies had no woman TD at all. Neither was there even one woman among the 13 government ministers at the cabinet table. It is a shocking exercise to read Oireachtas debates and media reports about the Mother and Child Scheme from that time. In the cacophony generated by an exclusively male hierarchy, an almost entirely male obstetrics profession and an obsequious male body politic, there is hardly a woman to be heard, even though the scheme dealt predominantly with women's health and medical entitlements.

The day after Bishop Staunton wrote to the Taoiseach, Browne was summoned to meet McQuaid at the Bishop's Palace in Dublin. He ultimately resigned as minister in April 1951, some of his most important reforms for the provision of women's healthcare following him into political oblivion.

Even as the public debate was raging over the Mother and Child Scheme, pregnant women were having their pelvises deliberately and routinely sundered in Irish maternity hospitals as a method of childbirth designed to encourage big families, compliant with Catholic teaching. This barbaric practice was considered preferable to Caesarean section in cases of complicated births or big babies as repeat delivery by section can limit the number of babies a woman can produce. From the 1940s into the 1980s, non-Catholic doctors were recommending sterilisation for women who had undergone three Caesarean sections. However, sterilisation was unavailable in the health service because many Irish doctors refused to perform it and the use of artificial contraceptives was banned by law.

Symphysiotomy involved the surgical separation of the ligaments of the pubic symphysis. The practice had been outlawed in Paris in 1798. It was supposed to be performed under anaesthetic but, in Ireland, many women were awake throughout the procedure. Their feet were hoisted into stirrups and, often, their arms were physically pinned to the bed while a gallery of male student doctors looked on. Some survivors have recalled seeing the obstetrician come towards them armed with a hacksaw.

About 1,500 women and girls were subjected – many of them unknowingly – to the procedure in Ireland over 50 years. They were never asked for their consent or, in numerous cases, were not retrospectively informed that symphysiotomy had been performed on them. They were sent home hardly able to walk or to look after their babies and older children. They suffered incontinence, immobility, chronic pain, depression, painful sexual intercourse that affected their marriages and difficulties in bonding with their children.

Searching for any mention of symphysiotomy in historical Oireachtas debates is like looking for the proverbial needle in a haystack. When stories eventually began to emerge in the 1990s, it was the first time most people had heard the word 'symphysiotomy'. More than

60 years after Browne introduced the Mother and Child Scheme, advocates for symphysiotomy survivors had begun campaigning to have the women's rights vindicated. Finally, they took their case to the UN Committee against Torture (UNCAT), where some of the women told their personal stories, which were invariably gruesome and sad. One woman recounted how her obstetrician, Eamon de Valera, a son of one of the State's founding fathers, had told her:

> I normally do a Caesarean section but, because you're such a good Catholic, I'll do a symphysiotomy. You're a Catholic family. You'd be expected to have at least 10 children. If you have a Caesarean, you can only have three ... The baby is as big as yourself. Why do small women marry big men? I'll have to stretch your hips and straighten your pelvis.

When, at last, the Irish State came up with a redress scheme for symphysiotomy survivors, it provided for a sliding scale of *ex gratia* payments of €50,000 to €150,000, without any admission of liability. Women accepting the deal were required to abandon any court cases they had already instigated. At the time, 154 cases were pending in the courts.

One woman who continued her case was Noreen Burns. Gravely ill in hospital and aged 82, she received a letter in 2014 from lawyers representing the National Maternity Hospital saying they would apply to the High Court to have their legal costs awarded against her if she applied for an early hearing date. Noreen, a native of Cobh in County Cork, died less than a fortnight after that letter was sent to her.

The question must be asked if symphysiotomy would have continued as an accepted clinical practice in Irish hospitals until the 1980s if there had been more women in the Dáil. Had 60 or 70 TDs been women, legislators who had actually experienced childbirth, it is unimaginable that they would have acquiesced to the continuance of the brutal practice or that it would have remained a national secret in the first place.

Some of Ireland's most haunting scandals have been inextricably linked with women's health and maternity. Noreen Burns' case has echoes of the tragic case of Bridget McCole, a mother of 12 from Donegal who died in 1996, aged 54, from Hepatitis C. She had contracted the disease from a contaminated blood product called Anti-D immunoglobulin, which some women receive during pregnancy to protect their babies from rhesus disease. Bridget received Anti-D in 1977 but did not discover until nearly two decades later that it had been contaminated by the negligent manufacture of the product by the Blood Transfusion Service Board (BTSB), a state agency. She was one of 1,600 Irish women who were poisoned by Anti-D.

By way of compensation, the government offered infected women an *ex gratia* payment conditional on them signing away their legal rights. There was to be no inquiry to establish how the fatal product was put into circulation, leaving women with basic answers to their, literally, life and death questions. When some women instituted High Court proceedings, the State threatened to pursue them for costs which, it warned, they could not afford.

Bridget initiated her case in June 1995. She was refused an application in June 1996 to have a full hearing of her case, which she had requested because she was in failing health. Instead, the action was set down for 8 October 1996, but Bridget died six days before it.

State records would later show that the government knew by the time she issued the proceedings in her test case that the BTSB had been negligent. The government also knew the State could mount no reasonable defence against the women's cases. Yet lawyers for the State adopted an aggressive, no-surrender approach. They tried to stop Bridget's case by claiming it was out of date under the statute of limitations. Just weeks before her death, they were still threatening to fight her tooth and nail. Even when the State capitulated and made an out-of-court settlement two weeks before Bridget died, she was threatened with pursuit of legal costs if she tried to seek aggravated damages.

By then, there were more than 20 women TDs in the Dáil but the total number of seats had increased to 166. Twenty-four of 41 constituencies had no woman TD whatsoever. Niamh Bhreathnach, the education minister, and Nora Owen, the justice minister, were the only women in the 15-member cabinet. It is not possible to say if Bridget McCole and the other women who received Anti-D would have been treated better if there had been more women in power but it is likely that they would, at least, have been treated differently. It is noteworthy too that Michael Noonan, who was the minister for health at the time, and was severely criticised for what the State did to Bridget McCole, subsequently became the leader of his party, Fine Gael. Later still, in 2011, he was appointed Minister for Finance during the Troika bailout of the Irish economy and was acclaimed by commentators in Ireland and abroad. Noonan's career after the Bridget McCole case says most, perhaps, about the priorities of a male-dominated political class.

The fate of women at the hands of the Irish State in the 20th century is as much a testament to the inadequacy of women's political representation as it is evidence of a country dictated to by one church and run by an obedient male elite. The constitutional catastrophe created by the eighth amendment in 1983, which inserted a ban on abortion in *Bunreacht na hÉireann*, is the ultimate example of how women's political powerlessness has damaged women's lives, their health and their loved ones.

Article 40.3.3 has produced a tragic parade of females who have been ensnared by its inflexibility – Miss X, Miss C, Ms D, A,B and C, D, Ms Y, NP. All of these girls and women have been before the Irish or European courts for no other reason than they were pregnant. Three of them had been raped. One had cancer. Another had lost a twin she was carrying and was told the remaining twin's unformed brain would kill it before it was born. Another of these young women was already dead and being kept artificially alive in the futile hope of saving the foetus that was 15 weeks in gestation when she died.

All this because Charlie Haughey, as Taoiseach, acquiesced to anti-choice campaigners on the eve of the collapse of his 1982 government. Abortion was already outlawed under the Offences Against the Person Act 1861 but there had always been a fear among conservatives that a court judgment could open the way to it, as happened in Roe v Wade in the USA. Remember how, back in 1950, in his letter to the Taoiseach objecting to Browne's Mother and Child Scheme, the Bishop of Ferns has warned that it could be interpreted as a 'provision for birth limitation and abortion'.

The political landscape was extraordinarily volatile when Haughey caved in to demands for a constitutional abortion ban. There had been three general elections in 18 months, repeated attempted putsches against Haughey within Fianna Fáil, and unprecedented turmoil in and around Leinster House. Though Haughey lost power in November 1982, before he could honour his promise to anti-choice campaigners, the new coalition government of Fine Gael and Labour put the abortion issue to a referendum on 7 September 1983, which was approved by 67% of those who voted. The people had spoken, but only after Dáil Éireann had had its say – a Dáil in which just 13 of the 166 TDs were women. Of those women, three were the daughters of former TDs and two were the widows of former TDs. The preponderance of 'inherited' seats held by women since the State's foundation has weakened the potential for women's equal involvement in parliamentary politics to make a real difference. In many cases, those women would never have had political careers were it not for the seats left warm by their husbands or fathers, leaving them somewhat indebted to their patrons in the leadership of their parties. It goes without saying that there is a strong tradition too of male TDs inheriting their seats but because they are part of a larger pool of TDs, it is less glaring. Besides, if so many women had not inherited their seats, there would have been even fewer female TDs.

It is no accident that the cruellest treatment meted out to female citizens by the State has been bound up in matters of pregnancy and maternity. Since time immemorial, churches and states have tried to control women's reproductive function. With a parliament so lacking in women, that was an easier feat in Ireland than elsewhere. The 1983 referendum, in effect, gave an equal right to life to a woman as to her foetus or embryo. Even after Mr Justice Niall McCarthy admonished the Oireachtas for failing to legislate in his masterpiece judgement in the X Case, Leinster House failed to act. In the intervening years, politicians have consistently cowered from addressing the constitutional timebomb that is article 40.3.3, citing inevitable political fallout, and threats to their Dáil seats, as justification for failing to do their legislative duty. It was only when the European Court of Human Rights told the government it had to legislate that the Oireachtas passed the highly-restrictive Protection of Life During Pregnancy Act.

Recourse to the law courts has been a safety valve for Irish women since the 1970s. In October 1979, Josie Airey from Cork won the right to free legal aid for her legal separation from a violent husband when the European Court of Human Rights ruled that the Irish government was obliged to provide her with free legal services. Six years earlier, the Irish Supreme Court established the constitutional right to marital privacy in a case taken by Mary McGee, a 27-year-old mother of four children. She had been warned by doctors that if she became pregnant again she risked death or crippling paralysis. She sued the State after it confiscated spermicidal jelly she had ordered from England on medical advice. Both women were represented by Mary Robinson, the senior counsel who would make history by becoming Ireland's first woman president in 1990. It is illustrative of women's inability to pierce the patriarchal edifice of Leinster House that a private member's bill Robinson drafted as a member of the Seanad, designed to end the ban on the sale of contraceptives, was never even officially published.

The Magdalene Laundries were one of Ireland's most abhorrent secrets, which only began to leak out at the end of the twentieth century. The laundries were asylums of shame, run by Catholic nuns, where unmarried and poor girls and women were sent when they got pregnant. Some were incarcerated by their families; others by the law courts or transferred from other religious-run institutions where their mothers had given birth to them. No questions were asked about their impregnators: were they rapists, eminent members of the local community, or fathers and sons within the family's four walls? The women were despatched to work as unpaid slaves, doing laundry for state agencies, commercial hotels and religious orders. They were deprived of their own names and were addressed by made up names, or numbers. They were forbidden to speak to each other or to hold their babies, who, in many instances, were taken from them and sold to adoptive parents.

The Irish State denied any culpability for the laundries. When a group of academics campaigning for justice for the women took the women's case to UNCAT, Sean Aylward, Secretary General of the Department of Justice, told the committee that the vast majority of the women went to the laundries voluntarily or, if they were minors, they went with their parents' consent. Reluctantly, the government established an inter-departmental committee, led by Senator Martin McAleese, which found the State did have a role but the report was subsequently criticised by the UN for failing to fully investigate the scandal. In February 2013, the Taoiseach, Enda Kenny, gave the women an emotional apology in the Dáil, having prevaricated for a week:

> As a society, for many years we failed you. We forgot you or, if we thought of you at all, we did so in untrue and offensive stereotypes. This is a national shame, for which I again say I am deeply sorry.

But would those stereotypes have been so easy to adopt if women had been encouraged to play a full role in Irish public life? If the men running the country had been doing their work alongside female colleagues, would they have been able to turn a blind eye to the victimisation of so many women, simply because they were women? In the aftermath of Kenny's apology, the State set up a redress scheme for the women which, like the other schemes before it, required them to disavow any potential court challenges if they accepted the *ex gratia* payments on offer. By this time, there were 26 women in the Dáil and two of those were in the cabinet (Joan Burton, Social Protection, and Frances Fitzgerald, Children and Youth Affairs). Not what you would call an abundance. Despite assurances by Kenny that, if re-elected Taoiseach after the 2016 general election, he would ensure women comprised half the cabinet, the old ways are dying hard. And yet, there are reasons to be hopeful.

Samantha Long's mother, Margaret Bullen, was placed in Gloucester Street (later re-named Sean McDermott Street) Laundry in the late 1960s and was still there 35 years later when she breathed her last, never having been released back into society. She died of an illness known as Goodpasture Syndrome, a disease of the kidneys and liver which can be caused by exposure to industrial-strength chemicals such as those used in the laundries. Samantha stood as a Fine Gael candidate in the 2014 local elections but did not take a seat in what was a dismal outing for the government party. Long's failure in a climate of anti-government sentiment did not diminish her reputation as a potential future TD. Four months later, however, she quit the party after it emerged that Enda Kenny, the leader, had ignored a list of three nominees – all women – to fill a Fine Gael vacancy in Seanad Éireann. By a stroke of magic – or just a stroke, perhaps – the man Kenny chose for the Seanad, John McNulty, had been freshly appointed to a State cultural board by the Minister for Arts and Heritage, Heather Humphreys, thus qualifying him for the Seanad election. Samantha Long, one of the three women recommended for the seat, had had enough, and walked away from Fine Gael. A year later, though, she was back in Leinster House, this time working as a parliamentary assistant to Lucinda Creighton, the founder and leader of a new political party, Renua Ireland. Creighton, a former Fine Gael junior minister, had also left the party, having defied the whip by voting against the Protection of Life During Pregnancy Bill.

The extent of Irish women's isolation from the political system is often understated, mainly because the country produced two consecutive women presidents whose combined terms of office ran for 21 years. The fact remains that there has been no woman Taoiseach. Nor has there been a woman minister for finance, a pertinent historical fact considering how women continue to occupy Ireland's lowest-paid jobs, have few seats on company boards, are paid less than male counterparts – often when doing the same job – and are consistently shown to be the poorest in society.

Feminists may despair when they look at the Dáil and its lack of enthusiasm for reforms that would enhance women's lives. A case in point was the government's decision to hold a referendum in 2015 on the Constitutional Convention's recommendation to lower the age threshold for presidential candidates, while quietly shelving the proposal to abolish women's quaint constitutional status in the home. Articles 41.2.1 and 41.2.2 state:

> In particular, the State recognises that by her life within the home, woman gives to the State a support without which the common good cannot be achieved. The State shall, therefore, endeavour to ensure that mothers shall not be obliged by economic necessity to engage in labour to the neglect of their duties in the home.

Of course, article 41.2 is entirely aspirational, as any young mother struggling to work and rear her children knows first-hand. So why have it there at all? Because there are not enough people in Dáil Éireann who have never felt the shame, frustration and anger it engenders in many women.

In May 2014, 195 women were elected to local government and six of 11 politicians elected to the European Parliament were women. By the end of that year, the Dáil boasted two women party leaders (Joan Burton, Labour, and Creighton, Renua) and one deputy leader (Mary Lou McDonald, Sinn Féin). Some of the most effective and notable TDs in that Dáil were women. So why, some wonder, do we need a gender quota for general elections, which required parties to nominate 30% women as candidates or face losing half their State funding in the February 2016 election.

The benefits quickly became visible as some aspiring male TDs bleated that they were being sacrificed in order to promote women candidates. They failed to recognise that, until now, they automatically benefitted by virtue of their gender, fitting a male-generated political culture. Fianna Fáil, which had no woman TD in the 2011–2016 Dáil, established the Markievicz Commission to report on its gender equality problems. Yet another advantage of the quota is that it provides an opportunity to test – and to debunk – the myth that people do not vote for women candidates. It may also lead to the creation of a working schedule in Leinster House that is more conducive for people with young families, both women and men.

To anyone still doubting that an increase in the number of women TDs will make a difference, I challenge you to go into Leinster House any day the Dáil is sitting and come back out with the names of eight male TDs who impress you. A tough challenge, isn't it, despite having a pool of over 130 men to fish from? Even if you manage to muster eight names, you will find that most of your choices, if not all, are either current or former cabinet ministers or party leaders; people whose ability has been recognised and put to the use of the State.

Now return to the Dáil and pick eight women who impress you. You might expect this to be a harder challenge, given that there were only 27 of them in the last Dáil. But it's not quite so hard, is it? The difference is that most of these women have never sat at a cabinet table or led a political party or had their talents fully used for Ireland's benefit. Up in the gods of the opposition benches sits Clare Daly, who jointly exposed the garda penalty points scandal, and Catherine Murphy, whose questions about the sale of Siteserv led to the establishment of a Commission of Investigation into Irish Bank Resolution Corporation. While Murphy, the Independent TD for Kildare North, was asking her pesky questions, the spin being whispered against her was that the poor misguided woman simply didn't understand high finance – she is, in fact, an excellent bookkeeper. Up in Leinster House's back row too sits Roisin Shortall, who resigned as a junior health minister in 2012 because she felt her attempts to introduce measures promised in the programme for government were being scuppered by the senior minister, James Reilly. Add Maureen O'Sullivan, who persuaded the Garda Commissioner to reopen an investigation of multiple child rape allegations against former swimming coach, George Gibney.

A small number of women have been elevated to high positions. Joan Burton was Tánaiste in the last Dáil, despite having been passed over after the 2011 general election for the finance ministry; the portfolio for which she was the outstanding contender after the economy imploded on a bed of cronyism and greed. Frances Fitzgerald as justice minister, held one of the cabinet's traditionally macho portfolios, but only after first proving her credentials in the inaugural Department of Children and Youth Affairs.

It is no coincidence that, over in the Seanad, which continues to thrive as an archaic talking shop, the proportion of women members, at 32% in March 2016, was double the Dáil's. Nothing says quite as unapologetically as does Leinster House that, in Ireland, a woman's place is in the back row, gagged.

There have always been feisty women in the Dáil. In the early years, many of them made the transition from insurgency to democracy alongside male colleagues. Dr Kathleen Lynn refused to take her Dáil seat in 1923 in

Dublin North. Kathleen Clarke, a founder of Fianna Fáil, opposed the Conditions of Employment Bill of 1935 to guard against women taking jobs from men and the 1937 constitution because it limited women's rights. It is worth noting that some of the most successful Irish women politicians have been non-party TDs, not dependent on selection for elections by traditional, male-dominated parties. Many commentators have remarked that the current Dáil has proven that Independents, though backbenchers with restricted speaking rights, can be highly effective in opposition. Few have mentioned that most of the Independents who have made the biggest waves are female. That success needs to be built upon by creating the critical mass that is essential if women are to be properly represented both in the Dáil and by it.

With the arrival of the gender quota, there is a sense now that Ireland may be on the brink of a gender equality breakthrough. If it happens, the whole of society will be the better for it.

MISSING VOICES:
WOMEN'S VOICES STILL NOT HEARD OR VALUED ON THE AIRWAVES

Lucy Keaveney and Dolores Gibbons

Women's voices, experiences and expertise continue to be regarded by news industries as less important than those of men.
– Ross and Carter, *Women and News: A Long and Winding Road*[1]

INTRODUCTION

In Ireland women currently comprise 51% of the population yet they are marginalised both in politics and the media. Steps have been taken to address this problem in the political arena with the implementation of gender quotas which were introduced with modest success in the 2016 general election. However, there is no evidence that the corresponding imbalance in the media which sidelines women's voices and opinions is being redressed, particularly in the area of current affairs programming.

Seventy one countries took part in the first Global Media Monitoring Project in 1995. This project examines the role and representation of women in the media and takes place every five years.[2] At that time, only 17% of the people heard or read about in print/radio and TV news were female. In 2005, the survey concluded that women were virtually invisible in terms of news and media content. While there has been some progress over the last ten years, findings from the 2015 survey (involving 130 countries) show still only 24% of the voices heard or read about were female. This figure demonstrates very little improvement since the project began in terms of women's visibility and at this rate of progress it will clearly take a very long time to achieve gender equality.

To ascertain the situation in Ireland, six week-long surveys have been carried out which tracked the voices of women in current affairs programmes on our three national stations, RTÉ1, Newstalk and Today FM. The original concept for these snap surveys – recording women's voices – originated at an International Women Empowering Communication conference in Bangkok in 1994. In this article we explain areas of concern we observed as we carried out our surveys and we draw attention to other relevant research and points of view. Finally we try to show what is needed to redress gender imbalance in media organisations here.

THE IRISH CONTEXT

The first of these snap surveys was carried out in September 2010. This was followed by a second in March 2012. The third was carried out in October 2013. A fourth survey was conducted in April 2014 while the fifth was conducted over 5 days in June 2015. The most recent survey was carried out during the week beginning 4 April 2016. These were snapshot surveys concentrating on female representation on current affairs programmes, focussing on the voices of women as heard without reference to the time allotted to their contributions. Women's presence as guests on panels, interviews with women and reports by women were monitored for all six surveys. The results are outlined in the following table:

Women's Voices on the Airwaves 2010–2016

RTÉ Radio 1	2010	2012	2013	2014	2015	2016
Morning Ireland	14%	14%	27%	27%	36%	19%
Pat Kenny/ S.O'Rourke	22% (P.K)	31% (P.K)	15%	44%	28%	21%
News at One	N/A	14%	18%	35%	31%	31%
Drive Time	21%	15%	23%	34%	27%	27%
Late Debate	N/A	N/A	15%	34%	20%	17%
Marian Finucane	18%	23%	25%	35%	23%	25%
This Week	N/A	N/A	N/A	12%	20%	16%
Saturday with Claire Byrne	N/A	N/A	N/A	17%	20%	23%

Newstalk	2010	2012	2013	2014	2015	2016
NT Breakfast	21%	25%	19%	32%	27%	26%
Lunchtime	N/A	22%	29%	30%	47%	26%
Pat Kenny Show	N/A	N/A	35%	17%	27%	34%
The Right Hook	11%	31%	20%	5%	20%	26%
The Sunday Show	17%	22%	21%	23%	29%	16%

Today FM	2010	2012	2013	2014	2015	2016
The Last Word	14%	16%	19%	28%	24%	23%

In our article 'Voices of Women – Still Missing in 2014',[3] we credited RTÉ with making progress in the following programmes: *Morning Ireland, Today with Seán O'Rourke, News at One, Drivetime, Late Debate* and *Marian Finucane* noting the increased female representation between 2010 and 2014. However, looking at the survey carried out in June 2015 this progress was not sustained, with the exception of *Morning Ireland*. The most recent survey carried out in April 2016 confirms that progress made in one year can fall back in a follow-up survey. As the table shows, far from making progress, half of the programmes monitored regressed in terms of participation of women, while two others remained unchanged. There is no doubt that the dominance of men on the airwaves is the direct result of the key issues which were part of the public discourse for the week – the formation of government and the Panama papers leak. This is a cause for concern and indicates a need to develop strategies and policies to increase and maintain the presence of women in this area, irrespective of the burning issues of the day.

The programme which improved most in 2015 was Newstalk *Lunchtime* presented by Jonathan Healy. His programme went from a low of 22% in 2012 to 47% in 2015. However in the most recent survey this programme slipped back to 26%, a figure which is worse than the 2013 survey. The 2015 survey was carried out during the week when Catherine Murphy was prominent in the Dáil on the IBRC inquiry. It was also the week of the resignation of Sepp Blatter as President of FIFA. This particular scandal, as well as dominating sports' reports, also made its way into current affairs and was robustly debated from a male perspective only.

On Tuesday 3 June 2015, Kathy Sheridan wrote in the *Irish Times* about sexism in sport in general and in FIFA in particular. She quoted sexist comments made by Blatter at board meetings which were not challenged by fellow board members. She also quoted a figure from a UK study which showed that 'Two thirds of women working in British football had experienced sexism'.[4] If the author had been invited on to one of these programmes to tease out the issues cited in her article, this would have widened the debate around the gender issues that FIFA and other sporting organisations need to address. However it appears that the male anchors and their backroom teams are so steeped in the prevailing macho culture that they could only see the issue from a male perspective.

The most recent survey was carried out during the talks for the formation of the next government and also the Panama Papers' revelations. *Morning Ireland* over the course of the week had just one woman commenting on the formation of the government with no women commenting on the financial scandal. *Drivetime* had two female politicians and their political correspondent commenting on government formation over the five days while a female academic was also interviewed. The only female voice commenting on the tax avoidance scandal was heard on the *News at One* programme. A similar pattern was also noted on the other two stations. These are prime examples of how our radio stations are stereotyping women.

In September 2012 journalist and commentator Alison O'Connor, as part of an academic thesis, met and interviewed some of the 'gatekeepers' (producers and editors) in a survey she carried out focusing on *Morning Ireland*. From those discussions she concluded:

> It appeared to this researcher that they were aware the issue of gender balance was something that had not been adequately addressed by their organisation but they did not wish to be quoted on the record criticising this policy.[5]

Another feature noticed in our media monitoring is that of the 'token female' being a regular feature of programmes such as *The Late Debate, The Marian Finucane Programme* and *Saturday with Claire Byrne*. The problem with this, apart from it being tokenistic, is that women are often shouted down and their voices drowned out especially during heated debate. This constant interrupting is frustrating to listen to and the one woman is often the very last to be invited into the discussion. Male presenters frequently interrupt as do male guests. Indeed getting a woman into the studio or on to a panel is no guarantee that her voice will be heard. In most cases the woman is just there to tick the gender box. This demonstrates the urgent need for gender equality training. Male guests who are usually on friendly terms with the presenter because of the frequency with which they appear also get longer speaking times. This pattern was also observed in the National Women's Council of Ireland (NWCI) *Hearing Women's Voices?* study of the under-representation of women in Irish current affairs programmes at peak listening times which was launched in November 2015.

A pattern emerged during the surveys showing that the gender balance deteriorated on Fridays. In 2010 *Morning Ireland* interviewed their highest number of men for the week on Friday 17 September with a ratio of 14 men to 1 woman. That same day *Drivetime* interviewed 17 men and 1 woman. On Friday 2 March 2012 *Morning Ireland* had 11 men and 1 woman, while on that same day Pat Kenny had his highest number of male guests (9 men and 2 women). In the 2015 survey Sean O'Rourke interviewed 12 men and 1 woman on Friday 5 June. On that same day, *Drivetime* had 12 men and just 1 woman. In the 2016 survey Seán O'Rourke interviewed 12 men and 5 women on Friday 8 April while Jonathan Healy interviewed 8 men and no women. Bobby Kerr, who was standing in for Pat Kenny, interviewed 7 men and 1 woman.

Similarly the dominance of male presenters on Fridays was also noted. In September 2014 Una Mullally wrote about the 'glass ceiling' for women in broadcasting:

> Anyone familiar with Marconi House on Digges Lane in Dublin, which houses Newstalk, TodayFM and TXFM, will notice that one of its design features is an actual glass ceiling – perhaps a message to women looking to get on air.

In the article Mullally focussed on the dominance of men in presentation across the three national stations (RTÉ, Newstalk and Today FM) concluding that 'There are basically no opinionated – not to mention even vaguely adversarial women presenting primetime weekday shows'.[6]

In 2015 we also monitored the figures for female presenters in RTÉ. Figures for *Morning Ireland* for April and May 2015 showed that men presented 73% of the time while women only presented 27% with a trend of two males presenting on Fridays. Likewise Áine Lawlor and Richard Crowley were co-presenters of the *News at One* programme. However this programme was hosted by both Richard Crowley and Jonathan Clinch for 72% of the time over 43 days in April and May 2015, while Áine Lawlor presented 28% of the programmes. All the Friday programmes were presented by Richard Crowley. Also weekday current affairs presenters on Newstalk and Today FM are male, ie. Ivan Yates, Chris Donoghue, Pat Kenny, Jonathan Healy, George Hook and Matt Cooper.

Matt Cooper who presents *The Last Word* responded to the NWCI submission in an article in *The Irish Examiner* on Friday 13 April 2012. This programme, which runs from 4.30–7pm, was the only programme monitored on Today FM. He robustly defended the policy they had on his programme for selecting guests. Over the six surveys this programme increased its presence of women from 14% in

2010 peaking at 28% in 2014 but slipping back to 23% in the latest survey. He was critical of the fact that he gave a lengthy interview to a female psychologist over three weeks and he was not credited with this. The survey was carried out over one of those weeks:

> When it comes to the news and current affairs of the day we try to get relevant participants on air, not commentators. Our criteria are that the person we ask to contribute should be involved in such a way to present relevant information and, if necessary, engage in debate. It is only when we fail to get principals that we fall back on commentators and then we try to achieve a 50/50 balance.[7]

He also cited the number of women in the backroom team – missing the point that it was male dominance of voices in presentation and contributions which we were surveying.

PROGRAMME GUESTS

Another pattern we have noticed over the six surveys is that all three stations draw on the same pool of Dublin journalists and broadcasters for expert opinion. 'Public service broadcasting is not well served by the narrow pool of Dublin journalists, economists, lobbyists and PR people who are invited on to panels in all stations', journalist Rónán Lynch commented in *Village Magazine*, November 2014:

> Broadcasters are obliged to represent diversity of voices from different geographical regions and backgrounds ... all too often radio hosts reflexively turn to authoritative-sounding experts and commentators drawn from Ireland's elite effectively narrowing public discourse and closing down debate.[8]

In the July/August 2014 edition of *Village Magazine* he gives a breakdown of guests on the *Marian Finucane Show*, both by profession and gender, which was monitored over the course of one year. Journalists/broadcasters were the highest profession represented with a figure of 74. Politicians were represented on the programme on 26 occasions; PR professionals 28; legal professionals 26; academics 25 and business people 18. Charities, security analysts, doctors, actors/writers and economists were in single figures.[9]

In December 2011 journalist and blogger, Gerard Cunningham, listed the names of 24 men and 7 women who feature regularly as panellists across all three stations:

> Fine people all of them but here's the thing. I've heard each one of them so many times on panel discussions, talking about everything from the latest euro-crisis to the mysteries of twitter, that I can pretty much predict their opinions on the topic of your choice ... and every time they share their now-predictable worldviews, they do a little bit to limit everyone else's worldview too.[10]

This opinion confirms our observations that programme makers across all three stations rely on a very narrow range of sources – most of whom are white, middle-class, middle-aged professional men. It does take an effort to seek out a broader range of people with opinions – there are a lot of young women (and young men) out there who are more than capable of discussing the issues of the day on these current affairs programmes.

In 2012 Mark Tighe (*The Sunday Times*) raised the question of where it is most of these panellists actually come from and he concluded, 'Journalists from the *Irish Times* accounted for almost half of the €120,000 that RTÉ paid its 10 most-used external correspondents in the past 3 years'.[11] This article was written as a result of a freedom of information request submitted by Eamon Ó Cuiv who also noted that 'the same faces' were used repeatedly and 'a huge concentration on *Irish Times* reporters'. Ó Cuiv stated:

> The payments aren't the biggest issue, it's the frequency with which some organisations and journalists are used. Does

regional spread, gender balance and a variety of views come into it? Or are we getting a concentration of views around the value system of one or two media outlets.[12]

To date neither of these questions has been answered.

SOLUTIONS

The results of the 2010 and 2012 surveys became part of a National Women's Council of Ireland (NWCI) submission to the Broadcasting Authority of Ireland (BAI) on fairness and accountability in news and current affairs. However when the BAI delivered their report they said that they had no jurisdiction over stations when it came to gender balance. In the 2015 Marriage Referendum it ruled that balance must be maintained between the Yes and No sides and found against the then presenter Derek Mooney for breaching this balance. Stations ensure that political balance is maintained in their current affairs programme and the BAI can also rule on this. Is there a very narrow interpretation of what constitutes 'Fairness, Objectivity, and Impartiality' in news and current affairs with gender balance being the major casualty?

Dr Tom Clonan provided us with a good insight into the prevailing macho culture in Irish current affairs programmes in an RTÉ documentary broadcast in 2015. Retired army officer Clonan, who became a whistleblower on bullying of women in the army, said on *The Media Programme* (RTÉ1) on 19 April 2015 that:

> The military would be constructed as a very hyper masculine environment with a very robust canteen kind of culture in it ... the research I conducted revealed unacceptably high levels of discrimination, harassment and particularly bullying and sexual violence against women in the army.

In his role as security correspondent he has been on many programmes across the media. On his encounter with the culture within Irish media he found:

that many workplace settings within the media would make the army's eyes water in terms of the masculine, casual sexism and quite a lot of bullying in this environment ... I have been contacted by female journalists in Ireland who have repeated similar stories of harassment, sexual harassment and bullying ... I think there is a requirement for major investigation and further analysis in order to remove those obstacles.[13]

There was no follow up debate on the points made by Tom Clonan. He wasn't invited on to any panel to substantiate his allegations. This would have been an ideal opportunity for Irish media to debate the macho culture so starkly outlined by him. On that same programme Alison O'Connor made reference to the fact that at media news conferences 80%–90% of people who set the agenda for the day's news are men:

It's the macho culture to stay late and be seen to stay late ... if you have an exclusively male environment, if decisions are taken at a level where it is testosterone driven with no oestrogen feeding in, then the balance is all wrong.

In her *Irish Times* article on 20 September 2012 journalist Laura Slattery wrote that at an evening news conference 'a typical ratio of men to women is 15:1. When there are two women present, I count it as *a good day for the sisters'*.[14] At a TV50 event in Cork in September 2012 the panel was asked what plans RTÉ had to address the gender imbalance problem over the following years. Panellist Steve Carson replied:

I agree there are not enough women on air. I don't buy the argument that it's hard to find women. Well, doing hard things is what we're all paid for.[15]

That it is difficult to find women is an argument which has been used too often in the past by senior management to excuse the inexcusable. Another defence RTÉ, Newstalk and Today FM management have used in the past was to point to the high numbers of females behind the scenes –

females engaged in editing, research and production. This is a weak argument and is not a good enough explanation for the absence of women's voices on the airwaves. A mindset seems to exist in the higher echelons of all three national stations which is ensuring that women are still marginalised.

The Gender Equality Task Force Progress Report to the National University of Ireland Galway (NUIG) was published on Tuesday 23 June 2015.[16] Initially they made a number of recommendations to address the lack of women at senior levels in the university, including the appointment of a Vice-President for Equality and Diversity and also that all senior management should go through 'unconscious bias' training. It was speculated that the final draft of the report would recommend that mandatory gender quotas be introduced to bring a 50:50 balance for senior posts at the university. The Final Report, published in May 2016, does not clearly specify this. The figures from our surveys show that the recommendations need to apply more widely as NUIG is not the only offender – just the one which was challenged and forced to address the issue.

In a documentary titled 'Leading Women' broadcast on Newstalk in 2014, Angie Mezzetti, former RTÉ newsreader and documentary producer, says that global companies such as Microsoft, Google, PWC and Accenture are now focusing on unconscious bias training to understand the obstacles preventing women from progressing in larger numbers into leadership roles in their companies. They have made gender equality 'not just a nice thing to have but a key business agenda item'. She interviewed Dr Melrona Kirrane, Dublin City University Business School, who stated:

> It all starts with stereotyping. When you see somebody that you think belongs to a certain category ... you ascribe a whole load of traits that go with that category to that person, simply

because it reduces cognitive load ... they are generalisations and they utterly blind us to the individual and we fail to see their unique characteristics.[17]

In her study of 11 episodes of *Prime Time* during the 2011 General Election, Maynooth University lecturer Dr Anne O'Brien found that:

> women's engagement with politics was gendered through processes of numeric underrepresentation, gendered visual practices, the use of predominantly male sources and by structuring the content of women's contribution to political debate.

She found that filming of outside broadcasts, looking for the opinion of the public showed that women were absent from the dominantly masculine public spaces where filming took place, such as a cattle mart, GAA grounds and a pub. In the report, the women interviewed were located at a housing estate and at a rowing club. Visually the reports carried 86 shots of men and only 29 shots of women.[18]

CONCLUSION

After completing the six surveys it is evident that policies, training and mentoring are needed to change the tired existing formats and to reflect the diversity of voices which should be heard on the airwaves. All media organisations need to provide pathways for women until 50/50 parity is achieved. It is unacceptable that any public broadcaster could function without having a robust gender equality policy permeating the whole workforce from managing directors down to new trainees. The stations should immediately introduce training for all presenters and have guidelines for all guests invited onto current affairs programmes.

If a task force has recommended unconscious bias training for NUIG management, and if global companies are providing training in it for their workforce, surely then our media outlets in radio and TV should also be aware of the need for training to improve gender balance at all levels of their organisations, but particularly for presenters and panellists. For training purposes opportunities should be given to women to present in the absence of the male anchor rather than bringing in yet another male.

A *Guardian* editorial published on 7 November 2014 stated that:

> The BBC has a special duty, through the universality of the licence fee, to lead the way. It has identified gender equality as a priority ... What we see matters to all of us; equality cannot be left to chance.[19]

In the Irish context RTÉ has that same 'special duty' to lead the way because it is also the recipient of the Irish licence fee. Like the BBC, RTÉ and the other two stations have a lot to do.

There has been a big increase recently in the popularity of local radio. According to Rónán Lynch in *Village Magazine*, 19 August 2014:

> When Community radio stations run training courses, they teach journalists to talk to the 'people on the ground' recognising that the voices of ordinary people are rarely heard on national radio unless they have suddenly become newsworthy because they've been the victim of a crime. The community radio approach is not found on national radio, as professional training teaches journalists to seek out authoritative voices, particularly people who speak for others: politicians, fellow journalists, and spokespeople for causes or movements ... it's an almost unconscious pattern of privileging upper-middle-class voices.[20]

With the introduction of gender quotas we have seen a modest rise in the representation of women in Dáil Éireann. Our low representation in the past is certainly one of the consequences of what Úna Mullally often refers to as the 'intentional sexual bias that side-lines women's voices on the airwaves'. Political parties have been forced to address this issue by the introduction of quotas as outlined by lecturer and researcher Dr Fiona Buckley.[21] Thanks to the gender quotas which were imposed for the recent election the female representation in the Dáil has now reached 22%. It is well beyond time for media decision makers and managers to seriously address the issue of 'missing voices' in current affairs programming. As Tom Clonan concluded in his *Media Programme* interview:

> It's incumbent on the NUJ and all the media organisations that they put in place very clear and explicit policies, goals and objectives that are measureable with regard to the participation and promotion of women and female voices at all levels of our media.[22]

Change will not come without the culture being challenged by an appointed authority. Perhaps the Broadcasting Authority of Ireland should have a much wider remit and a key role in all of this? As Aidan White, General Secretary of the International Federation of Journalists (1987–2011) said, 'Fair gender portrayal is a professional and ethical aspiration, similar to respect for accuracy, fairness and honesty'.[23] There is a moral imperative for management to address the issue of gender balance in current affairs so that 'fair' gender representation becomes a reality. This has not happened and so a body such as the BAI should have a stronger role in monitoring and regulating in order to ensure gender equality policies are drawn up and implemented on the national airwaves.

Referring to the dominance of males in current affairs panels on Sunday 6 September 2015, Booker Prize winner, Anne Enright said on the *Sunday with Miriam* programme:

> They (men) are so busy jostling with each other and putting each other on pedestals and knocking each other off pedestals that they don't have time to notice women ... You might want

to undo the sense of hierarchy that we love so much which is so masculine.[24]

Finally we feel that quotas are urgently needed to address the unconscious bias problem and the poor representation and stereotyping of women in the media. The BAI should have a role in setting guidelines for the introduction of quotas and, as with the implementation of the political quotas, sanctions should be imposed if programme makers fail to meet set targets. Journalist Alison O'Connor has strong feelings on the absence of female voices on the airwaves. She has also come to the conclusion that gender quotas are needed to bring equality to the airwaves. In an article published in the *Irish Examiner* on 13 November 2015 she wrote:

> My pride has taken a back seat on the issue of gender quotas and if legislation and penalties are what is needed to ensure that women get heard on the airwaves or have their plays staged in our National Theatre, or indeed their say in our boardrooms, well then let's bring them on.[25]

Getting women's voices and opinions heard on the airwaves, on a par with men, must be a priority. We shouldn't have to wait for another six years for change to occur. We have highlighted the problem with the under-representation and stereotyping of women. It is now time for radical change, policy formation, new thinking and unconscious bias training in order to achieve fairness for women on the airwaves. The research is there and the time has come for action.

SOURCES
1   Ross and Carter, 'Women and News: A Long and Winding Road', *Media Culture and Society*, 2011, http://mcs.sagepub.com/content/33/8/1148.abstract.
2   Global Media Monitoring Project (GMPP). http://fujomedia.eu/2015-global-media-monitoring-project-gmmp-report/.

3   Dolores Gibbons/Lucy Keaveney, 'The Voices of Women – Still Missing in 2014'. Published on http://www.nwci.ie/index.php /learn/blog-article/lucy_keaveney_the_voices_of_women_still_ missing_in_2014.

4   Kathy Sheridan, 'FIFA may have met its match in US Attorney General', *Irish Times*, Wednesday, 3 June. http://www.irish times.com/opinion/kathy-sheridan-fifa-may-have-met-its-match-in-us-attorney-general-1.2234932.

5   Alison O'Connor, 'A Man's World? An Examination of the Gender Balance of Spokespersons/Experts in Irish Media and Implications for our Public Discourse', (unpublished thesis, September 2012). Reference 5.

6   Úna Mullally, 'Women need to raise the volume on radio exclusion', *Irish Times*, 8 September. http://www.irishtimes.com/ culture/tv-radio-web/lack-of-women-on-irish-radio-is-an-intentional-bias-1.1921049.

7   Matt Cooper, 'Yes, we do try to strike a balance for women's voices in broadcasting', *Irish Examiner*, April 2012. www.irish examiner.com/viewpoints/columnists/matt-cooper/yes-we-do-try-to-strike-a-balance-for-womens-voices-in-broadcasting-190370.html).

8   Rónán Lynch, 'How to get on the Pat Kenny Show', *The Village Magazine*, November 2014. http://villagemagazine.ie/index.php/ 2015/02/how-to-get-on-the-pat-kenny-show/.

9   Rónán Lynch, 'Marian Finucane Show: professionals over weekend brunch'. August 2014. http://villagemagazine ie/index .php/2014/08/marian-finucane-show-professionals-over-weekend-brunch-by-ronan-lynch/.

10   Gerard Cunningham, 'Roll Call' http://faduda.ie/tag/today-fm December 2011.

11   Mark Tighe, 'RTÉ in the spotlight for using "same faces" as commentators', February 2012, www.thesundaytimes.co.uk/ sto/news/ireland/News/article878386.ece.

12   Eamon Ó Cuív, 'You May Detect A Pattern', February 2012. www.broadsheet.ie/2012/02/26/you-may-detect-a-pattern/.

13   The Media Show presented by Conor Brophy, 19 April 2015. www.rte.ie/radio1/the-mediashow/programmes/2015/1419/6952 09-the-media-show-sunday-19-april-2015/.

14   Laura Slattery, 'Media content needs a sex change', *Irish Times*, September 2012. www.irishtimes.com/business/media-and-mar keting/media-content-needs-a-sex-change-1.534302.

15 TV50 event, Cork, Saturday 8 September 2012. www.irishtimes.
.com/opinion/organised-campaign-needed-to-get-more-women
-s-voices-on-radio-and-television-1.548057.

16 Gender Equality Task Force, NUIG Progress Report to Údarás
na hOllscoile. www.nuigalway.ie/media/nuigalwayie/content/
files/aboutus/Gender-Equality-Task-Force---Progress-Report-
June.pdf.

17 Angie Mezzetti, 'Leading Women Documentary, www.women
inleadership.ie/2014/12/women-in-leadership-on-newstalk/
Newstalk, July 2014.

18 Anne O'Brien, 'It's a Man's World: Mediations of Women and
Politics on Prime Time (RTÉ)', The Irish Politics Forum, March
2015.

19 *The Guardian*, 'View on Women in Broadcasting: Still the Second
Sex'. Editorial. November 2014.

20 Ronan Lynch, 'Marian Finucane Show: Professionals over
weekend brunch'. *The Village Magazine*, August 2014. www.
villagemagazine.ie/index.php/2014/08/marian-finucane-show-
professionals-over-weekend-brunch-by-ronan-lynch/.

21 Fiona Buckley, 'How Ireland legislated for candidate sex quotas
to increase women's representation', Democratic Audit UK.
November 2013. http://www.democraticaudit.com/?p=1848.

22 Tom Clonan, speaking on the Media Show (RTÉ), 'Balancing
act: are women getting a raw deal in the media?' www.
rte.ie/radio1/the-media-show/programmes/2015/0419/695209-th
e-media-show-sunday-19-april-2015/?clipid=1860216#1860216.

23 Aidan White, General Secretary of the International Federation
of Journalists in 'Getting the Balance Right: Gender Equality in
Journalism', UNESCO 2009. www.portal.unesco.org/ci/en/files/
28397/12435929903gender_booklet_en.pdf/gender_booklet_en.p
df.

24 Anne Enright on *Sunday with Miriam*, 13 September 2015. www.
rte.ie/radio1/sunday-with-miriam/programmes/2015/0906/72604
1-sunday-with-miriam-sunday-6-september-2015/?clipid=19697
55#1969755.

25 Alison O'Connor on Gender Quotas in the media. http://www.
irishexaminer.com/viewpoints/columnists/alison-oconnor/its-
fair-to-implement-gender-quotas-and-get-the-balance-right-
364666.html.

WOMEN AND THE ARTS

Úna Mullally

When the Abbey Theatre's 1916 centenary programme was announced in late 2015, the impact was immediate. But it wasn't the impact the national theatre wanted. With just one female playwright programmed for a stage that was set to commemorate the birth of a republic, the discrepancy was instantly obvious. The set designer and arts manager Lian Bell called it out, and a hashtag was created: #WakingTheFeminists.

When the Abbey director Fiach Mac Conghail took to Twitter to answer some questions about the programming, the writer Belinda McKeon, Lian Bell, myself and others queried the exclusion of women. Mac Conghail's tweet that 'thems the breaks' resonated bitterly with many women who have felt that exact brush off, not just for much of their artistic or professional lives, but for their lives as women in a country and a world that assumes their exclusion as a default position.

I wrote this piece in the early days of the #WakingTheFeminists movement, and what a movement it would become. It has to be said that this movement did not occur in a vacuum. An increasingly amplified conversation about gender inequality across institutions, professions and life in general allowed this to happen. As journalist and broadcaster Nadine O'Regan said at a talk at Other Voices in Dingle in December 2015, this year would be seen as one where we began to acutely recognise this problem and begin to deal with it.

It's easy for me to commentate in newspapers, but it was much harder and far more brave for women in theatre, and their male allies, to take a stand within their industry. So many did. So many theatremakers, playwrights, designers, festival managers, mentors, actors, writers, directors, producers and so on took that stand. These are the women we should salute. Because now, when a theatre programme emerges, we will be more conscious than ever of a bias it may have. Now, it will not be acceptable for theatre programmes – and much more besides – to project that idea of 'thems the breaks'. The feminists have been awake for some time, but now, many of us are braver and louder and have more solidarity to call out inequality when we see it.

If the Abbey Theatre announced that 90% of its 2016 programme was made up of plays written by women it would be viewed as extraordinary. It would be a 'statement'. Yet when the national theatre announced its programme celebrating the 1916 centenary, 90% of the plays programmed are by men. That is not a 'statement', it's just the norm. Out of the ten plays that the Abbey has scheduled for 2016's 'Waking the Nation' programme, just one is by a woman. Take a bow, Ali White, whose *Me,*

Mollser made the cut, a 'specially commissioned monologue for children'.

I spend my life listening to great records by women, going to great plays by women, watching great films by women, and reading great books by women. Yet time and time again the selection of arts programming – especially in Ireland – is overwhelmingly male-focussed. Why? I am tired of having to bang this drum, but every music festival lineup that disproportionately features male musicians, every theatre disproportionately programming male playwrights, every film festival screening mostly films by men, every literature prize shortlist being mostly male, shows that we are not beyond this most basic of conversations.

Here are some statements you hear when pointing out gender imbalance in an arts programme. More men than women make art. Men make better art. Women don't come forward to submit their art. Even if those things were true – Why? What these statements really want to insinuate is that women themselves are responsible for their exclusion. Women are historically not the gatekeepers to cultural institutions, record labels, publishing houses, theatres and film studios. The problem isn't women making art, it's men not letting it in. When people – it's nearly always men – say things like 'do you expect plays to be programmed just because they are by women?' Such statements are designed to shut down the conversation and assert male ownership over art. Funnily enough, you'll find that it's those who benefit from the status quo who seek to maintain it. People who refute exclusion are generally ones who are rarely excluded. We are often told that women don't put themselves forward enough, but this magical thinking ignores the discriminatory environment within which women are making art. And so the cycle goes: male-made art gets seen, therefore is perceived as better, therefore more men make art when they continuously see their perspective reflected and have male role models to aspire to, therefore more male-made art gets made, therefore more male-made art succeeds, and so on.

I do not know the behind-the-scenes complexities of programming 2016 at the Abbey. But with the greatest respect for the director of the Abbey, Fiach Mac Conghail, no matter what the reasons for its shortcomings, the end result is the same. The audience doesn't see the process of programme-making, it sees the programme; a programme largely excluding female voices, which is hugely disappointing.

When Mac Conghail took to Twitter to answer questions and criticisms, which was a welcome act of engagement, he said that the Abbey has produced nine plays by women since 2008, and that plays aren't programmed on a gender basis. 'I'm sorry that I have no female playwrights next season. But I'm not going to produce a play that is not ready and undermine the writer', Mac Conghail tweeted. That's all well and good, but how come so many men made the cut and women didn't? If there were issues with plays being ready, or funding being in place, why did men benefit and women not? Is there really not one more play written by a woman, old or new, fit to be programmed?

Is this just an Irish problem? No, however a cursory glance at the National Theatre in London's current programme sees 20 featured productions listed on their website. Amongst those there are seven plays with female writers, a series of debates featuring seven women and seven men, and a performance festival featuring four female artists and three male artists.

Gender equality in Ireland's artistic institutions is not about tokenism, it is about redressing a historical imbalance, it is about representing the population, it is about showcasing multiple perspectives, not just male ones, it is about reflecting the whole audience and not just a part of it. If art is about how we see ourselves, then why are we only getting one half of the picture? The Abbey Theatre receives taxpayers' money, which does not discriminate on gender, yet most of the work it shows is by men. Why? If there is such a dearth of female-made theatre, what is it doing to address this? Are there female mentorship schemes? Female commissioning schemes?

Conversations about women in the context of 1916, and the fierce battles they so bravely fought for their republic and their suffrage are gaining traction, and not for want of trying. One of the reasons why it's so important to shine a spotlight on the female aspect of the birth of our republic is because of how extensively it was erased, not least by our subsequent constitution. One hundred years later, much has changed for the better, yet the conversation about gender equality is just as relevant and perhaps even more heated. What an opportunity the Abbey has missed to not just represent the artistic output of women in Ireland, but also to acknowledge that conversation. Naturally, *The Plough and the Stars* features in the programme. Maybe it's time for another riot.

VOICES FROM THE FRONT LINE

GENDER EQUALITY: ONE MILLENNIAL'S EXPERIENCE

Laura Harmon

Some of us will have a catalyst moment where it becomes abundantly clear that we are facing a barrier or being treated as lesser, purely because of gender. My catalyst moment came when I was in college and I began to really see for the first time that most of the people in power positions in the world around me were men. Across the board in society, whether it's politics or business, education or in the media, men still hold the majority of power, even though half of Ireland's population are women.

The overall representation of women within students' unions has hovered around 20%. I was president of the Union of Students in Ireland (USI) in 2014/2015 and it had been twenty years since the last woman president, Helen O'Sullivan. How could two decades pass in student politics without electing a female leader? The same situation is reflected in many students' unions in Ireland. In St Pat's College, for example, where women account for over 66% of students, just four students' union presidents were female over the past 20 years.

During my three years in the student movement as an officer in USI, there was always a motion at our annual congress about encouraging and supporting women running for election. Each and every year, we would debate for over an hour (sometimes two hours) with heated arguments on both sides. The debates were never about introducing quotas but training and supporting women to run. There would be men and women on both sides queuing up to speak. Some of the opposing women felt it was insulting that they would need any support to run for election – after all they themselves got elected so why would they need any support? The debates always hit a nerve and became more about emotional responses and personal stories as opposed to facts. We spoke more about the women who were already at the decision-making table as opposed to those who weren't. Each year winning the debate to support women running for election became that little bit easier but there was still massive opposition.

Not once did I speak about my gender when running for election, yet it was one of the main aspects that was covered when I was elected as USI president. During my time as USI president, just four SU presidents were women. If they were absent from our presidents' working group meetings, I ended up being the only woman in the room. Not once did I experience any sexism from my male colleagues, in fact, they were extremely supportive and most were running their own campaigns to promote women in leadership on their campuses. I suspect they might have shared my feeling that it felt really odd having such a huge gender divide in the room.

On my last year in USI, I brought a motion that I knew wouldn't pass – I was just stirring debate. If it passed, it would mean that member colleges of USI would have to attempt to bring delegations comprised of at least 40% of both genders to USI Congress. I knew the motion would be controversial and unlikely to pass because USI just wasn't ready for anything that resembled a quota. I proposed the motion and it was vetoed from the floor – we never even got to have the debate.

I spoke to Helen O'Sullivan when writing this chapter and she doesn't think we have made as much progress in the last twenty years in relation to women's rights as we might think and I agree with her.

One of the biggest mistakes the student movement made, in my opinion, was to abolish their Women's Rights Officer (WRO) position. Helen had been one of the last full-time USI WROs before she became USI President in 1994/1995. If we look back at the history of the student movement I think it's fair to say that the movement has been strongest on women's rights issues when women have been in leadership roles. In the late 1980s and early 1990s the women's rights action committee was strong in USI and during that time USI led major campaigns on abortion rights for example.

Without a specific officer designated to work solely on gender issues, it meant from year to year there were varying degrees of emphasis on women's rights within the student movement. It was hard enough to get motions passed in 2014 and 2015 to invest in campaigns to support women running for election and I think it will be an uphill battle for the student movement to ever get back their national WRO position unless there is a concerted campaign from the membership. Many students' unions have adopted campaigns to encourage women to run and, working with Women for Election, there has been a promising increase in women running this year. Let's hope this trend continues.

In 2013, USI published the Say Something study – the first study of third-level students' experiences in Ireland on harassment, stalking, violence and sexual assault. Over 2,750 students of all genders responded. The study was supported by Cosc (the National Office for the Prevention of Domestic, Sexual and Gender-Based Violence) and the Department of Justice and Equality.

The study found 16% of respondents experienced some form of unwanted sexual experience during their time as a student at a higher education institution.

One in five women who responded experienced some form of unwanted sexual experience, with 11% experiencing unwanted sexual contact. 7% of men who responded had some form of unwanted sexual experience. 5% of women students were survivors of rape, compared with less than 1% of men. These figures were even higher for lesbian, gay and bisexual students and higher again for transgender students.

These results are not dissimilar from the 2002 national *Sexual Abuse and Violence in Ireland* (SAVI Report) findings where one in five women respondents had experienced contact sexual assault as adults and one in ten men experienced the same.

Less than 3% of respondents to the Say Something study who had an unwanted sexual experience reported it to college officials or to An Garda Síochána. Some common reasons given included a fear they would be blamed; shame or embarrassment and not wanting friends or family to find out. Some 51% of the women surveyed discussed sexual violence with their friends, but only 38% of men did.

The largest proportion of survivors of unwanted sexual experiences identified the perpetrator as an acquaintance. Trinity College Dublin Students' Union surveyed over 1,000 students in December 2014. They found one in four women and 5% of men who responded had an unwanted sexual experience during their time as a student.

The Say Something survey revealed a worrying lack of awareness about sexual consent campaigns, with only 31% of women and 32% of men saying they had heard of any consent campaigns before.

None of this is unique to Ireland. A similar study of women students conducted by the National Union of Students in the UK in 2010 called 'Hidden Marks' found that one in seven women had experienced serious physical or sexual assault during their time as a student. The 2007 Campus Sexual Assault (CSA) study funded by the US Department of Justice found one in five women respondents and 6% of men were survivors of attempted or completed sexual assault during their time in college.

In September 2014, President Barack Obama launched the 'It's On Us' campaign. The campaign resulted from the White House Taskforce to Protect Students from Sexual Assault, which published a report in April 2014 outlining how colleges can prevent and address campus sexual assault. Some recommendations include the need for colleges to conduct systematic surveys; the need for bystander intervention to be promoted to encourage witnesses to step in when misconduct arises and for colleges to identify trained people who can provide emergency and ongoing support. The administration also published a sample reporting and confidentiality protocol, as well as best practice for the formulation of sexual misconduct policies. These recommendations also serve as food for thought in an Irish context.

So what can be done in Ireland to help address these issues?

It was great to see USI team up with the Dublin Rape Crisis Centre and Cosc in autumn 2015 to develop the #AskConsent campaign – the first campaign of its kind to be rolled out nationally in Ireland that focused on consent and the need for consent. Of course this is something that affects all genders and the campaign is gender inclusive.

It's great to see that Trinity College Dublin are following the lead of Oxford and Cambridge by introducing consent workshops for first year college students in September 2016. This will apply to undergraduate students living in Trinity Hall in Rathmines. This is a very positive step which I believe should be implemented across the board for third level colleges in Ireland. A recommendation that came out of the USI Say Something survey was that the Government should produce standardised protocols for higher education institutions on reporting and support procedures when cases of sexual assault occur.

Ultimately, comprehensive sex education needs to start much earlier. This should be introduced to the curriculum from primary school and reinforced all the way through Ireland's education system. As it stands, religious ethos is an impediment to this occurring in our schools and until we address the issue of school patronage and develop more non-denominational schools this will likely remain a barrier to delivering proper sex education to our young people.

The Eighth Amendment is another huge issue for young Irish women and women of all ages. Enacted in 1983, no woman under fifty years of age in Ireland has had the opportunity to vote on this issue. It's about time we had a referendum on this issue.

A quarter of those who avail of abortion services in the UK who give Irish addresses are under the age of twenty-five. That's a lot of young people. Between January 1980 and December 2013, over 150,000 women travelled from Ireland to access termination services abroad – on average twelve women per day. The cost of travelling and missing out on work or study means that this is a class issue also as it is even harder for women who are less well-off to travel.

There is a lot of work to be done to bring about gender equality in Ireland. It is heartening to see the surge in feminism that we have seen over the last few years. It's also important that while women are leading the fight for their own equality, that men have a space within that movement too, because gender inequality affects all of us in society.

STILL LOCKED OUT:
THE EXPERIENCE OF COMMUNITY DEVELOPMENT IN IRELAND

Cathleen O'Neill

Constance Markievicz was an Irish nationalist, suffragist and trade union activist. Her journey brought her from soup kitchens in Liberty Hall to the chambers of the Dáil. When preparing to write this article I couldn't help but wonder what Markievicz would make of the values that she held dear in terms of equality and rights for women – would she recognise them in today's Ireland? Markievicz was present when the Republic got off to a promising start vowing to *cherish all of the children equally*. Would she believe that a century later in 2014 that 11% of children (aged 0–17) were living in consistent poverty.[1] Is this how the State practises cherishing all of our children equally? How would she rate the trade union movement and the erosion of workers' rights and pay? What score would she give to our recent Tánaiste and Minister for Social Protection for her *achievements* in cutting back services to the most vulnerable in our society – people with disabilities, pensioners, travellers and payments for the children of lone parents without any review of their circumstances. What comments would Markievicz make about those women in power and the role they played in the recent war on the poor, the closing down of essential equality and human rights organisations and other practises that we view as *hostile cultural action* including shutting down community development projects, drugs rehabilitation projects and the total silencing of the dissenting community voice. I can almost hear her scathing comments echoing through the last one hundred years.

During the recession in the mid 1980s I was a very young mother with 5 children who had been forced onto social welfare after a marriage breakup. The combination of recession, depression and poverty made for a fast feminist learning curve as I battled week after week with one State or political official or another for survival. At no stage of these battles did the State attempt to make my husband responsible for paying maintenance. He ignored court orders for payments and ultimately left a well-paid job rather than comply with an attachment of earnings order. He received three times the amount on Social Welfare that we as a family of five was granted as his dependants.

As an accompaniment to this article I will start with a poem that I published during those battles. Sadly those same feelings evident in the poem are as unchanged today as the day it was written, both for me and for thousands of other women. This poem is dedicated to SPARK, and to those lone parents they represent and the struggles they are facing at present.

THE CAOIN

I started to scream again today
A slow sad scream of frustrated anger
Today I wailed at the wall of officialdom!
Smug, smiling, filing cabinet face
Closed to my desperate entreaty
Social justice is a right
Don't dole it out like charity
I stood there, dead-locked, mind-locked
Helpless in this sightless one dimension world
With dignity in danger, I turned and
Slowly, silently I walked away
And my mind screamed a slow, sad caoin for the
Us and Damned their social welfare.

WOMEN AS CAPACITY BUILDERS IN THE COMMUNITY

Yet, there was also hope to be found as a woman living in the 1980s. The second wave of feminism was still having an impact, particularly in the media, as women journalists debated the issues and produced a raft of TV and radio programmes to raise awareness of the issues facing women. Working-class women were setting up community-based daytime adult education centres. Politics, feminism, women's publishing houses and community-based writing groups gave a voice to women. It was possible in those days to meet with and lobby your local TD or government minister to advocate on behalf of your community or group. Out of this space many voluntary projects and community development projects were funded by the State.

Yes there was poverty and social class discrimination; yes there was huge inequality in the State, in schools, in work and politics. But there was a hope that between the women's movement, the community-based groups, the voluntary sector and our friends in Europe, we could bring about change. We became experts at writing and costing funding proposals, writing business plans and finding European partners.

Whilst the Celtic Tiger roared, we concentrated on community development. We worked with our communities to build capacity. In some cases we entered into private/public regeneration partnerships, building houses, community halls, schools and other essential community needs. Three decades of vibrant community development saw many positive changes for community groups and women's groups. In all of these endeavours we carried the values of gender equality and social justice forward.

And then, at a stroke, we watched as the economists and politicians and the whole neo liberal structure swept us off the table. We lost our own advocates in the Equality Authority, the Combat Poverty Agency, the Irish Human Rights Commission and we lost our own community development projects. More crucially, we found that our lobbying tactics were falling on deaf ears as 'They' closed their ears and doors to our pleas for social justice. And the media completely turned its back on us as they danced to the neo liberal tune. On reflection, it feels like we slipped seamlessly from one recession to the next, and that our feminist ideology and perspectives took a heavy battering along the way.

We were battling on the ground to save our projects and communities, to support women who were experiencing domestic violence, persistent poverty, the care crisis, the disability crisis. We marched and protested to draw attention to the fact that women make up the majority of people living in poverty. Households headed by women are at the greatest risk of poverty. Women with a disability are twice as likely to live in poverty. Cuts to social welfare were life and death issues and affected women more than men. We screamed as loud as we could that the State was conducting a war against the poor; that it was actively engaged in hostile economic and cultural actions against women – to no affect. Our protest went unheard even as we continued the fight.

NEW PARTNERSHIP COMPANIES AND THE DEMISE OF
COMMUNITY DEVELOPMENT PROJECTS

The economy is being blamed for the changes currently being made in the community and voluntary sector, but we activists know that more than 14 years ago (prior to the recession) that there were plans to close down the sector. The sector was getting too strong, too assertive, too successful at educating the grassroots and empowering people to claim their rights. All that the economic collapse provided was a sure-fire excuse to get rid of us.

Community development as we know it ceased to exist on 14 December 2009 when the government closed 29 CDPs (community development projects), deeming them to be non-viable after an unequal, hidden and unclear review process. Two thirds of these groups were Dublin based. The remaining 150 projects are being merged with Local Partnership Companies, along with their transfers of undertaking.

Partnership Companies *are* about providing labour intervention and training. They are *not* community development led and there are real fears that they will follow a labour market agenda only – no more possibility of meaningful engagement for social change or of building local capacity. We, as workers and activists, will be neutered and domesticated by local partnerships. The loss of community development projects, and process, ethos and principles, will have long term consequences for marginalised community groups in Ireland.

We are worn out articulating the dangers that communities face if they lose their CDPs – telling and retelling what will happen to elderly members of our community, to women, and women's groups, men's groups, children with special needs, communities with special needs! What the government doesn't seem to *get* is the powerful role that a small two or three worker project can play in community cohesion, in leveraging funding far in excess of the small grant it receives, in enabling community groups to become viable, in empowering communities to articulate their own needs from the bottom up.

CDPs are key community anchor organisations, who challenge for and with people who are left behind, discarded and dismissed. All of this was happening during an era when a little over 20 men (politicians, property developers and bankers), were playing a giant Monopoly game with our country and our people. A wink and a nod here, a tilt of the eyebrow there, a quiet phone call late in the evening, a sharing of information from all the key boards they sat on – as they bartered our futures and our children's futures to buy and sell the most expensive land in the world.

Or maybe they do *get* it. They certainly seemed to *get* the role played by the Equality Authority and Combat Poverty Agency in reaching for equality and social justice when they closed them down. Perhaps they do realize the role played by CDPs in helping people to name their own worlds and identify their own needs. Maybe they do know – hence the savage attack on the sector and on CDPs, and on working class communities.

Where can the justification be, for example, in purporting to 'save' an average of less than €95,000 per year per project in these areas by removing supports that the most vulnerable and disadvantaged people depend upon? The fact that this will generate the need for significant increased service spending in redressing the effects of individual and community breakdown demonstrates a reckless disregard for accountability in public expenditure.

If none of these considerations were taken into account by the enlightened elite in our government, then there is a clear case to be answered – at the very least in relation to incompetence leading to yet more waste of public resources in the longer term.

What if this is not incompetence? Is it possible that even our own particularly challenged and overpaid political leaders cannot grasp the damage and cost associated with their decision?

We think they do know. And that is why they decided more than 14 years ago to close us down. The reality is that sustainable communities – based on equality of opportunity – are not on the Irish political agenda. It is not so long, after all, since a certain Minister for 'Equality' 'Justice' and Law Reform reminded us all that equality is bad for the economy. We must not confuse this madness with incompetence. Tell them that you know! Tell them you are aware that they are attacking the most vulnerable and it has to stop! Tell them that our communities, and community development, and equality and social justice are rights, and that our rights cannot be bartered or sold to the highest bidder.

KILBARRACK COMMUNITY DEVELOPMENT PROJECT:
RETAINING OUR INDEPENDENCE
My own project is the Kilbarrack Community Development Project. We decided not to sell ourselves to any bidder, opting instead to remain as an independent CDP. This decision was made at a huge financial cost for workers in the project – a cost they were happy to make to remain independent.

The KCDP was founded in 1994 at the request of people living in the catchment areas of Grange A and D, particularly those parts that experienced economic, social and educational disadvantage. We became a company limited by guarantee, and we remain as such. We were set up by the people of Kilbarrack, not by any State department. Our board of directors is made up of members of the target population who experience the aforementioned deprivation and we hold a public AGM each year. The project is responsible for a number of key initiatives including the Kilbarrack Children's Centre – an after-school facility catering for 74 children funded by POBAL. We also have strong links with, and are funded by, the School Completion Programme and the National Education Welfare Board. We provide exam support to the Department of Education in Athlone by giving tutorial support and by hosting Junior and Leaving Cert exams for those young people who are out of school.

In addition we run the Kilbarrack Women's Health Project, a community arts project, an internet café, an information and support centre and we provide administration support to the St Benedict's Resource Centre. We run addiction programmes for young people. We are twinned with the Kilbarrack Youth Project and we also run an outreach support project for women experiencing domestic violence.

The KCDP applied for and successfully received a grant from the Department of Community, Rural and Gaeltacht Affairs (CRAGA) in 2001 to run a number of community development programmes. The KCDP was one of 180 similar CDPs to receive this funding. During the last number of years CRAGA made a number of changes to how the projects developed, including its recent decision to merge CDPs and local area partnerships.

The key role of any CDP is to work with those most removed from the decision-making process and build capacity at a local level. The KCDP has been very successful in this regard and enjoys a good reputation within the community and voluntary sector. Our board held several planning days in recent years trying to change the CRAGA agenda and our manager spent the last three years lobbying at a local and national level to have this decision overturned. She did this on our instructions, along with other key groups who form the National Community Development Forum.

In December 2009 a review of all CDPs was carried out and a number of these had their funding discontinued. Our own review was deemed to be successful and our funding *was* continued, but some months later we gave our grant back to the department so that we could retain our independence.

In mid 2010 all CDPs were instructed to transfer those staff who were paid under the CRAGA grant to the local partnership, along with a transfer of undertakings and the assets of the company. The staff in question was our manager and our administrator. After a long and painful consultation the board and staff of the KCDP, in consultation with the community, made a unanimous decision not to merge with the partnership and to hand back the CRAGA funding. We did this to retain our independence and to continue supporting the local community. We remain firm to the principled stand that we took then and we believe it was the only position to take that allowed us to retain our integrity as a CDP.

In the present crisis we totally need to push our feminist perspective. I firmly believe that is what Countess Markievicz would advocate. We need to end the gender blind nature of government and social policy. We must educate ourselves and the policy makers about the fact that women make up the majority of the working poor, that they mostly work in low paid jobs, zero hour contracts etc. The whole nature of 'Care Labour' or 'Solidary Labour' needs to be debated in political and public forums – for without 'Solidary Labour' capitalism cannot continue to grow. We must promote the work of feminist writers and economists. They have produced fantastic research and recommended policies.

It is clear to us all that capitalism relies on the existence of unpaid work – 'Love Labour' – that is done by women in order to satisfy its greed and growth. We should demand that the feminist voice be included in mainstream commentary on the current economic crisis. And we must ensure that our own values and ethics offer new ways of naming our own world and bring about positive change for all. Patriarchal structures and capitalism will not be changed without a massive battle being fought. There are very positive signs emerging such as the recent Marriage Equality referendum and the desperate battle being waged by the anti-water campaigners and those communities who support them. It will be a long road but we are able and ready to win this challenge. Be very clear about this, there is no room in Ireland for the dissenting or critical voice. There is no room in Ireland for the community project that tries to bring about change or inform people about the implications of cuts in social welfare or to lobby for equality and social justice. They have done their very best to silence us but we must 'Insist, Resist, Persist' and be as awkward as we can about making our demands heard. After all, that is what Markievicz was all about! This is why she supported the working classes in 1913. These are life and death issues for ourselves and our communities and our world. Otherwise we will find ourselves still locked out in another 100 years.

SOURCE

1   EU SILC 2014 accessed from http://www.barnardos.ie/what-we-do/campaign-and-lobby/the-issues/child-poverty.html

A CAGED ESCAPE

Pamela Kpaduwa

2015 JULY
I heard a lady's voice talking to my children, but I couldn't make out who it was, so I stepped out from the sitting room and peeped through the door. It was my friend Janet [pseudonym]. I hadn't seen her in fifteen months and I didn't recognise her as she had changed so much. She was screaming abuse at me and, in a split second, before I could say anything, she pounced and tore off my nightdress. Before I could recover she was outside running towards the gate.

I was so shaken. My children were crying because they had never seen anything like that in their lives. They refused to sleep in their room that night thinking she was coming back. Then it dawned on me that Janet's mental illness had taken a turn for the worst and yet no one was taking her seriously. It was at that point I knew I had to do something. I called the guards, not to have her arrested, but to get her help ...

2006 JANUARY – THE BEGINNING OF MY JOURNEY

On a good day it takes courage to leave one's home and family. How much more when you have to leave in a hurry, leaving behind years of memories that you can never replace.

Coming to Ireland has been both liberating and inhibiting. I have a happy picture in my head that I always go back to when I want to escape from the present reality of things, a picture of me and my sister sitting outside my mum's stall in the market. I can remember their chatter as they call out to each other and their customers: 'come and buy from me ... mine is fresh and cheap ... I will give you better discount ... try it out and you will be convinced'. On and on and on. I could never imagine not having that sense of security like a blanket wrapped around me.

I never expected to have things handed to me but then I never expected to experience the high level of distrust and disbelief that follows one around, especially if you come from my country Nigeria no matter your personal circumstances.

2015 JULY

Nearly 10 years on and we are still suffering from that stigma of distrust and unbelief. Janet can't get the help and care her illness requires, simply because she is an asylum seeker and therefore a liar.

The system of direct provision has robbed me of every sense of worth and replaced it with a kind of mediocrity that has also worked hard at keeping me down perpetually. It has become almost impossible to raise my head up. My original qualifications have become obsolete, skills are not utilised and poverty germinates.

I have done nearly all the courses available to us – which is FETAC levels 1 to 4 – and they have all expired with me still in direct provision and not utilised at all.

When I eventually leave here, instead of joining the labour force, I will have to use a few more years to update myself. The cycle keeps going on – from one open prison to a bigger open prison. How can one raise the next generation of upstanding men and women in such conditions? Whatever happened to all children are born free and equal? And all the purported rights of a child and the best interest of the child? Direct provision has robbed these children of vital parts of their childhood and will still stretch its ugly hands into their future if we let it.

I came here in 2006 excited at the prospect of a new life and a secure future, devoid of fear and conflict, only to be trapped in a maze of mirrors where each turn leads to the same place and everyone in the system mirrors your personal frustrations and dashed hopes. Escaping from personal situations and conflict to be caged in a collective situation and conflict with people from different cultures and language and religion is nothing but a caged escape.

After my encounter with Janet, I realised that every one of us in direct provision has a degree of Janet in them; depending to what degree we can manage it and keep the lid on or else explode under the slightest pressure.

My children have been my saving grace as I occupy myself trying to raise them as best as I can given the circumstances. I am hardly a good role model for them as they see me do little or nothing day by day. I feel extra pain when I see them being denied the opportunity to grow up in a normal family setting, living with just family members and not strangers from different parts of the world with different religious beliefs.

My daughter often comes home from school trying hard not to cry because they were left alone outside their school as they were waiting for the bus from the centre to pick them up. Little things like this tell the children how unequal they are to other 'normal' children. Over the years, my children have lost many of their friends to deportation. I suppose in a way we are still lucky to be here.

What answers do I give my children as they look to me with questions in their eyes, looking for answers, direction and hope? They do not know any other home and as much as I want them to have a happy childhood they see the fear in my eyes and that's when the questions come.

'Mummy are we going back to Africa?'

'Mummy please I don't want us to move, I like it here'.

'Why was "Chioma" taken back to Africa?'

'Will they take us back?'

And on and on.

I pray that one day we will all look back and marvel at how far we have come.

A Personal Experience of Political Activism

Ruth Riddick

When the Countess Markievicz School extended its generous invitation to participate, we agreed that, given the communications issues which consumed my activism in the 1980s and 1990s, it would be particularly appropriate to leverage contemporary media – in this case, a video link – to bridge the geographical challenge presented by my unavailability to travel from the US to Ireland for this event.

My colleagues from the days of our 'freedom of information' campaigns will remember my exasperation that we were even having a legal argument about who could say what to whom when satellites were bouncing unfiltered images and messages around the world in real time. (Yes, that would be the Eurovision Song Contest!)

I've been asked to outline my 'personal trajectory' as an activist. Hmmn. That would be: I was born into a repressive society. I yelled 'no'. I found others who yelled the same. We figured out how to make the kind of noise that results in legal reforms while also helping some women in crises we identified as patriarchally engineered. I made a sort-of difference, and I've left a legacy of sorts. I fulfilled enough of my self-imposed personal debt to my mother – who died young – of being a woman who came of age in mid-century Ireland, and my family-identified debt to the country which provided me with a free and rather fine education. I got on with my life, finding new adventures and more age-appropriate issues to engage my eldering time and energy.

And what was it that I did exactly?

I asserted that women in Ireland have a right to information about lawful extra-territorial services – including abortion – successfully arguing the point before the European Court of Human Rights (Open Door Counselling 1992). This right is now enshrined, somewhat haphazzardly, in Irish constitution and law.

I codified principles and procedures for non-directive pregnancy counselling which were adopted by the Irish Family Planning Association (IFPA) when it introduced its nationwide service in 1993. These protocols continue to be implemented and taught as best practices.

In support of these goals, I ran a formal counselling service from 1981–1986 (founding Open Door Counselling in 1983), managed an informal informational hotline and counselling referral service from my home phone from 1986–1993, and consulted with the IFPA in 1993. All in all, my colleagues and I responded to many hundreds of women with pregnancies they described as presenting a crisis in their lives. And we did it within the framework of the law because we had a duty of care to our clients – even as, in our personal capacities, we campaigned for change.

And, of course, I spent countless hours writing, speaking, touring, lecturing, broadcasting, editorializing, publishing and generally droning on about the philosophical urgency of our slogan, 'a woman's right to choose'.

I didn't do any of this on my own and I didn't do any of it perfectly, and I certainly didn't realize my personal agenda for feminism in Ireland. I did make lifelong friendships with people I love and admire, and I didn't make a dime.

As planned, I aged out of frontline activism at age 40. I remain convinced that reproductive rights requires the leadership of young women and that it's the responsibility of younger generations to identify their priorities and strategise accordingly.

If I can help you, I'll be delighted.

Nowadays, I write for *Conscience*, the newsjournal of Catholics for Choice (CFC), an international non-profit advocacy organisation headquartered in Washington, DC. The longterm CFC President is a Dubliner, a friend from his early work at the IFPA. (For those of you who remember the 1980s Case of the Virgin Condom – that was Jon O'Brien!)

Catholics for Choice was founded in 1973 to serve as a voice for Catholics who believe that the Catholic tradition supports a woman's moral and legal right to follow her conscience in matters of sexuality and reproductive health. It's a healing message with continued relevance.

How is it that I became so involved as an activist for reproductive rights in Ireland?

The roots of my feminism undoubtedly lie in the dreadful social conditions into which I was born. Who would now believe that women were forcibly retired from civil service careers on their wedding day, as my mother was? Or that women weren't allowed to serve on juries, even in trials of women? Or that you couldn't be served pints of beer in 'public' houses, or at all? Or a myriad of gender-based discriminations and daily humiliations from the seemingly trivial to the incontrovertibly egregious?

One of the linchpin outrages of the day to which I responded viscerally was highlighted by Nuala Fennell in *Hibernia* magazine in the late 1970s. In the absence of legal divorce, men in Ireland were empowered to lock away their wives in mental asylums; these committals were involuntary and interminable. I salute Fennell's crusading journalism and advocacy which led to a career in mainstream politics as Ireland's first ever Minister for Women's Affairs.

Or what about the nuns who told my class of barely menstruating young females that, if it came to foetal distress in childbirth, the attending physician is required to privilege the baby even at the sacrifice of the mother? This message was delivered in the context of a complete ban on contraception.

Thus, the nuns may take their share of credit for my activism and, indeed, in the early years, they claimed me for their own for all that they likely disputed my opinions.

Also radicalizing was Paul VI's encyclical on contraception, *Humanae Vitae*. Still a schoolgirl when it was published, I read the English language version in one of the 'quality' English Sunday newspapers and it was extensively discussed at the family dinner table. My parents thought the encyclical a terrible mistake and a betrayal of Vatican II, the source of hope for many distressed Roman Catholics looking for modernisation in the church.

I just thought it was nonsense.

In due course, I was on the streets of Dublin marching for legalized contraception, a political goal which I also wanted to achieve for personal reasons. I was young; I was in love; I was sexual; I was sexually active.

However, in my story, the true nexus of the personal and the political was spontaneous and unplanned. You might say that I was in the right place at the right time: a public meeting of the grassroots Women's Right to Choose Group, held at Liberty Hall in 1981. The meeting was chaired by Mary McAleese, already a force in Irish public life. (Not that we expected then that she would be our second female President!)

Journalist Mary Holland, whose work I had long admired, spoke from the platform about her abortion. After Mary excused herself for family reasons, anti-choicers present spoke very abusively about her. I was incensed. Naturally, I spoke up, identifying myself as both Irish and a woman who'd recently had an abortion. In that passionate moment, the purpose and practice – the destiny – of my next fifteen years was set.

Thus, some of the personal roots of political activism.

'The personal is political' is a slogan popularised in the heady days of so-called second wave feminism. In the throes of idealistic youth, this is a hard message. It seems to undercut the high mindedness of our cause. We prefer to highlight the justice of our mission, the selflessness of our commitment. When I found feminism as both politics and philosophy (thank you, Germaine Greer and *The Female Eunuch*), I was energised by the possibilities for world betterment. So much to change, so much time, a whole generation in which to do it!

In a generation, there's no doubt that we succeeded in making a lot of necessary change, at least at a superficial level. And I don't say that lightly – it's way more comfortable to live with superficial improvements than without. Check out television's *Mad Men* for further information.

For those of you not yet twinkles in your parents' eyes, the 1980s in Ireland may be reasonably characterised as a period of 'second partitioning' or what we now know as 'culture wars'. The implicit struggle for Ireland's future was between the waning authoritarianism of the State's founding patriarchs (McQuaid and de Valera), who both died in the early 1970s, and an increasingly cosmopolitan culture simultaneously focused on America and the European Union.

The (Roman Catholic) centre couldn't hold, but a frightened laity retrenched around issues they found deeply threatening – explicity, abortion and divorce; both subjects of 1980s referenda so deeply divisive as to bear hallmarks of civil war. Those feminists, such as myself, who had spent our youngest days working to mainstream hitherto silenced issues such as domestic violence, rape, unwanted pregnancy, were obvious targets for a generally inchoate anger simmering to the surface.

When I was formally interviewed by a very senior Garda in the mid 1980s, I asked why a complaint against Open Door Counselling was made under the law – specifically, the 1861 Offences Against the Person Act – when the same paths of social protest were open to my complainants as to me. The memorable reply was an eye-opener:

> You may not like some of the ways our society does business, Ruth, but you believe that, by-and-large, society functions and that your political representation and rational argument can have an improving effect; in short, you belong. Your complainants, by contrast, believe their whole existence is under mortal threat from people like you. When you're under threat, you call the guards.

Well! This was news to me; a lesson from the inside on the nature of democracy as played out at senior levels of modern Irish society. I understood in the moment that, at a fundamental level, Irish society had already moved on, not per my feminist agenda, to be sure, but away from the dark ages. Not so long later, the President of the High Court referred to me and my colleagues as 'well intented and highly-qualified professionals ... providing much needed services'.

It occurred to me that, notwithstanding that the High Court shut down my service agency, our efforts had – ineffably? – moved into the halls of the establishment.

Thus, it was unlikely that I would see the inside of a jail cell on contempt charges, for all that I broadcast my availability to convey taboo information via my listed home phone number, and this on the front page of *The Irish Times*.

Equally, it was highly likely that I would get a positive hearing in the European Court of Human Rights. But not before Open Door's Senior Counsel read, without interuption, the feminist-inspired principles and procedures of non-directive pregnancy counselling into the record of the Irish Supreme Court.

These days, I often refer to the period of my sustained activism as one in which I made a public nuisance of myself. I'm only half-joking. My insistence on arguing the point through the courts was, at best, *unladylike*. For all the contemporary editorial referencing my characteristic pearls and red nail polish, I was a determined, polarising figure and my uncompromising rhetoric was uncomfortable to many colleagues.

Further, writer Ronit Lentin once told me that our work relies on tremendous, and often hidden, support from our nearest and dearest. It's not enough to be politically committed, we must be personally resourced. Thus, the domestic and emotional support of my family-of-adoption was key to my availability in the public square. In the arrogance of my political moment, however, in the conviction that I was doing the right thing, I had neglected to explicitly recruit my partner and his family to the stresses of my mission. The unforseen demands on them over a decade were hellacious. Credit for the patience and generosity of the extended OBrolchain family is way overdue.

Additonally, it was only the pro-bono contribution of my voluntary legal team, in both the domestic courts and at Strasbourg, that could give teeth to my assertion that I would fight forever for the right to disseminate information as a reputable pregnancy counselling service provider.

As Hillary Clinton's favourite cliché reminds us – it takes a village. A personal and political community, not an ideological isolate. And so we speak of movements, even as we recognise (and honour) the individual energies that animate them.

So much for all that. What can it serve emerging activists to rake over these old coals? Those of you historians who enjoy such stories will find the details fresh in newspaper and television archives.

Like you, I'm more concerned that each generation of feminists needs to reinvent its political consciousness along with its agenda. Our stories are purposefully lost in projects of ideological forgetting. Filmmaker Lelia Doolan, herself no stranger to controversy, speaks of the difficulty in securing funds for her exemplary 2012 documentary on 'forgotten' Bernadette Devlin, once among the most famous people on the planet – a mere forty years ago.

These truths demand that we document our history in our own time.

That history, in turn, contextualises present struggles: we don't look back to marinate but to understand that we carry our foremothers' incomplete and imperfect work forward into new challenges.

I appreciate that these remarks may not be the benignant trip down memory lane which may have been anticipated in your kind invitation. I'm not great on 'my greatest hits'. And this writing hasn't been a particularly pleasant experience; my memories are, at best, emotionally mixed.

It was the feminist theologian, Mary Daly, who observered that the deeper we get into women's history, the worse the news. Why should I be any different?

So, my advice to the younger activist:

OWN YOUR AGENDA

You are not obliged to pick up my unfinished business, unless we explicitly share your mission and want to work together.

DO NOT CURB YOUR ENTHUSIASM

Politics is a longterm process dotted with events, some of which turn in your favour.

GET A LIFE

You can only save the world if the people who love you, yourself included, are right along there with you.

KEEP YOUR ACTIVISM IN PERSPECTIVE

Your cause will not keep you warm in that dark night of the soul which is the price of admission to our humanity. Only your radical honesty can do that.

KNOW YOUR ENEMY

The dualism that's so much a part of our philosophical framework is a lie. We're all in this together, but power relations are unbalanced. Our mission is always to serve the powerless, ourselves included, however and wherever we find our authentic cause and can deploy our talents; but not at the expense of our precious humanity.

REMEMBER THAT LIFE IS MULTI-CIRCULAR NOT LINEAR

with surprising opportunities for a redo. You will enjoy these adventures and epiphanies if you keep faith with your principles.

TAKE COMFORT FROM THE FACT THAT NOBODY AND NOTHING IS PERFECT

Perfection is the fanatic's lie, and it's particularly attractive when you're young and untested. You don't have to be victim to the lie.

In closing, I can only hope a meditation such as this, that reflecting on 'the personal is political', helps you navigate the next chapters in your personal stories and in the necessary political campaigns of today and tomorrow.

Learn from me, by all means. Learn from my mistakes. Forgive me, and move on. Thank you. Good luck!

Ruth Riddick's participation in the Countess Markievicz School was underwritten by Catholics for Choice.

MIGRANT DOMESTIC WORKERS' EXPERIENCES

Mariaam Bhatti

In my five years of working in Ireland as a domestic worker I have seen a lot to consider myself an expert on the issue among many others whose place of work is behind closed doors of private homes. I also think when there are any reforms in the sector, domestic workers themselves should be consulted and be at the centre of discussions to be able to contribute as they know best how to make their workplaces better.

In this article those I refer to as domestic workers are people who work in private homes as childminders, housekeepers, nannies, au pairs, gardeners, personal drivers and carers (for the elderly or for people with disabilities). Their workplace is usually someone else's home. Some of these workers work and live in their employers' homes (live in), but many live outside their place of work (live out).

This can be a great setting in terms of cutting transport costs and time spent travelling to and from work. And some domestic workers and employers refer to this as 'free accommodation and meals' but it isn't such. Simply because one hasn't seen a deduction on the payslip (if they get one) or 'touched' the money first before paying it back to the employer for food and accommodation provided to them, doesn't mean they are not paying for it. But based on how little pay that many live-in workers get, their food and accommodation costs are already deducted from the overall pay or at least considered before net pay is decided on. This is not always clear to many domestic workers as many people don't get contracts or payslips so they may not necessarily understand this. The breakdown stated clearly by the National Employment Rights Authority (NERA, now merged with other bodies to be the Workplace Relations Commission) explains it clearly. It also further states that all employers are required by law to keep records of employment at the place of employment (such as contracts and agreed working times) which many employers behind closed doors are not aware of or choose to ignore.

What I find really worrying is that many people do not consider care work or work traditionally done by women such as looking after the home and caring for children as work. I know from my own experience as a woman and more relevant to this as an au pair in my first job in Ireland back in 2010 as well as working as a childminder and a cleaner in the last four years. If I were to describe my day's work, this is how it would be.

My day started at 7am and it usually started by getting the room set for a bath for two girls – a toddler and an eight year old. I would get all I needed ready (nappies, clean clothes, hair accessories etc) and mix water to the right temperature. Then I would bring the toddler from her nursery (as soon as she was awake) and give her a bath while monitoring the older child to wash herself. This morning bath routine was also accompanied by multitasks such as leaving the bathroom washed and clean in the process and taking dirty clothes and nappies to the nappy bin and laundry basket respectively.

This was followed by breakfast which was usually a selection from various types of cereal. Usually I would then get lunch bags ready after the children had had breakfast and before leaving. Then coats would be on, followed by a quick walk to a local primary school which was 10 minutes away. I would leave the older child to school and then hurriedly push the pram with the toddler in it to a creche which was another 15 minutes fast walk from the school in another direction.

The toddler was in creche for three hours and this was the only time I had to go back to the three storey house (4 bathrooms, 4 bedrooms and a nursery) to do everything else I could not do in the morning. Tidying the house, sweeping and mopping the floors, hanging laundry, doing the dishes and preparing lunch for the kids. This took so much time that sometimes I would be on my feet from the time I would have left the kids to the creche and school respectively until it was time to collect the little one from creche three hours later.

As soon as she was home I would feed her lunch and change her nappy and by the time we were done the two of us had to leave to collect the older child from school. We would bring her home, give her lunch, empty and clean her lunch bag and clean her lunch box and juice bottle for the following day. I would also get her uniform and jumpers properly hanged for the following day. Most afternoons we would do activities together for an hour or so before getting late afternoon snacks ready and embarking on homework. Usually by the time homework was done it would be time to tidy the house from all play and activities. If we had been to the park, it would be time to head home, change nappies and give the children a snack while preparation for dinner started.

The children's mother usually arrived between 8.30 and 9pm when the children were having or had just had dinner and an evening bath and were in their pyjamas. She would normally take over from there and I would get myself a shower, get into my own pyjamas and have dinner in my room before passing out from tiredness. Sometimes I would go online and have a moment on Facebook to see what the world was up to during the 12 or 14 hours that I was 'away' from the world. This happened six days a week with the sixth day, a Saturday, slightly different in that I worked 'half' a day from 7.30 to 3pm which was a full day (8 hrs) on its own, but because my employer had called it a half-day I also called and believed it was that too.

Saturday was a day I dreaded. I slipped into anxiety of some sort from late Thursday to Friday because I knew Saturday was around the corner. On this day as soon as I woke up I had to deep clean the whole house from bottom to top. I had to start with the kitchen and living area so that by the time the family were awake they would be able to have breakfast while I moved to the floor above which they would have just woken up from. By the time I finished eight hours later my muscles and every part of my body would be sore. Eight hours of deep cleaning not only every room but every appliance and every cupboard is huge tiring work. Mostly I would not have eaten anything or had a break during those hours unless it was a nature call break.

Sundays were my only day off but I spent most of it catching up on sleep. Sometimes when I woke up I was sad to realise it was almost the end of the day and the same cycle was a few hours from beginning again. So what is called light household duties for au pairs was the opposite to me. Minding children is hard work but it was different because children are fun to be around and make a long day pass by eventually, but cleaning all day is a different story.

For all of this work I was paid a flat €400 a month. There was no extra pay or day off in lieu of working on bank holidays. And of course I did not know I had any rights as a migrant worker as I was new in the country and did not have access to such information or local media. The place where I worked in Dublin was isolated with just a small new business centre. I was discouraged from meeting other people outside the family I worked for so I wouldn't have had access to other domestic workers or local people. I even had to ask for permission to go outside the house on my day off. Back then I was very naive, too trusting and didn't know about my rights as a human let alone as a worker.

When I left the family I was introduced to a member of the Migrant Rights Centre Ireland's Domestic Workers Action Group. This person is now like a sister to me. My life changed completely. I saw a new Irish society that I had never seen before. I had lived in this society already for a while but it was like a different world within Irish society. I became human again, a smile began to visit my face from time to time and I started to have a good posture, even when walking. I started to project myself and my voice better. I was no longer isolated and most importantly I had been empowered through being educated about my rights as a worker.

However I still found it challenging to find another family to work for despite having experience and having done a six month childcare course and work experience in a creche. I know I did not have a reference from the family I had worked for due to the circumstances that led to my leaving, but I had upskilled myself and had even done

Garda vetting and first aid, but a year later I still had no job. I later got a childminding job through word of mouth and it became an amazing journey. I was treated totally the opposite of how the first family treated me. I was paid a little above the statutory requirement of €8.65 an hour and I felt respected and valued as a worker. Here I did not live with the family and my role and responsibilities were clearly outlined. I did not have a written contract or payslip, but the verbal agreement was kept as agreed. I have moved on to working part-time as a community worker since I completed a university degree in Community and Youth Work but I still occasionally babysit and mind children from the second family that I worked for for four years. Working for this family taught me that it is possible to treat people right and it can work very well in addition to workers themselves knowing their rights as workers.

HISTORY MATTERS

Rita Fagan

I was fortunate to be asked to speak as a working-class community activist at the Markievicz School in 2013, the year commemorating the 1913 Union Lockout. I spoke about housing and community issues and also about working-class women's resistance. I gave a case history of our struggle for the regeneration of a public housing project on St Michael's Estate, Inchicore in Dublin. I briefly mentioned the deep history of this public land and its place in Irish history. This 'Promised Land' housed the English military in what was called Richmond Barracks. It is one of seven identified State sites for the commemoration of the 1916 rebellion. It is where 3,000 volunteers, including members of Cumann na mBan and the Irish Citizen Army, who were fighting for independence were taken following their surrender in Easter week 1916. It was where they were court-martialled before being taken to Kilmainham Gaol for whatever punishment was handed down. Of those 3,000 volunteers,

77 of them were women who played significant roles in the rebellion and the fight for equality. Countess Markievicz, Rosie Hackett, Brigid Lyons Thornton and Winnie Carney were included in these women. These women made up the six battalions at the GPO, the Four Courts, City Hall, the College of Surgeons, Jacobs Factory and Marrowbone Lane.

Historians Mary McAuliffe and Liz Gillis documented these women in a book called *We Were There*. This was launched by President Michael D. Higgins on International Women's Day 2016 as part of the Richmond Barracks Project. The project got me thinking about working-class women being written into history and why it is so hard to find them in the history books. Women like my own mother who is 50 years a tenant and community activist like me and other sisters out there in grassroots community struggles – marginal voices. Often times it is because they are so caught up in the struggle to survive or defending community projects against cuts that those struggles and their roles within them don't get written down and archived. So it is of vital importance that we who are working class, traveller, black etc, women leaders look to our own communities to find, write and tell our stories. Such stories of women's activism from the grassroots on issues such as housing, welfare and community infrastructure which is being dismantled as I write and stories about the fight back against racism and poverty and today's fight to prevent water being privatised.

It took years to have Richmond Barracks acknowledged as a lost chapter in the history of the fight for independence and within that raising the profile of women's role before, during and after the rebellion. Parallel to documenting their stories is the story of the public land which housed Richmond Barracks. In the late

1960s this land became the community of St Michael's Estate, a community with a very active tenants' history. However, by the mid nineties the estate became very neglected, undermined and unheard. It was abandoned by the State and its institutions. The tenants, who were mainly women and children, were silent witnesses as their homes, blocks and community disintegrated around them. St Michael's Estate became a den for dealers and drug takers. It became a social ghetto. The tenants organised because they had had enough. Women leaders like Nellie Kinnane, Margaret Sommerville, Mary Sommers and Ann Marie Brennan, along with the support of us, the Family Resource Centre Community Development Project, led the fight for regeneration. It was a really interesting process and struggle that achieved three different sets and types of public housing and community facilities which John Bissett has documented in his book, *Regeneration: Public Good or Private Profit?*

However, it was a war which went on for 16 years; 16 years of persistence, determination and passion – the spirit of doing the right thing. It was a battlefield of defending the land and the vision for public housing. Other women at the heart of the battle were working-class local leaders; Caroline McNulty, Natasha Farrell, Nicky Fahey and Jo Kennedy along with Eilish Comerford, Eadaoin Ní Chlerigh and myself who worked closely building their capacity to fight back. The community was let down four times by the State – but we would not give up and we would not go away. We used creative protest and the media and we also joined with O'Devaney Gardens and the Dominic Street areas of Dublin who were also let down by the developer Bernard McNamara in 2008.

It has always been my view that poor people live on very rich land in this city. The then Fianna Fail government and the recent Fine Gael and Labour government through their policies of 'Public Private Partnership' were involved in the land grabs of these three communities. We in St Michael's Estate saw it, as described by John Bissett, as the 'Collective Eviction' of whole communities such as St Michael's Estate and O'Devaney Gardens. We have never given up. We won two more acres which now houses 75 families. As the suffragettes would say; we are going forward with a plan to get the next two acres for 50 senior citizens' accommodation developed and to ensure the remaining ten acres of St Michael's Estate gets public housing during this housing crisis where over a hundred thousand families are on waiting lists. It is outrageous.

Without a consciousness of what has gone before, it is difficult to imagine a different future. I guess what I have tried to do in this piece is remember, recount and document. As I read somewhere: 'As long as someone controls your history, the truth shall remain just a mystery' – (Ben Harper).

History does matter! It is our business to go forward. You must on no account turn back – ARISE!

La Lucha Continua.

WOMEN'S STATUS IN IRELAND:
WHERE ARE WE 100 YEARS ON?

Micheline Sheehy Skeffington

We want equal pay for equal work, equal marriage laws, the
abolition of legal disabilities, the right of women to enter the
hitherto banned learned professions, women jurors and
justices, in short, the complete abolition of various taboos and
barriers – social, economic and political – that still impede
women's progress.

– Editorial, *Irish Citizen*, October, 1919[1]

My grandmother Hanna Sheehy Skeffington had a vision
of an independent Ireland emerging where Irish women
would achieve equality in all aspects of life and would
play an equal role in the governance and decision-making
of the new State. In the event, she was to struggle many
times throughout the first decades of the new Irish State in
order to even preserve what dignity and equality women
had so far achieved. Though in more recent times there has
been much progress, women in Ireland continue to endure
violence, discrimination and lack of opportunities. They
still occupy very few senior decision-making positions. My

grandparents, and later my parents, were to play a strong role in those battles for equality, so I am proud that I too have recently had the opportunity to strike a small blow for women in highlighting injustices within Irish universities.

Francis Sheehy Skeffington and Hanna Sheehy Skeffington

Ireland of the early 1900s was entering a new era. The nineteenth century had left poverty in the cities and a tough and relentless rural life, with evictions a recent memory. These were the conditions that led to the formation of the Land League – and indeed the Ladies' Land League – to start a revolutionary campaign for tenants' rights. The Fenians were the active rebellion group of the late nineteenth century and Hanna's father, David, and uncle Eugene Sheehy were imprisoned many times for Fenian activities. But in the Ireland of the early 1900s there was also a growing scholarly class. Women had been attending university for some years and were easily the match of their male colleagues in intellect and wit. Attending the then Royal University in Dublin, my grandmother soon became appalled at her status. Not only had women to attend lectures separately from men, but they were debarred from attending university events and society meetings in the evenings. Much worse, Hanna Sheehy, as she was then, soon learned that as a woman she was ranked alongside convicts and infants in being denied the vote. She already possessed a strong sense of justice and a desire for Irish independence and this further stirred her revolutionary spirit.

Thus began the twentieth century, with almost two decades of revolutionary debate, discussion and agitation leading up to the Easter Rising of 1916. To my mind, it would seem to have been a more intellectual revolution, as scholars such as Thomas MacDonagh and Francis Sheehy Skeffington enthusiastically joined in debate and developed ideas alongside working-class socialists such as James Connolly. These three in particular were strong believers in the equality of women and MacDonagh and Connolly were two of the six signatories of the 1916 Proclamation who did support equal rights for women.

So where did the Easter Rising lead us? Much has, and will, be said about the 1916 combats and its revolutionary outcomes. But the history books still mostly deal with the men and with Constance Markievicz as leaders. To mark her as one of the 'leaders' there is an often-used portrait of her – clearly in a studio – posing in combat mode with a gun. But she too was an intellectual and had high ideals for women as well as men. She lived in Rathmines near my grandparents, and, as friends, they regularly visited each other and entered into hot debates regarding the relative importance of Irish independence and women's emancipation. Markievicz, like Maud Gonne MacBride and many of Inghinidhe na hÉireann, believed that once Ireland achieved independence, women would be granted equal rights and that therefore the national revolution should be prioritised – temporarily – over that of women. Those who know something of Hanna will not be surprised she took the view that women's rights were equally important and so she would not wait for independence, but continued her suffrage activities as a main concern. She must later have often reflected on just how right she was, since the emerging Ireland of the 1920s was, if anything, more repressive to women than under British rule. Indeed, that is the context within which she referred to the Proclamation as declaring women truly equal as citizens of the new State. Written entirely by men focused on the revolutionary ideal, it says something of the influence of the feminist debate that it resulted in a declaration of equality for women and men, as well as of independence.

So what of the Sheehy Skeffingtons? My grandparents met as students at the Royal University – there was ample opportunity to meet in and around the National Library and at public events – and soon developed their ideas and ideals together in friendship. As testimony to their feminist principles, when they got married in 1903, they took each other's name, both thus assuming the surname Sheehy Skeffington. Francis Skeffington was an ardent feminist, always wearing a 'Votes for Women' badge on his lapel. He wanted emancipation and independence for all Irish people equally and he was a strong, indeed 'militant' pacifist. Hanna never saw her position as a woman to be different from that of men and it outraged her that women were denied access to key decision-making roles, not least in the emerging revolutionary movement, where Cumann na mBan was seen as a support for the Irish Volunteers, from which women were debarred. For feminist reasons she never joined Cumann na mBan, nor did Frank join the Volunteers (he was later to say in his Open Letter to his friend MacDonagh that he was glad of this, as he disapproved of the increasingly military approach of its members). Hanna was less militantly pacifist, but abhorred killing; she was to play a role in attempting to stop the 1922–3 Civil War as she felt this was senseless bloodshed, despite being anti-Treaty herself. Both Hanna and Frank were also strong socialists and as such were firm friends with James Connolly, debating, both in public and at more private gatherings, their ideals, strategies and plans for emancipation and better working conditions for the poor, as well as equality for women.

Feminist activism was to take up much of the Sheehy Skeffingtons' lives in the decade or so following their marriage, little interrupted by the birth of their son, Owen (my father) in 1909. Impatient with the slow progress of petitions and letters requesting the granting of the vote for women, notably to the Irish Party (which Hanna's own father represented as an MP), Hanna founded the Irish Women's Franchise League in 1908 with her friend Margaret (Gretta) Cousins. Action stepped up, with the women heckling public representatives and addressing crowds in any public place available. I remember the wooden foldable platform at home with 'Votes for

Women' on a brass plaque at the front which the suffragettes used to address increasingly-large gatherings. There was also a magnificent banner in green poplin embroidered in gold lettering with the League's name in English on one side and in Irish on the other.[2] They adopted green and orange as the Irish suffrage colours – this in itself was a statement of independence from Britain and from the British suffrage movement which used purple and green.

In 1912, they determined to further raise their profile and several women chose to break windows in public buildings. Hanna selected Dublin Castle, for it was the seat of British power and thus she could have a go at the ruling forces at the same time.[3] She and her seven colleagues were arrested, variously tried and sentenced and went to prison. Frank supported her actions and the second time she was arrested (in 1913), he even refused to bail her, as he supported the use of imprisonment to highlight the women's cause. In 1912, five days before she was to be released, she went on hunger strike. The story is told in Margaret Ward's (1997) wonderful biography of Hanna, but I can certainly say it was an 'experience' for her. She used to say in fact that one has not been fully educated until one has had a spell in jail. The hunger strike was in sympathy with two English suffragettes who were imprisoned in Mountjoy Jail and who at once adopted the already-used tactic of hunger striking in Britain. It is interesting that when Hanna and her other hunger striking colleagues were released they immediately force-fed the English women. The authorities never dared to force-feed Irish women in Irish jails. It is curious to also reflect that – at least in relatively recent times – the first people to go on hunger strike in prison in Ireland seem to have been these two British women (followed at once by my grandmother and three of her colleagues).

As a journalist, Frank felt that press coverage of suffrage activities was not sufficient, so typically, he founded a suffrage newspaper with Gretta Cousins' husband, James. This was the *Irish Citizen*, itself a statement of independence, since no Irish were yet citizens but still *subjects* of the British crown. Below the title in every edition was a banner heading: 'For men and women equally the rights of citizenship. From men and women equally, the duties of citizenship'. This, to my mind was pure Frank as he had a very high sense of duty towards his fellow people and indeed, attempted to inculcate that to all who would listen (James Joyce, famously, was one not so inclined to listen!).

Thus ran the years that led up to the tragedy of 1916. And that, to my mind, is what it was, a tragedy, not only for my family – for Hanna and her son Owen – but for the nation. Ironically the pacifist Frank was to be one of the first to be executed, indeed murdered, by a British firing-squad. But the 'success' of the 1916 Rising was in part due to the tragedy of losing so many fine leaders and the brutality with which they were eliminated after they surrendered. Remembrance of that time should be a time of reflection, not one of celebration. What kind of a nation would we have should those leaders have survived? To my mind, almost certainly, women would have played a stronger role in shaping and running the emerging State.

This would not have been hard, since one of the first things in the 1920s that the Free State government did was to withdraw women from jury service, one of the few public roles they had at the time. There followed a litany of repressive measures down to the 'marriage bar' enacted in 1933 which lasted for some women until 1973, where women, especially in the public service, had to cease employment on marriage. Hanna rallied her suffrage friends in 1937 to fight de Valera's proposed new Constitution which was particularly patronising towards women. They succeeded in part by having some of the more offensive sections removed (such as reference to women's 'inadequate strength'!). She publicly denounced de Valera saying he showed a 'mawkish distrust' of women; a description that might apply to many of his contemporaries on both sides of the Treaty.[4] The *Irish Press*, a Fianna Fáil mouthpiece, gives some idea of how these opinions were framed by very conservative Catholic doctrine in a piece published in 1937. It said that women in opposing the Constitutional reference to their 'proper sphere' being in the home were actually 'deliberately' opposing the 'advice' of none other than Pope Pius XI.[5] Indeed, had women not got the vote while still part of

Britain in 1918, one wonders would it have taken much longer to grant it in independent Ireland.

The decades following independence were ones where women were expected to stay in the home and bring up families, supporting their husbands in their lives and careers. There was a very strong and narrow view of the world that was dominated by the Roman Catholic Church. Successive governments bowed to the bishops' views when enacting legislation and only now are we learning the extent of cover-ups, child abuse and condemnation especially of women during those times. Politicians such as Noël Browne and indeed my own father, Owen Sheehy Skeffington who was a Senator, brought the wrath of the clergy and its supporters down on them for daring to propose a more egalitarian society. Involving the State in family matters was tantamount to communism, but this elevation of the family to such a sacred place resulted in the entrapment of women in the home, with more children than they could afford and sometimes with violent husbands. Women who became pregnant outside this 'norm' were condemned virtually to imprisonment and their child taken off them. None of this is now news, but the shocking reality of those decades only started to come to light towards the end of the twentieth century. It is an indictment of the newly-emerging State that so little care or support was actually afforded to its female citizens.

It is for historians to analyse just how the sea-change came about from an outgoing progressive and egalitarian vision (encapsulated in the 1916 Proclamation) to the repressive narrow-minded governance of the early decades of independence. It may be that those 1916 leaders were a minority and that most men did not believe in granting women the freedom to express their ideas. John Dillon MP for the Irish Party alongside Hanna's father, was said to have believed that it would be the 'end of western civilisation' were women to be granted the vote.[6] It was also true that in post-war Europe there was a groundswell of opinion that believed women's primary role was to produce children and look after their husbands. It also suited the emerging fascist governments' objectives. In Ireland suffice it to say that the achievement of the vote in 1918 did not bring about much immediate change in women's role and status.

However, Ireland has come a long way since Hanna first went to prison over 100 years ago for suffrage activities. The path to social change for Irish people, notably female citizens, was slow and tortuous to the point of turning back on itself at times and it was not until the late twentieth century when the tide began to turn in women's favour. We've had two mould-breaking female Presidents, many female ministers, female Tánaiste and laws enacted to grant gender equality as well as social and labour rights for women. But would Hanna be satisfied? I am sure she would not. Nor indeed would Frank. They would be at the forefront of the twenty-first century feminist movement highlighting just how society continues to let women down and agitating for true equality and justice for all. Women are still far from playing an equal role in Irish society, and continue to suffer discrimination in all aspects of life, not least in employment.

As institutions, universities are generally considered seats of learning where the development of mould-breaking ideas is a key principle. One would expect that female emancipation would be at the core of such institutions and that young female undergraduates would have many role models to aspire to and would see women and men playing an equal role in university governance. But they do not. Most Irish universities have boardrooms or public places lined with ponderous images of former male presidents and governors and it is rare to find even a building or a lecture theatre named after a woman. These are mere symbols and images, but they are powerful and reflect a thinking that for the most part does not include women. The boards and heads of Irish universities are still almost entirely male. The criteria for selecting these positions of power inevitably are coloured by a male view of what comprises 'leadership' qualities. The systems are hierarchical and, by and large, leave no room for flexibility of viewpoint, let alone in structures or even working hours.

It is no surprise therefore to learn that Ireland has the second-highest Glass Ceiling Index (GCI)[7] for academia in all of Europe, after Malta (which has one university).[8] This EU report, covering all of Europe, not just EU countries, is issued every 3 years. But in 2012, GCI data for Ireland (as for Malta) were 'unavailable'. This suggests that the worst countries become reticent in providing data when ranked so poorly. The Irish Higher Education Authority (HEA) that supplies those figures would seem not to want Ireland to appear in such poor light. As well as supplying the data, it would be even better to actually address the problem. I very much doubt that our position has changed even now. The situation is not good in any Irish university (though marginally better in the Institutes for Technology), but NUI Galway is the worst, with 13.5% females at Professorial level.[9] This means that NUI Galway is potentially the second worst university in Europe for its GCI. It also means that there is a very real chance that undergraduates will never see, let alone be taught by a female professor throughout their degrees – and this is in 2016, not 1916. If one includes Senior Lecturers the percentage rises to 21% female, but this is still worse than any other Irish university. See the figures as follows:

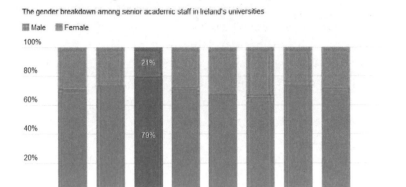

Proportion of female to male senior academics (including those at Senior Lecturer level) in Irish universities, averaged from HEA table published that day. Irish Times, 3 December 2014.[10]

So when in 2009 I enquired as to why I had not – yet again – been promoted to Senior Lecturer (SL) after 22 years lecturing in NUI Galway and learned that only one woman (6% of female candidates) was promoted compared to 16 men (50% of male candidates), I immediately set about seeking redress, not just for myself, but for all the other women like me, stuck below this thick and very opaque glass ceiling. I got very good advice and support from my SIPTU shop stewards and was able to lodge a complaint with the Equality Tribunal within the six months deadline.

The reason I took this major step was partly because of my grandparents' and parents' legacy. I knew that, far from being criticised by them for putting my head above the parapet, they would *expect* me to do so and question why I had not were I to remain silent and accept my lot. That sense of duty to one's fellow citizens so widely promulgated by my grandfather and taken on by both my parents, Owen and Andrée, was coupled with some of Hanna's revolutionary, dogged determination to achieve justice for women. I was also encouraged by the idea that, win or lose, I could probably make use of my family name, specifically my grandmother's, to publicly highlight injustices against women in my institution and further afield.

To focus here on my case and situation is not to disregard the often much greater discrimination suffered by women in other spheres. But my win at the Equality Tribunal in November 2014[11] obviously had to concentrate on my own academic career and situation. The ruling, however, did not specifically focus on myself, but listed some twelve points that refer to flaws and discrepancies in that whole round of promotions. It stated *inter alia* that the 'same criteria' were 'applied differently' to favour men over women; that one male candidate was not even eligible and that by eliciting statements about leave taken for childcare, the university had discriminated against many of the (6 eligible but unpromoted) women (especially as there was no evidence that the inevitable dip in productivity had been taken into account).

The decision was to spark much on-going debate and protest in academic circles in Ireland. And my hope is that it will bring about real change for all women, not only in academic institutions (the situation for non-academic female university staff is even worse, for they have less voice and influence), but in Irish society in general. What spurs me to continue campaigning is that society and the universities in particular are very slow to actually bring about change. NUI Galway has set up a Gender Equality Task Force (I believe as a result of my Tribunal ruling) that will make recommendations to ensure greater opportunities for women in the university. But this, I believe, is a smokescreen to conceal the fact that nothing tangible has changed for women in NUI Galway. I know from my case that I was not the only woman to be better than several of the successful male candidates in 2008/09.

There are five other women whom I know to be as meritorious as me. But the university publicly says on the one hand that there was a mere 'blip' in the promotions in 2008/09 and on the other that as soon as it saw the results it 'knew there was a problem'. I have no wish to dwell on NUI Galway, but the attitudes it publicly displays are symptomatic of closed minds, fear of change and a cronyism that is rife within the higher echelons of Irish institutions. *Plus ça change, plus c'est la même chose.*

In the 1980s I was on the then UCG (University College Galway) Equality Committee which compiled a report that showed UCG to be ranked last in Ireland for the number of females in senior academic posts and made recommendations to rectify this.[12] Now, nearly 30 years later, we have not moved in rank, even if more women do occupy senior posts. At the time of my case, 84% of my academic superiors were men. The Academic Council, the chief academic decision-making power in NUI Galway, currently comprises 81% men. The Equality Tribunal ruling summarised the chances of female candidates being promoted to SL in NUI Galway in the previous decade at less than one in three, whereas men had a one in two chance. In the 2013/14 round of SL promotions, though for the first time nearly 50% of the 104 candidates were women, just nine of the 28 promoted were women. The proportion was even lower at Professorial level (e.g. in 2009–2014, three women out of 26 in total were promoted to Personal Professor).

So the facts belie the rhetoric. Women still do not have an equal chance to men of being promoted in NUI Galway. The reasons for this are many – as they are for Ireland's low GCI ranking in Europe. One reason is the government drive for universities to raise much of their own funds. The Higher Education Equality Unit (HEEU), within the HEA, promoted equality for women and other disadvantaged groups in the workplace for just over a decade, but in 2003, inexplicably, it was disbanded. Focus is now on a more corporate image and universities are expected to attract substantial funds themselves, a situation that inevitably favours male privilege.

Coupled with this is an obsession with world ranking, not in terms of the proportion of senior female academics, but for a numerically measureable set of criteria that conform to a corporate high-end research image. These metrics are part of a neoliberal managerial approach to education which fail to address the more human aspect of education and thereby discriminate against a whole sector of academics where women comprise a significantly high component.[13] These rankings effectively favour men who find more time to travel abroad to important meetings, who openly state that their priority is their research and not their lecturing role and many of whom rely on the support of their partners to rear their family. These rankings select for a particular type of person in particular fields of research, thus effectively reducing universities to industrially-oriented research institutes that just happen to have an intake of students.

The underlying point of my case was not that there was a 'problem' with women, but that the selection criteria favoured a particular type of lecturer; one who would demonstrate leadership, help boost the university's international rankings and bring in more money. This system selected for men overwhelmingly over women and thereby discriminated against women. It is not, therefore, that women need 'fixing' (in the words of a female colleague 'we are sick of being put under the microscope to find out what's wrong with us'), but the whole culture of the organisations needs changing. In a cogently-argued paper Coate and Howson[14] demonstrate that a 'prestige economy' exists in universities and that rewarding of prestige achievements (such as chairing departments or key committees, editorship of journals or delivering keynote addresses) further advances men, who benefit from male-centred social activities and personal favouritism that gives them greater access to these prestige positions. This also results in cumulative disadvantage for women, who, by having less access to this 'prestige exchange', are then perceived as less meritorious.

Therefore the suite of training in assertiveness and strategic planning offered to women in NUI Galway following the 2008/09 outcry will not suffice to ensure that women's actual qualities and achievements are given true recognition. Added to this is a lack of provision for evaluating staff on leave for caring duties. Consultants were brought in to re-assess the 2013/14 SL promotion round who demonstrated there was 'no significant difference' between successful and unsuccessful candidates in terms of leave taken. But they appear not to have distinguished between sabbatical leave (that very much enhances an academic's career) and leave taken for caring duties. This was deduced from feedback to many of the 20 appellants, as the report itself remains unavailable for consultation. Where a lack of clarity exists regarding criteria, or where transparency is poor regarding the selection and scoring processes, it leaves the system open to abuse and discrimination against candidates.[15]

Were the above 'corporate syndrome effect' not sufficient in effecting discrimination, it has been shown that men regularly get higher recognition for equal achievements than women (the 'same criteria … applied differently' of my Tribunal ruling).[16] One fascinating account relates how, on delivering a seminar, a transgender person's research was judged 'much better than his sister's'.[17] It is also important to be flexible in an organisation. The use of very male-centred selection criteria is one area that needs addressing, but also recognition is required of different work patterns and availabilities of staff who have caring roles – still very much left to women, so childcare is still strongly a women's issue. In a university in the UK where greater flexibility was introduced across all sectors, women occupied a much greater proportion of senior posts than in other more 'traditional' universities.[18]

Educare in Latin means to draw out, so in its truest sense it means that students should be encouraged to develop their minds, to widen their perspectives and to hone their thinking skills. In the current global environment of financial and climatic crises, it would strike me as important to train and develop young minds, not just in how to succeed in highly-specialised and well-funded careers, but in how to think laterally and globally to develop alternatives to current mindsets. In an age of mass communication and instant information, it is vital to develop our critical minds, such that alternatives to increasingly global problems can be debated and evaluated.

Therefore, though universities form only one aspect of our society they should maintain their independence of thinking and recognise the value of all their staff equally. Female academics bring a different perspective to research, study and governance. A university that truly recognises the importance of diversity amongst staff as well as students will provide an example of a more just and egalitarian society that can be rolled out to the wider community. My grandfather, Francis Sheehy Skeffington, welcomed opponents to his views and encouraged lively debate and discussion. He believed this was the only way to resolve conflict, while also developing new ideas and thinking. My grandmother, Hanna would be horrified at how little women are still valued in our society, just how little they are allowed to contribute and how rarely their voices are heard. I owe it to my grandparents to continue the struggle – in however small a way – for an egalitarian society where women are integral to its formation and development.

ACKNOWLEDGEMENTS
I am very grateful to Joanna McMinn for reading and commenting on an earlier draft of this chapter and to Rosemary Cullen Owens for setting me right on a historical point.

SOURCES
1   Cited in Rosemary Cullen Owens, *A Social History of Women in Ireland, 1870–1970* (Dublin, Gill and Macmillan, 2005). Hanna Sheehy Skeffington was Co-Editor of the *Irish Citizen* with Louie Bennett at that time. This piece would seem to me to be almost certainly Hanna's writing.
2   Both platform (along with 2 others) and banner are now in the National Museum in Dublin.
3   I am left-handed like she was and I remember my father telling me with pride of how, as she was being arrested, they immobilised her right arm – and she got another shot at the windows with her left hand before being led away.
4   Margaret Ward, *Hanna Sheehy Skeffington: A Life* (Cork, Attic Press, 1997).
5   Maria Luddy, *Hanna Sheehy Skeffington* (Dundalk, Historical Association of Ireland and Dundalgan Press, 1995).
6   See Cullen Owens, 2005.
7   The Glass Ceiling Index (GCI) is the proportion of women in senior posts here taken as being at Professorial level – relative to the total number of female academic employees (European Commission, 2009).
8   European Commission, *She Figures 2009: Statistics and Indicators on Gender Equality in Science* (Brussels, DG Research, European Commission, 2009).
9   HEA (Higher Education Authority), *Gender and Academics*, 2014. http://www.hea.ie/news/gender-and-academic-staff.
10 P. Duncan, 'Women under-represented in senior university posts HEA finds', *The Irish Times*, 3 December 2014,

http://www.irishtimes.com/news/education/women-under-rep
resented-in-senior-university-posts-hea-finds-1.2024458.

11 See https://www.workplacerelations.ie/en/Cases/2014/Novem
ber/DEC-E2014-078.html for the full text of the ruling.

12 Anon, *The Position of University College, Galway, Regarding
Implementation of the Recommendations on the HEA Report (1987)
on 'Women Academics in Ireland'. Report to Academic Council of
UCG by the Group Established in May, 1989 to Consider the Above*
(Galway, University College, Galway, 1990).

13 K. Lynch, 'Carelessness: A hidden doxa of higher education',
Arts and Humanities in Higher Education, 9 (2010), 54–67.

14 K. Coate and C.K. Howson, 'Indicators of Esteem: Gender and
Prestige in Academic Work', *British Journal of Sociology of
Education*, 2014, online: DOI: 10.1080/01425692.2014.955082.

15 L. Barrett and P. Barrett, 'Women and Academic Workloads:
Career Slow Lane or Cul-de-Sac?' *Higher Education*, 61 (2011),
141–155; Coate and Howson, 2014.

16 J. Mervis, 'US Study Shows Unconscious Gender Bias in
Academic Science', *Science*, 337 (2012), 1592.

17 B.A. Barres, 'Does Gender Matter?' *Nature*, 442 (2006), 133–136.

18 See Barrett and Barrett, 2011.

Leabharlanna Poibli Chathair Baile Átha Cliath
Dublin City Public Libraries

The Countess Markievicz School would like to thank each of the contributors for their support for this project which has taken some time to be realised. The School has many friends but in particular we would like to thank Pauline Conroy for her encouragement, enthusiasm and advice throughout without which the project would not have commenced. We also remember Sarah Lundberg who gave several lunchtimes, freely sharing her publishing expertise and Catriona Crowe who put us in touch with Sarah. As editor Alan Hayes has been a true friend to the School in his selfless commitment in bringing this publication to fruition and supporting the School to realise this ambition.

We are grateful to the Department of the Arts, Heritage and the Gaeltacht for their support with a special word of thanks to Stephen Brophy who was the very patient and always available liaison person within the Department. Thank you to our other sponsors the INTO, ASTI and SIPTU who are long-standing supporters of the Markievicz School's work. Thanks to Ken Drakeford and Ailish McShane for their help with the School logo.

Finally a big thank you to the School Committee, and the Publication Working Group for all their voluntary work in getting this project over the finishing line in this the centenary year of the 1916 Rising.

– Máire Meagher

Thanks to Diana Copperwhite for her wonderful cover painting and to the Kevin Kavanagh Gallery. Therese Caherty's indexing work is much appreciated. Special thanks to Máire Meagher for her tireless work. Thanks to the NLI for the Frank and Hanna Sheehy Skeffington photo.

– Alan Hayes
October 2016

IVANA BACIK is a barrister and Reid Professor of Criminal Law, Criminology and Penology at Trinity College, Dublin. She is a Senator for Dublin University (elected 2007, re-elected 2011 and 2016). Her research interests include criminal law; criminology; feminist theory of law; human rights and equality law. She co-authored a study on gender in the legal professions (Bacik, Costello and Drew, *Gender InJustice*, 2003), and her other publications include *Kicking and Screaming: Dragging Ireland into the Twenty-First Century* (O'Brien, 2004).

MARIAAM BHATTI arrived in Ireland in 2010 to work as a live-in fulltime childminder and housekeeper although the role was titled 'au pair'. She is a member of MRCI'S Domestic Workers Action Group and was one of the 23 founders of the Forced Labour Action group that successfully campaigned for two years for criminalisation of forced labour in Ireland. Through a scholarship, Mariaam studied and graduated with a BA (Hons) in Community and Youth Work in 2015. She has just completed a Masters in Social Science (Rights and Social Policy). Both degrees are from Maynooth University. Mariaam now works as a Community Development and Outreach Worker and continues to be active in the community.

PAULINE CONROY is a social scientist who has worked and studied on gender issues in London, Paris, Florence, Brussels and Dublin. Her most recent publications are 'Women in the Revolutionary Decades' in *Theory and Struggle*, the Journal of the Marx Memorial Library, London (2016), 'Dúirt Bean Liom: Punishing the Productive and the Reproductive' in *The Abortion Papers Ireland*, Vol. 2 (2015) and 'Searching for the Disappeared: The Richmond Asylums at Grangegorman and Portrane' in the *Medico-Legal Journal of Ireland* (2015).

CLARE DALY is an independent socialist TD in Dublin Fingal. She served on Fingal County Council for 13 years and as a Shop Steward during her time as an Aer Lingus worker. As President of the Students Union in DCU, she was a leading member of the campaign for abortion information and the battle against SPUC in the 1990s. Clare, a leading campaigner for women's rights, was the first TD in the history of the State to introduce pro-choice legislation to the Houses of the Oireachtas. She continues to campaign on international and national human rights issues. Clare was re-elected to the Dáil in February 2016.

RITA FAGAN has been involved in Community Development for the past 25 years and is the Director of the St Michael's estate Family Resource Centre. In December 2009 Rita received the first ever John O'Connell Award from NUI Maynooth for her continued dedication to community development. She was a member of the team who pioneered the first grassroots response to Violence Against Women collaborating with the Irish Museum of Modern Art and artists to deliver the renowned art exhibition 'Once is too much'. Rita was chosen as one of the five change makers to speak at the Possibilities Event for the Dali Lama's visit to Ireland in April 2011.

DOLORES GIBBONS formerly taught at Greendale Community School, Kilbarrack, acting as a Guidance Counsellor for many years. She completed the Equality Studies Masters in University College Dublin in the mid 1990s; served as a committee member of the Countess Markievicz School, and is active in the 50:50 Group (Women in Politics) and the Teachers' Union of Ireland Retired Members' Association.

ANN LOUISE GILLIGAN (PhD Boston College) is the director of The Centre for Progressive Change, Ltd. She lectured in the Department of Education at St Patrick's College (DCU) and is author of publications on creativity in education and educational disadvantage. She was appointed by the Minister for Education to establish and chair the National Education Welfare Board, and was appointed by the Minister for Education to join the board of Quality and Qualifications Ireland. She is co-founder of An Cosán, Ireland's largest community education organisation located in Jobstown, with her spouse Minister Katherine Zappone. Since 2004, Katherine Zappone and Ann Louise Gilligan advocated to have their September 2003 Canadian marriage recognised by the Irish State. They are co-founders of Marriage Equality and both worked tirelessly in the successful Referendum on Marriage Equality in 2015.

LAURA HARMON is an equality campaigner and former president of the Union of Students in Ireland. Some extracts from this chapter have previously been published in opinion pieces by Laura in *The Irish Times*.

ALAN HAYES has been involved in feminist, women's studies and equality activism for nearly 30 years. He has written articles on women's biography and feminist publishing. Among his publications are *The Years Flew By: The Recollections of Madame Sidney Gifford Czira* (Arlen House, 2000); *The Irish Women's History Reader* (Routledge, 2001); *Irish Women's History* (Irish Academic Press, 2004); *Pauline Bewick at 75* (Arlen House, 2010) and *Hilda Tweedy and the Irish Housewives Association* (Arlen House, 2012).

GORETTI HORGAN is a lecturer in Social Policy in the School of Criminology, Politics and Social Policy at Ulster University, where she is a member of the Institute for Research in Social Sciences and Deputy Director of Policy with ARK [www.ark.ac.uk]. She has been active in the fight for abortion rights in Ireland since 1980, in the South with the Women's Right to Choose Group and Anti Amendment Campaign and, since 1986 in the North where she is a founder-member of Alliance for Choice.

LUCY KEAVENEY is the joint founder of the Countess Markievicz School. She was the school's Chairperson for three years and is now its patron. Passionate about politics, current affairs and equality she noticed on retiring from her teaching career that most current affairs programmes on radio were dominated by men in both presentation and panel formation. To ascertain the degree of this dominance she initiated a series of surveys to highlight the problem. Articles pertaining to the surveys have been published in the *Irish Times*, the *Journal* and on the NWCI website.

PAMELA KPADUWA was born 5 August 1974 in Enugu, Nigeria, the fourth in a family of six. Obtained a Higher National Diploma in Mass Communication from the Federal Polytechnic, Oko Anambra State Nigeria. Has a Masters Degree in International Relations and Strategic Studies from Lagos State University, Lagos. Married with 4 children and has lived in Ireland since 2006 in Mosney, a direct provision hostel. Currently lives in Ardee, County Louth.

MARGARET MARTIN is Director of Women's Aid. Women's Aid is the national organisation supporting women experiencing domestic violence in Ireland since 1974. We work to make women and children safe, offer support, provide hope and act for justice and social change. The Women's Aid National Freephone Helpline 1800 341 900 operates 24 hours a day, 7 days a week. We offer a one to one support service, court accompaniment and run the Dolphin House Domestic Violence Support and Referral Service.

MÁIRE MEAGHER is a graduate of UCD where she also completed a Masters in Equality Studies in the School of Social Justice. As a disability advocate, her research work focuses on the recognition of rights and improvement of services for persons with an intellectual disability and their families. *The Distant Voice* working paper published in 2015 and co-authored by Pauline Conroy examined the first 50 HIQA inspection reports of residential services for persons with a disability in relation to quality of life outcomes. As an Expert for Ireland in a European Fundamental Rights Agency Report, she examined homophobia in Irish post-primary schools: *Professionally Speaking: Challenges to Achieving Equality for LGBT People* (Fundamental Rights Agency and Trinity College, 2016). She has been a member of the Countess Markievicz School committee since 2012 and is currently the School's Chair.

UNA MULLALLY is a writer and broadcaster. She is a columnist for the *Irish Times*, and co-founder of The Women's Podcast. She has presented and produced television series and documentaries for RTÉ and TG4. She is the author of *In The Name Of Love*, an oral history of the movement for marriage equality in Ireland, and founded the queer spoken word night Come Rhyme With Me. She has won numerous awards for her work including the GALAS Journalist of the Year 2015 and the Praeses Elit award 2016 from Trinity College. She lives in Dublin.

MARY P MURPHY lectures in Irish Politics and Society in the Department of Sociology, Maynooth University. She has research interests in gender and social security, globalisation and welfare states, activation, the politics of redistribution, and power and civil society. Recent publications include *Careless to Careful Activation: Making Activation Work for Women* (Dublin, NWCI 2012) and (co-edited with Fiona Dukelow), *The Irish Welfare State in the 21st Century Challenges and Changes* (Basingstoke, Palgrave, 2016). An active advocate for social justice and equality, she is a part-time Commissioner on the Irish Human Rights and Equality Commission.

NIAMH MURRAY is principal of a primary school in inner city Dublin. She holds a Masters in Equality Studies from UCD. In 2011, whilst a part time student on the course, she co-founded the Countess Markievicz School and was its chairperson from

2013–2016. She has written a forthcoming book, *Countess Markievicz and the Women of the Revolution.*

JUSTINE MCCARTHY is a journalist and columnist with *The Sunday Times.* She is a multi-award-winning journalist, including awards for campaigning and social justice, the Journalists' Journalist Favourite Feature Writer, Public Interest Reporter and Columnist of the Year. She is the author of two books, *Mary McAleese: The Outsider* and *Drowning the Truth: Scandals in Irish Swimming.* She was appointed an adjunct professor of journalism at the University of Limerick in 2013 and is a frequent broadcaster on radio and television.

CATHERINE MCGUINNESS was born in Belfast, and was educated in Northern Ireland and in Alexandra College Dublin, Trinity College Dublin and the King's Inns. She was called to the Bar in 1977 and to the Inner Bar in 1989. She served as a member of Seanad Eireann 1979–1987. In 1994 she was appointed as the first woman judge of the Circuit Court. She subsequently served as a judge of the High Court and of the Supreme Court 2000–2006. She was President of the Law Reform Commission 2005–2011. In 2012 she was appointed to the Council of State by President Michael D. Higgins. She has served on a number of State boards and voluntary bodies, and in particular was Chair of the Forum for Peace and Reconciliation in the early years of the Peace Process. She is at present Chair of the Governing Body of National University of Ireland Galway.

An award-winning journalist and broadcaster, MARIE O'CONNOR has been a birth activist since the 1980s. A health correspondent with Raidió na Gaeltachta, she is the author of several non-fiction books on the politics of health care. She has been at the helm of Survivors of Symphysiotomy, the national membership organisation for survivors and their families, since 2010, when she was elected chairperson of this all volunteer group. O'Connor led the delegation to the UN Human Rights Committee hearing in 2014: the UNHRC found that women who underwent symphysiotomy in Ireland had been subjected to involuntary medical experimentation and torture.

Feminist, mother, academic, researcher and training specialist committed to creating more equal worlds of work CLARE O'HAGAN holds an MA and PhD in gender equality areas and also holds a BA and MSc in Human Resource Management. She has written *Complex Inequality and 'working mothers'* (Cork University Press, 2015), published several peer reviewed journal articles and presented at numerous conferences. Research interests include motherhood, equality, gender, employment, childcare and intersectionality. https://www.linkedin.com/in/clareohagan www.theequalitybusiness.ie

CATHLEEN O'NEILL is a community and equality activist. She believes in the power of people and community as the way forward for social change. Positive changes in her own life happened as a result of the values and practice of the community development process. If Markievicz were alive today she would be involved in community development and in taking it back from the State.

JANE O'SULLIVAN practices as a human rights solicitor in an independent community law centre in Dublin. She also works in law and policy reform in relation to access to justice, and particularly in the areas of housing, employment, equality, social welfare and community care. She has an undergraduate degree in Law and French from UCC and an LLM in International Human Rights Law from NUI Galway.

MAEVE O'ROURKE is a barrister at 33 Bedford Row, London. She was an Advisory Committee member of Justice for Magdalenes from 2009 to 2013 and is currently an Advisory Committee member of JFM Research.

Reproductive rights activist and service provider, RUTH RIDDICK led a successful appeal at the European Court of

Human Rights against Ireland's restriction on information about extra-territorial legal abortion (Open Door. 1992), resulting in Irish constitutional reform. Author of *The Right to Choice: Questions of Feminist Morality* (Attic Press), selections from her pro-choice polemic appear in the *Field Day Anthology of Irish Writing*. She is a regular contributor to *Conscience*, newsjournal of Catholics for Choice (catholicsforchoice.org). Ruth Riddick is a 2015 Irish America Healthcare and Life Sciences honoree.

MICHELINE SHEEHY SKEFFINGTON, a recently retired plant ecology lecturer at NUI Galway, is Hanna and Francis Sheehy Skeffington's granddaughter. Both grandparents were ardent nationalists, pacifists, socialists and were very active in the early 20th century campaigns for women's suffrage. Micheline was inspired by them when taking a case in 2009 against NUI Galway for gender discrimination in failing to promote her to Senior Lecturer. She won the case in November 2014 and is currently engaged in a campaign, supported by NUI Galway students, staff and many others, to redress the gender imbalance in senior posts in that university.

JAMES M SMITH is Associate Professor in the Department of English and Irish Studies Program at Boston College. He was an Advisory Committee member of Justice for Magdalenes from 2009 to 2013 and is currently an Advisory Committee member of JFM Research.

SONJA TIERNAN is a Senior Lecturer in Modern History at Liverpool Hope University and the Peter O'Brien Visiting Scholar in Canadian Irish Studies at Concordia University for the fall semester 2015. Sonja previously held fellowships at the National Library of Ireland, Trinity College Dublin and at the Keough-Naughton Institute for Irish Studies, University of Notre Dame. She is author of a number of publications including the biography, *Eva Gore-Booth: An Image of Such Politics* (2012) and *The Political Writings of Eva Gore-Booth* (2015), both published by Manchester University Press.

MARGARET WARD is the author of a number of books, including *Unmanageable Revolutionaries: Women and Irish Nationalism* and biographies of Maud Gonne and Hanna Sheehy Skeffington. Until her retirement she was Director of the Women's Resource and Development Agency in Belfast. She is currently Visiting Fellow in History at Queen's University Belfast and is editing the political writings of Hanna Sheehy Skeffington. In 2014 Margaret was awarded an honorary Doctor of Laws by Ulster University for her contribution to advancing women's equality.

KATHERINE ZAPPONE is an Independent member of Dail Éireann and a former Independent Senator (2011–2015). Dr Katherine Zappone has spent her life campaigning for social justice and human rights. Dr. Zappone was a commissioner with the Irish Human Rights Commission (2002–2012) and has held leadership positions in the NWCI and the Centre for Progressive Change. She is co-founder of An Cosán, Ireland's largest community education organisation, with her spouse Dr Ann Louise Gilligan. Minister Zappone holds a PhD from Boston College, an MBA from the Smurfit Business School and an Honorary Doctorate of Laws from UCD School of Law.